THE FLOWER ORNAMENT

TAKING THE BUDDHA'S TEACHING

MASTER LAUGHING CLOUD

An Nlite Book
www.flowerornament.com

Copyright © 2013 Paul Frederick Martin
All rights reserved.
ISBN: 1482717328
ISBN 13: 9781482717327
Library of Congress Control Number: 2013904642
CreateSpace Independent Publishing Platform
North Charleston, South Carolina

Contents

Before Beginning .... Page 1

Receiving Good Fortune .... Page 4

My First Teachers .... Page 6

Johann Sebastian Bach .... Page 14

Physics as a Religion .... Page 20

Master Han Shan .... Page 25

American Zen .... Page 28

Not Getting Through .... Page 44

Pastoral Life .... Page 53

Furry Teachers .... Page 74

A Change in Practice .... Page 78

A Great Responsibility .... Page 85

Getting What I Wished .... Page 87

Opening a Portal to The Flower Ornament Sutra .... Page 93

Family Practice .... Page 96

A Hint of Something Rotten .... Page 99

Angie .... Page 100

Snow .... Page 104

The Crushing of Dreams .... Page 107

Moving Into Church .... Page 117

The Universe Aflame .... Page 121

Home to Trouble .... Page 126

Building a Timber Frame .... Page 132

The Beginning of the End .... Page 136

Hell's Portal Opened .... Page 142

Talking to Head Office .... Page 156

A Gun to His Head .... Page 162

The Last Indignation .... Page 171

Sayonara .... Page 175

A Dizzying Spin .... Page 178

Burying The Three Jewels .... Page 182

Master Sheng-yen .... Page 188

Queens .... Page 192

Opening Mind .... Page 207

A Man of No Rank .... Page 211

A Bodhisattva	Page 216
Dissolving a Horrid Affliction	Page 218
Another Retreat	Page 223
Practice is Enlightenment	Page 228
"You Must Take Your Teaching From The Buddha"	Page 231
A Fusing of Minds	Page 234
Pinebush	Page 242
An Opening	Page 244
A Hut to Myself	Page 251
49 Days	Page 260
Electric Toilets	Page 272
Becoming a Pirate	Page 277
Finding Nothing	Page 279
Receiving Upia	Page 290
A Dharma Goose	Page 292
The Bodhisattva Retreat	Page 293
Returning With Nothing	Page 303
A Voice From The Past	Page 305
911	Page 307
Secret Transmission Locked in Neutral	Page 308

New Vistas .... Page 321

Solitary Retreat .... Page 317

A Dream .... Page 325

"There is no wisdom or any attainment.

With nothing to attain, Enlightening Beings relying on Prajna Wisdom

Have no obstructions in their minds.

Having no obstructions, there is no fear

And departing far from confusions and imaginings

Reach Ultimate Nirvana."

- SHAKYAMUNI BUDDHA.

Before Beginning

The matter of birth and death is not trivial.

It is not diminished nor resolved by circumstances of having and not having, giving and getting.

Between the boundaries of birth and death we experience the dualities of pleasure and pain as functions of having, not having, giving and getting all framed within the impermanent tossing sea of life. It is inherent in human nature to seek a way beyond suffering and impermanence. Thus we crave emancipation in this life by getting something or receiving something.

To have a body is to crave. The most fundamental craving is the need for our next breath. Therefore, craving whatever is needed for continuing life is the cause of maintaining a body through which we experience affliction.

If all things are impermanent, then how can something generated out of craving, getting and receiving possibly be absolute lasting freedom from affliction, birth and death?

The Great Way cannot be given or received. It is beyond the natural mechanism generated by craving.

And yet, it is only through craving freedom from affliction illuminated by The Buddha's Teaching that we can realize The Great Way beyond craving and suffering.

The circumstances that led me to be a disciple of Great Master Sheng-yen would have been of little consequence had he given me something that I could say I got, and yet I deeply craved to get something from him.

Things happen.

Dividing them into good and bad, giving and getting is standing outside phenomena when there is no place to abide. If the nature of this is realized, then everything that emerges in life no matter how painful or undesirable is an opportunity born of the deepest compassion.

This is the teaching of the Universe.

This is The Teaching of The Tathagathas.

Over 20 years ago I came to Great Master Sheng-yen deeply troubled by a series of cataclysmic events that were thrown in my path to realize The Way. He told me I should not take his teaching, but that I must take my teaching from The Buddha.

Although it was painfully unclear what he had told me at that time, the teaching I received from him from that point onward was The Teaching of The Buddha.

I have lived a very fortunate life.

It has been an unending emersion into the practice of Buddhadharma that at first I was not aware of, and later, when I began formal lay practice, was not always within the circumstances I would have preferred, nor the stability and security that people generally crave.

I have had the great good fortune to receive The Teaching in this way. This great good fortune sometimes took the form of being attacked by demons attempting to destroy me.

Why was this good fortune?

It was because I eventually made it a practice that everyone and everything is a teacher, no matter how painful or difficult the interaction. Thus a compassionate and liberated Universe beyond preferences is born. This very Universe abounds with Bodhisattvas, without changing anything.

Is this Universe any different than yours?

Receiving Good Fortune

The foundation to realise the wonderful truth that lies beyond affliction through the afflictions of life began before I was born.

My mother, nine months pregnant, was visiting her parents when my unbalanced 11 year old cousin ran up to her, pointed to her swollen belly and laughed, "Why is that sticking out so far?" He then kicked the protrusion so hard she collapsed.

From the circumstances of birth I have been given a lot.

The town where I grew up was situated within a pleasant sea of farms within an economic setting that appeared to have no bounds. Southern Ontario in 1950's Canada was a garden of opulence. People there worked very hard and were rewarded for their labours.

This setting of peace and prosperity was in opposition to the horrors of The Second World War still fresh in people's minds that consumed the youth of my parents' generation, one way or another. In Canada, we observed the day marking the end of this human slaughter as a funeral service.

Beyond the superficial explanations found in controlled history texts and media we grew up with, the conflict was created by the highest echelons of a cabalist secret society controlling vast wealth and therefore human volition. The point in time they decided to end the previous phase of the slaughter called "The First World War" was set as the eleventh hour of the eleventh day of the eleventh month. In cabbalist numerology eleven is the number of the turning point following massive death. This magical spell is very much in effect to this day. It had the reverse intention of ending "The War to End All Wars". Thus World War 2 followed, and a progression of hidden and not so hidden wars were inseminated right up to this present day slaughter generated by 911.

Although created by the self-righteous numerological magic of occult bankers, the spiritual nature of the services conducted across Canada and elsewhere on this hour was deeply Celtic. Unlike the United States, Canada was drawn into both World Wars from the very beginning and all those who were slaughtered on the fields of Flanders and the beaches of Normandy were volunteers. Small town kids and farm boys sucked into a vortex of something very different than church and media had told them. It was a religious right of sacrifice that had secret intent and power.

I felt the spirits whose names were cast in the town cenotaph that we marched to as school children on that day. Present in the silence that followed the bag pipes and drums, they were not "the fallen" as is common to say these days amongst the spiritually false and experientially removed. They had been ripped apart, drowned in mud, cremated alive in flaming Spitfires or 109's. They experienced the speechless terror of sacrifice in a religious economic blood ritual that was intentionally created by those who practice greed, hatred and ignorance, and then profit from it.

These wars were in a distant land and fought against a vilified people. The same is true today. Only the names of the places have changed. Afghanistan, Iraq... The same forces that have caused this infinite suffering using lies and false pretences of supporting the common good is now in the process of bringing war once again to North America.

My First Teachers

I was very fortunate to have two excellent teachers that gave me no choice but to enter The Way. They were my Mother and my Father.

My father was my hero. He was a veteran of the Second World War.

For him, the war was the best time of his life. He got to fly supplies and mail cross the North Atlantic in some of the most sophisticated aircraft of the time. They were burnt out, shot up B 17's "pre-loved" by the U.S. Army Air Corps then sold to the Royal Canadian Air Force at a really good price. The limitless expanse of the icy North Atlantic consumed without a trace one in seven of his squadron. This was attributed to mechanical failures and snorkel submarines. However, these were far better odds than flying a brand new Rolls-Royce powered Lancaster with a belly crammed with white phosphorus incendiaries to drop on German homes at night. There the odds of not coming back were one in three.

My Dad never talked about how dangerous it was or that he was part of some great cause. Instead he spoke of his love of flying and the aircraft he flew.

None of this remotely prepared him for the battle to follow; marriage to my mother and family life.

My mother too was a veteran. She had survived an ongoing war with her brothers having been trained in rural isolation by her French Canadian mother. Had my grandmother fought alongside Leonidas at Thermopile, the Spartans would have defeated Xerxes on the spot. She was a remarkably powerful woman.

Mom's true religion was the art of afflicting anything male, especially my Dad. As long as I could remember, Mom kept going in and out of mental institutions at the frequency of about once every spring or so, with the added bonus of experiencing electroshock and cocktails of the latest experiential psycho drugs the mental health industry doled out. They couldn't break her will to be unique. She was far too strong and intelligent for them to succeed.

The summer before my sister's birth, mother had a serious breakdown and had to be taken practically kicking and screaming to the psych ward. Before she was taken away, my grandmother fueled by a conviction that Mom should not go to such a place, openly battled all family members as well as the family doctor. The whole event was very disturbing, with Mom confused and crying a lot, my older compassionate female cousins taking me outside the farmhouse away from the battle going on, then my grandmother telling me that what they were doing to Mom was horrible and they were going to take her away.

They did take her away.

I stayed at the farm and was given my Mom's empty bedroom to sleep in. It was the end of the world for me. I was three years old.

After Mom returned home and everything seemed normal once again, my Grandfather became very ill.

I was left at the neighbour's house across the street while my parents stayed with my grandmother, a two hour drive from home. In the house where I stayed lived a boy who was four years older than me. I guess he had enough of me being a focus of attention in his own home.

One day his mother went shopping and left us alone playing in the basement. Sometime after she left, he quietly ascended the stairs and locked the basement door from inside. Returning to floor level, he picked up a long sharp piece of wood, fixed his eyes upon me and slowly approached. Holding the basement key in front of my face, he coldly said that there was no way I could escape, and that he was going to kill me. I ran to the top of the basement stairs screaming and tried to open the locked door in vain. He slowly climbed the stairs with the stick in front of him, point first. It was only when he heard his mother's car enter the drive way that he stopped terrorizing me, saying that if I said anything to anyone about what went on, he really would kill me. I had no reason to doubt his sincerity, so in the days weeks, months and years that followed, I didn't say a word about what happened. In fact, I even put it out of memory.

After my parents returned, they picked up that I didn't want to stay at the neighbour's house any more, but left me there anyhow. Having no choice in being left in such a precarious setting, I refused to sleep in the same room as my secret tormentor by flying into tantrums. Everybody thought I had suddenly become a weird troublesome little 3 year-old. However, I am sure the woman whose son was tormenting me must have figured out what was going on and chose to say and do nothing about it.

When not being in the care of the neighbours, I could not exhibit anything short of model behaviour. This was because my father couldn't understand anything beyond his mental concepts of what a three year old should be. This paradigm of parenting was augmented by a book in my Mom's library written by the shill Dr. Benjamin Spock on how to raise little children.

My father kept saying, "What's the matter with him now?" My Mom was concerned, but didn't have any idea what the cause was. So they left me at that house for overnight stays as grandpa's condition worsened.

This traumatic series of incidents disappeared from my memory until 16 years later when I chanced meeting my tormentor in London Ontario. He spoke through a smile while recalling a humorous childhood memory.

"Remember when we were kids and I scared the living crap out of you in our basement? I've never seen anybody so freaked out!"

When I replied that I didn't remember he couldn't believe it. It took me a long time for the memories of what happened to come into consciousness. Were it not for that chance meeting in a mall, they would probably not have emerged from my psyche as early as they did.

It wasn't long after Grandpa died that my sister was born.

I had just turned 4.

Our family doctor botched the delivery and my sister almost strangled. Although a healthy baby girl, she began to show signs of behaviour that indicated all was not well. This was the beginning of a chain of mental health industry diagnosis starting with possible brain damage, then later on retarded, then later on autistic, then schizophrenic, then a little later schizophrenic and dyslexic, then ultimately by the age of 16, a cocktail of all the above. She really exhausted the ancient Greek vocabulary of psychiatrists and psychologists who attempted to describe her.

As I got older I began to get the suspicion that although she had real problems, she was cleverly faking a great deal of them in order to get Mom's overreacting attention and protection (diagnosed as "postpartum", which is not Greek, but Latin)) by saying and doing things that she found really bothered people. Later on she used denizens of the mental institutions she frequented as mentors of behaviour. Thus not only was she inventive, she was able to become a "text book case" as well. It seemed that only I could see my sister having a direct pipeline to tragic self-generated never ending suffering and I began to lose faith in psychiatry and psychology as a cure for mental affliction.

The Church avoided us like the plague even though Dad fed it money.

My sister taught me in a very powerful way. She suffered greatly. Every moment of her life was an increment of mental torment that I lived in counterpoint with. The dynamics of my family run by my "post-partum" mother put her as the centre of attention and she naturally used this to gain whatever solace and security she could get. This made the natural interactions of a male four year old toward an attention demanding baby sibling supercharged. I got blamed for being evil and even the cause of my sister's problems.

My sister, on the other hand, although using these tools at her disposal, harboured an appreciation and caring for me as she got older. I tried to reciprocate this bond. From early on I was spiritually linked to the living hell she was experiencing and would beat the daylights out of any male (and there were many) who picked on her. This was something neither of our parents realized.

My mother made life living hell for my Father, and my Father, after returning the favour, buried himself in the basement of our house building an airplane, perhaps thinking it was a thing for him to escape in. This was not a model airplane, but a 2 seat 85 horse power fabric covered airplane with a steel tube fuselage and wood wings. It was begun when I was 5 years old, and successfully test flown when I was 18. I spent much of my childhood as a human clamp holding various parts in place while Dad fit them.

As sometimes happens under such circumstances, Dad began to blame me for the affliction that was going on at home and I developed a habit of getting clobbered a fair bit while holding parts for test fits. This I felt was due to my imperfections that he continuously pointed out to me.

When the airplane was finished and test flown, I was told he didn't want me flying it because I would smash it up. This lack of faith in me was at odds with the fact that, outside of Dad's awareness, I was capable of wringing out my motorcycle and not crashing it, a far less forgiving beast than a two seat home built airplane. Furthermore, I had never put a dint or scratch in the family car, let alone roll it in a ditch as did one of my friends. However, I thought that maybe if the airplane ballooned on a thermal at the end of a hot paved runway just before landing and I didn't catch it with the throttle, or some other natural occurrence that might cause ground looping and a dinged up wing tip or prop, I would be blamed for it. It would be better to stay away from flying even though I had a great love of airplanes. Because of this, I didn't get my pilot's license.

The airplane

My mother, a highly intelligent, compassionate, strong willed contrarian could be as tormenting as she was tormented. Despite the usual spring odyssey of being taken against her will by father to the nearest psychiatric ward to "treat" what they called depression with electroshock and the latest chemical cocktails, the drama of acting out, treatment and suffering actually fuelled this cycle that continued throughout most of her adult life. By giving her performances Greek and Latin names, the psychology and psychiatry industry bestowed upon them a reality similar to a physical ailment offering both vindication for her actions as well as an audience. In return, through her suffering, she vindicated their need to exist and obtain a hansom paycheck.

School was an exciting wonderful expanse that I graduated into. As a little guy I had a love affair with my kindergarten teacher and she always gave me glowing approval. It was heaven. Kindergarten was a strange word to call a place I spent a fair bit of time in, so I asked my Dad what it meant. He said, "I think it's a German word".

I would then sit in front of the TV and be subjected to frequent historical films consisting of R.A.F. Hurricane and Spitfire gun camera footage of German airplanes being ripped apart and blowing up as well as American footage of bombs falling on German cities from fairly high altitude. This was always accompanied by a most solemn authoritative narrative, its essence being that all this was O.K. because the German recipients were under the influence of evil and started the whole thing. Since I was by now familiar with the rules of playground conflict, I figured that there wasn't anything wrong with any of this and yet, here I was spending significant time in a wonderful place with a German name, and the wonderful ethereal Motherteacher who was the focus of my adoration's name was Mrs. Klienstiver.

This joyous heaven vanished at grade 1, never to return.

The abrupt ending of what had been an enjoyable and stimulating experience followed an unusual test administered to us after we had lunch.

Living in the beautiful little Southern Ontario town of Exeter, I had the privilege of taking executive lunches by walking home from school, eating, then watching cartoons or The Three Stooges until I had to go back. It was for this reason I was late for the spoken instructions belted out by my drill sergeant grade 1 teacher on how to approach this examination. It was not like the normal tests and questions I was used to. I wasn't sure how to proceed but was afraid to ask because, after all, I was late in coming back from lunch and that was a punishable offence in her books. I coloured some of the pictures, and left most of the strange questions unanswered.

The test was then collected and that was the end of it.

Or so I thought.

That was my first I.Q. test. We were given the next one seven years later. For all of grade 1 until late grade 7, I was assumed to be an idiot by my teachers. If I managed to do anything right, it was at odds with my abysmal I.Q. Of course I had no idea this prejudice was going on. Everyone including my Dad, seemed to think I was stupid. Dad often referred to me as a "dull tool" and my sister later attending the same public school as me certainly didn't help the overall picture. My constant show and tell reports of building a real airplane in the basement of our tiny bungalow cemented the idea in my teacher's minds that I was not only stupid, but delusional as well. I really began to detest institutional learning. There were more interesting real things going on at home in the basement.

I remember a day or two after completing my second I.Q. test in grade seven, the school principal entered our classroom with an air of urgency, easily picked up amidst the stultified boredom of grammar class.

In hushed tones he said to the teacher, "There has been a highly unusual result."

After that point onward, they started treating me as some sort of Einstein. However, that didn't change things much in my books. I still had an aversion to school.

Johann Sebastian Bach

It was my Spartan grandmother who insisted that her daughter's son take piano lessons.

One evening my Dad brought home a recording to play on his state-of-the-art high fidelity stereo. Usually it was either bag pipe music, Hawaiian grass skirt music or yet another rendition of "The Harmonicats"; gifted Italian mouth organ players of Ed Sullivan fame.

This record was different. On its jacket cover was an array of organ pipes with the word "Bach" emblazoned in gothic gold letters. I was 12 and had heard the name through my music teacher.

"This will really test the sound system!" he said as he lowered the disk onto the turn table.

He had absolutely no idea what he was doing.

What followed was life changing.

It was a recording of Bach's Toccata, Adagio and Fugue in C major, Toccata in F major and Toccata and Fugue in D minor performed by Doctor Michael Schneider on the Luneburg Organ, a restored Northern German 17th Century instrument that Bach himself had once played.

What I heard was a living dragon of powerful depth and clarity, its sword-edged speech timeless. This was not the church music of hymns and reassurance. What I heard was the urgent questioning of thunderous earth spirits resounding to ethereal voices glistening in higher register. It was a vast interplay of light and darkness that I did not associate with Christianity. Primordial, it spoke directly to me in a language I had not realized I understood until that moment.

Almost every day when I came home from school I would put that record on the turn table and crank up the volume. I also did so in the evening. This caused my Dad to shout from the depths of his basement workshop, "Turn that goddamned thing down!"

Mom suggested to Dad that perhaps they should throw the recording out, but the degree of my protest changed their minds. To their great credit, both endured, perhaps hoping it was a stage I would pass through.

It didn't.

At 16 I began building a harpsichord from a kit imported from New York City consisting of a plastic covered keyboard, nylon action jacks, tuning pins, a few strings, and a full sized drawing. Once it was finished I started a long process of learning Bach Inventions, Preludes and Fugues.

So here I was in small town Ontario Canada with Dad building an airplane in the garage and basement, Mom going in and out of mental hospitals, my sister a highly visible anomaly forced by Mom to go to the same school I attended, and the music I lived by was Northern German Baroque organ and harpsichord music while my classmates were dancing to the Beatles. I was too shy to go to dances and have a girlfriend, even though my hormonal tides and secret crushes on the goddesses of my high school were enormous.

This caused me to fend for myself in isolation, and arouse a very real desire to become free of affliction.

We always had enough to eat, and like pretty much everyone else at that point in time and space, lived in a centrally heated house.

Dad kept saying to me "I don't know what the hell is the matter with your mother. We're doing fine. We have everything we need!"

The crowning moment for my father arrived during an especially difficult and heart rendering incarceration of Mom. I was about 13 at the time, and all hell had broken loose. More so than usual, she had to be once again forced into the psyche ward.

From what I now know about what went on there, I really don't blame her for resisting. Treatment is exactly that: treatment. One's will is involuntarily surrendered. It is a form of possession.

A week or so after things had somewhat settled down, the Psychiatrist/God Figure in charge asked Dad to make an appointment with him. During that audience, my father was told from the highest authority that there was no cure for Mom, and that things would be like this for the rest of their lives. From that point onward, something in my Dad died. He became inwardly bitter and, more than ever, I became a very handy target for his frustration.

Although not in the least pleasant, this affliction turned into good fortune because it was my first fundamental question that the Chinese Masters called a Hua-tou; "Why is there such horrible affliction in such a life of abundance?"

This was a manifestation of the powerful driving force causing me to enter The Way long before I ever heard of Dhyana, Chan, Zen or Buddha.

In this timeless light not yet glimpsed, I was most fortunate to somehow have the ability to turn affliction into something converging to a point beyond affliction.

After reaching the age of 17, I had had enough. I let my hair grow a little long, bought a motorcycle and took to smoking cigars while riding it. They burnt a lot faster at 90 miles per hour. I used to skip class, pop a wheelie in front of the high school, then wring my bike out, dragging its foot stud on pavement in high speed acceleration lane turns.

As with many other male kids my age at the time, I became a lightning rod for the statement, "Get a haircut!" This supercharged my Dad's incessant attacks on me and my intelligence although relatively speaking I was really quite straight and conservative. Unlike my little circle of eccentric friends who referred to me as "guru", I never tried pot or other drugs, save the odd beer. I was a true anomaly.

Since my family was not musical, I got very little in the way of emotional support to continue musical training. I did so at odds to their wishes by riding my motorcycle to the city of London Ontario and taking private organ lessons from a music professor on a recently installed three manual mechanical action organ based on 17th Century building principals. It was excellent for Bach.

Although we were Catholic in what was an Orange town, the kindly ex R.A.F. minister of the Anglican Church in Exeter went as far as giving me a key to the church so that I could come in and practice the falling-apart 19th Century tracker organ any time I wanted, and at no charge.

This was as close to the organs that Bach played as I was going to get within a thirty five mile radius. Unfortunately, the organ was barely playable due to years of very reasonably priced Jack the Ripper style maintenance. However, more than other mechanical action organs of its genera designed for hymns and little else, it had a stop list that had upper work and clarity despite its Romantic 19th Century voicing. Its mechanical action was the standard sticker and backfall type, a cumbersome regression from the elegant and responsive roller actions of previous centuries. To placate the piano trained organists of the day, it had what was called a "nag's head swell" to create dynamic variations of loud and soft without registration change. For reasons still not clear to me, the heavy oak swell shutters were mounted horizontally, allowing their substantial weight to be experienced with one's right foot during the most meaningful of crescendos. When the shutters were fully opened, a long lever would drop into place on the swell pedal and the massive shutters would be suspended open. In order to revert back to pious softness, all one had to do was kick the lever and the whole contraption came crashing down with a heavy thud, much like the action of a guillotine. It was fun to improvise some heart rendering little soap opera melody that gained in tremulant intensity only to have the contraption crash down making the rest silence.

This church, more than any other in Exeter, was a sanctuary of spirits. These were the spirits I knew whose names were etched in the cenotaph and recalled on Remembrance Day. Hidden spells, written in pencil beside the spiral staircase leading up the bell tower or carved with a school boy's pocket knife inside the organ chamber were only seen by those like me who materialized and lingered within its realm. Spells like "In memory of Davy Johns, age 18, killed in the Great War 1915" were incantations echoing immeasurable human affliction. Above the large Union Jack flanked by regimental flags, the glorious hammer-beamed ceiling was illuminated during the day by a beautiful, large stained glass depiction of a robed Jesus. Unlike the Jesus' in the Catholic Churches I was familiar with, this one had little evidence of lacerations, nail wounds, and in fact, looked pretty healthy.

When this church was built, no expense was spared. It was funded by a wealthy Exeter business man and as a reward, both he and his wife were encrypted in the basement after they died.

Their names were "Trivitt", and the church had the unusual name, "Trivitt Memorial Church."

This stuck with my Anglican public school friends in a B movie horror film sort of way. They were either genuinely scared to hell of "The Trivitts" coming up out of the basement during church service, or wished them to do so out of boredom when their imagination wandered.

After the setting of the sun things became another story inside the church. The luminous Jesus faded into darkness and other things not relying on light came into consciousness.

I was one of those beings.

To get away from whatever was going on at home, and not be disturbed by wedding preparations, church officials and other things, I would go for a motorcycle ride until after nightfall, then park my bike away from the street lamp and enter the pitch dark church. I didn't turn on the lights because that would alert outsiders that someone riding a motorcycle was in the House of God and might cause them to phone the police, or give Reverend Anderson trouble, even though my sport bike was not quite the same species as those ridden by "Hell's Angels.".

I got so I could reach the organ console without falling into a church pew and pull the chain on the garish porcelain light socket mounted over the music desk. The large stained glass window facing main street that didn't depict Jesus was only faintly illuminated by the street lights.

I didn't feel afraid of this old place and the fact that the Trivitts were buried under its floor, just behind the organ console. In fact, like the old minister, they seemed to welcome me. Out of my back pack I would pull Bach's Preludes, Toccatas and Fugues and started practicing as best I could, given the instrument's medical condition.

Physics as a Religion

My father came from a long line of engineering and machine shop wizards, the most publically prominent being P.E. Martin, Henry Ford's first production manager. Henry had gone bankrupt twice before he hired P.E. It was probably P.E. who invented the modern assembly line.

Dad was a great inspiration to me. He was my hero, being the ultimate do-it-your-selfer. During the day he was an optometrist whose practice became quite successful. After hours of looking at people's retinas, he would come home, have dinner, then enter his subterranean abode to do things wonderful and mysterious. Where most people would talk of actually building something, he simply and quietly did it no matter how adverse the situation was, or how long it took. He loved technology. Having once apprenticed as a tool and die maker, he had a little machine shop in our basement. The Atlas metal lathe made in Kalamazoo Michigan in 1938 was magical. Some of my earliest memories were sitting in a cloth lawn chair Dad set up so that I could watch the shiny carriage hand wheel turn all on its own as ribbons of steel curled off the tool bit. It was an altar from which he caused things of great fascination to emerge. This was power.

It was at about the same point in time when Dad bought the organ record he deeply regretted that he told me that as far as flying machines went, conventional rocketry was absurd because there was very little control of flight path. All of this was within the time frame of the manned space program that had reached a rabid religious media-driven fervour.

"Antigravity is the ticket!" he would say. "If you could build an antigravity machine you would not have all the problems of primitive rocket thrust. You could fly anywhere and enter into space with ease."

The next intellectual leap was even more impressive, its source mysterious.

"Physicists are wrong. Gravity is electrical in nature and all you have to do is make a flying machine that generates an electrical charge to use for lift, instead of wings. This is something you should work on."

Of course his general understanding of the dynamics involved was overly simplistic, but his conviction was quite strong and since I was thirteen years old, it resonated with great amplitude within me.

Since he was building a flying machine in our basement and garage it seemed possible that I might succeed in creating a flying machine using high voltage fields.

The paradigm of the 1960's was that within the application of technology lay the salvation of humanity. As a thirteen year old kid I set my life's task to save humanity through the creation of a machine that could be free of what binds us to earth.

Dad helped me build a Van de Graaff electrostatic generator using a six inch diameter steel globe of the world kindly donated by a good friend, and an electric fan motor I salvaged. After sanding off all the continents, oceans and lakes, it made an excellent electrode. I then set up a little lab in the corner of our basement and spent countless hours in darkness watching three inch sparks leap from its surface to my knuckles. I observed that when the generator sphere was covered in fine dust, the point of discharge looked very much like the crater Tycho on the moon, and got little pieces of aluminium foil, styrofoam and anything else of the right mass to enter a rapidly decaying orbit and crash onto its surface, then leap off again when I brought my finger close. That was about as far as these basement experiments went. Although they were great fun, I realized that using electrostatics in this form was not going to produce anything that you could fly in. I needed to learn more.

Thus I was religiously drawn to engineering and especially physics. I dreamed of going to university and becoming a wizard of empirical knowledge absorbing myself and being absorbed by the Universe. This is what I thought I was getting into as I prepared at the end of high school to enrol in the honours physics program at The University of Waterloo.

During that time I was visiting my Mom while she took a spring stay in a mental institution. The English department of my high school slated that we study Macbeth, King Lear, Hamlet and T.S. Elliot's Murder in the Cathedral all in succession. I took to heart the great profundity of these tragedies. However, it might be said that the subject matter could be construed as being a little depressing. Then to top things off, after finally overcoming shyness and getting a girlfriend who offered everything a sexually overcharged young man could want, I was suddenly dumped for one of the high school gym teachers.

Questioning everything

In the fall of that year, broken hearted and boiling with affliction, I went off to the Honours Physics Program at The University of Waterloo. This was a technical university that is sometimes referred to as Canada's M. I. T. It prided itself in the fact that it had a high failure rate. In engineering they would say at the beginning of first year, "Take a good look at the guy sitting beside you. There's an over 50% chance you won't see him here after Christmas."

The Honours Physics program there was 15% worse. And this did not attenuate after first year, or second, or third. Those that didn't make it were absorbed into engineering (rarely), honours science as a physics major, or flunked out completely (the usual route).

I remember finding a graduate student working something out on a blackboard in the physics building and began to talk to him about physics.

He listened carefully, then burst into laughter exclaiming, "You don't know what you are getting into!"

As he kept repeating that statement while shaking his head, I could see his eyes welling with tears and his laughter verging on crying.

From the beginning it hit me hard. I saw that my professors were definitely very accomplished in their field and were to be admired. But a major component of their life-practice was burying themselves in a discreet branch of physics academia that through default had a unique position within the universe of University. They were the results of a Pavlovian exercise. Give what the institution wants in behaviour and get the reward in marks, degrees and prestige. I began to see that the definition of a Ph.D. being someone who knows more and more about less and less rang very true.

Yet I believed that physics was the true religion of current Western Civilisation and that this fusion of mind and nature was for me "a consummation devoutly to be wished".

But something was wrong. I began skipping lectures to practice Bach Inventions, Preludes and Fugues on pianos in empty practice rooms and chapels, and began to earnestly question the nature of observer and phenomenon. Physics bases itself on the a-priori assumption of separation of observer and phenomenon, and yet, to me it was a mystery how this could in fact be possible. How can you separate yourself from the Universe when your senses are all a function of it? How could the Universe stand apart from the senses when the senses generate the perceived Universe? Nobody in physics seemed to know, or care, although Heisenberg inadvertently touched upon it. It was all a wheel of study, tests and reward in the form of marks, degrees and prestige. This question was for me very deep and troubling.

As all this was happening, my mother, in denial there was anything wrong with her daughter, forced her to go to a technical high school when she turned 16. My Dad protested, and then resigned himself to saying that there was nothing he could do to prevent it. This move was catastrophic for my sister, and now I was visiting both my Mom and sister drugged up in the London psych ward.

Master Han Shan

It was at this point in early spring of 1973 that I bought a book entitled "Practical Buddhism" by a Chinese scholar and lay practitioner named Charles Luk. It contained the autobiography of Master Han Shan Deching. When I read this autobiography containing the words, "From the beginning, nothing is," and "All time and space is a cicada's wing and the Universe a horse's hair," a powerful deep joy filled me.

This Practice of Master Han Shan Deching was what I desperately wanted and needed to do.

The upheaval of a great spring of awakening began in reading this book. Even though it was exam time, I practically stopped studying physics and began attempting to immerse myself in the Hua-tou Wu after nearly breaking my legs to get into a full lotus on top of my dormitory bed.

That spring I threw myself into painting a Buddha image on a panel having never had any instruction in the visual arts. Its form was "Dali-ish", and I left it unfinished and unsigned, wondering where it came from.

My attempt at a painting of a Buddha

I don't know how I managed to stay in honours physics, but I did go on in the program. Although I loved the beauty of mathematics and the power of working concept derived from physical empiricism, for me this institutional setting was living hell. Socially, being in physics at Waterloo was very similar to being a monk. There was precious little time to do anything but learn concepts, go to lectures and do labs. I was too tormented to effectively study or have a social life with the goddesses that abounded in arts, philosophy and psychology (at that point in time, extremely few entered the honours physics program, or engineering for that matter).

However, this lonely hell was continuously punctuated by simple things of great beauty such as dew drops condensing from early spring mist upon campus willow branches. I appreciated these things in profound depth because they were experienced in poignant isolation, now framed within Buddhist Concept. This Concept was somehow deeply familiar to me. It was ultimate empiricism. There was nothing else.

Besides the book "Practical Buddhism" that I read and re-read, there were no Chinese books on Chan Practice in the University book store. There were, however, a great many on Japanese Zen and I filled my library with them. Out of incessant torment, my interest and longing to practice Chan or Zen Buddhism had reached a rabid fervour.

Early that summer I had an unusual lucid dream.

I found myself sitting before a Zen master. He asked me a profound question for which I had no answer. When I awoke, I could not remember what the question was. I thought it most peculiar that somehow I knew that this master was a contemporary university scholar and not that old. Although he was Asian, had a shaved head and wore a Buddhist monk's robe, he also wore glasses. I wondered why, given that it was a dream, the master took this unusual form and not something more classic and stereotypical.

American Zen

Words have dependent meanings. They emerge from events that in essence are empty and produce mistaken realities of things that have no fixed reality. This emptiness is the fountainhead of all that is blissful, painful, material and ethereal. It is the source of infinite meanings and interpretations that can be construed as truths or lies.

In order to tell you about what followed beyond this point, I will not use the convergent names of certain characters and places. To do so will swamp the mind with the polarities of marketed reputations versus hidden actions. From my perspective, it doesn't matter if the convergent names commonly associated with the peoples and places are used. I have liberated them. However, within the realm of blind perceptions, their names are strongly affixed to self and reputation that is taken by many as being real. It is better to illuminate their actions and steer around the names they use. The most important thing is that the reader's perception is illuminated to what has been hidden so that The Buddha's Teaching will not be lost and humanity will not be led into collective darkness.

I have liberated these people and places because I used the situations they offered without separation from Buddhist practice. For this I am grateful. It is without a doubt that I learned a lot from these people, and made their teaching valuable because I was eventually able to drop it.

To come to this place I had to be hit over the head.

I began earnestly looking for a Zen Master and made contact with a Zen Center in Upstate New York.

The year was 1975, and the teacher who had recently given himself the title "Roshi", was famous for writing one of the earliest books in English on actual Japanese Zen practice, or at least the form he had experienced.

In May of that year I drove alone from my home town of Exeter Ontario to Doorchester New York to take part in a one day workshop at this Zen Center.

For me, the whole experience was not like finding something I had longed for. It was not like finding a venue for the solution of all my problems. A formal 30 minute period of sitting meditation was conducted in the Zendo. In my entire solitary meditation sitting over the previous two years I had not experienced nearly the leg pain I did within that 30 minute period. But I was sensitive to the energy in the Zendo, and found the focus of the method of meditation of counting the breath within a structured setting exactly what I needed. For that reason I decided to enrol that July in what was called a "Training Program" that would last four weeks wherein its participants lived a monastic Zen Schedule.

It was during that first training program that one of the advanced students, who had been recognised by The Roshi as having experienced kensho (seeing the flash of the sword of enlightenment), was to give a Dharma talk on compassion. We were all instructed to ask a question.

That night, after her talk, people asked questions that took the general form of "My aunt is very sick, what should I do?" or, "How can I be more compassionate in daily life?"

In hushed, thoughtful tones she answered each question. It was a reverential affair.

When it came my turn to ask a question, my whole life experience of my mother protecting my sister to the point of destroying her, and the stream of doctors, psychiatrists and psychologists treating both my mother and sister under the guise of compassion yet clearly failing, could not be buried.

In spite of terminal shyness, I summoned up all of my courage.

"There has been a lot of talk about compassion this evening," I said, then asked, "Beyond words and images, what is true compassion?"

The Zendo filled with silence.

Then, like a wolverine with P.M.S., the speaker ripped into me.

"WHAT DO YOU WANT!" she yelled.

"A DICTIONARY?"

I sat in my place and said nothing.

The silence in the Zendo became deafening.

After a moment's lapse, she cooled and went onto the next question.

The next day I noticed some people viewing me with a sense of awe.

That evening The Roshi gave a talk.

"Sometimes silence can be golden, sometimes it can be yellow," he said.

I enrolled in two more training programs and was going to do another when The Roshi suggested that I either join the staff or at least start going to sesshins (intensive retreats).

By this time I had a very good look at the Zen lifestyle as embodied in staff life at the Center. This included cleaning seven toilets three times a day. These toilets were usually spotless to begin with. I felt that it would be far more useful to practice Zen while immersed in the real world and go to as many sesshins as I could. Unfortunately, the timing of the Doorchester sesshins were at odds with maintaining a career in anything physics or engineering related, as I later found out when I asked my boss at the aerospace company I worked at for a week off in October, then another in December during the period before the seasonal holidays.

Realizing I could not have a career in Physics or Engineering, from 1975 until 1977 I supported myself with minimum wage jobs while renting a room at The Toronto Zen Affiliate, a branch of The Doorchester Zen Center. This was so that I could go to Doorchester for as many seven day sesshins as I could, usually around four a year.

The first Zen sesshin I went to was four days long and took place at the Toronto Affiliate. It was unusual in that The Roshi was leading it. Usually four day sesshins, even in Doorchester, were led by his senior students. The longest formal meditations I had done previous to that point in time were one day long at the end of each training program. The leg pain I experienced in just that one day was enormous. I could scarcely get up after each round of sitting to hobble into the walking meditation line. I figured that since this sesshin was four days long I could multiply the pain coefficient by a factor of four and wondered if I would survive.

I was assigned the beginner's practice of counting the breath. In the evening after the first day we had our first private dokusan (interview) with The Roshi.

After prostrating, then stating what my practice was, he said, "Paul, there are four levels of attainment that can be aspired to. The first is improved health through meditation, the second is clarity and focus of mind during daily life, the third is awakening or kensho and the forth is becoming an enlightened being who appears in this world to help the suffering and transmutes to other realms. What level do you aspire to?"

"The fourth," I firmly said.

This answer caused The Roshi to pause.

In sincerity he said, "I am going to assign you the koan Mu."

My spirits soared. Mu (in Chinese, Wu) was the primary koan that people including The Roshi himself had been assigned and had realized kensho. Now I had a clear shot at ending the affliction that plagued me. Enlightenment was within my grasp. I returned to my seat in the Zendo burning with joy and determination.

Then things started to heat up. People began yelling their koans. Accompanying an incessant background of agonising leg and back pain was the strong use of the oak Kyosaku. I found getting firmly hit without warning twice on each shoulder two or three times during each round of sitting distracting and my shoulders began to ache.

During the next dokusan I related this to The Roshi.

"You'll get used to it," he said.

Hearing this I yelled and struck both my shoulders with my hands, bowed, got up, left the dokusan room and returned to my seat in the zendo. If this is what I had to endure to realize Enlightenment, I would gladly do it.

This determination did not go unnoticed. The two advanced students who were using the kyosaku began to give me extra attention in the form of getting hit harder and more often. Despite a living hell of leg pain and increasing shoulder pain, my concentration began to build exponentially. During the rounds made with the kyosaku, many practitioners yelled their koan. This was in the Japanese Rinzai tradition. I too did this, and also began growling and speaking words that were not English, or anything else for that matter. I felt electricity-like energy flowing through my hands accompanied by an overall sensation of unshakable power within this hellish environment. To concentrate on anything else but the koan Mu was for me unthinkable. Yet my mind easily wandered.

Suddenly something came to me in the form of an odd familiarity. This was little different than the sensation of being in battle in the Roman army. Terror, screaming and yelling, physical contact, pain and the ever present possibility of letting the worm of fear turn in your gut causing you to drop your sword and shield to turn and run, only to get killed on the spot by your own side, were overridden by an inexplicable self-generated energy that could carry you through anything. This was transcendent battlefield samadhi. It was what the Romans called "valour".

Before what was called "The dokusan rush," an inspiring oration was given by one of the monitors that built in crescendo, ending with a statement belted out at the top of his lungs such as, "The Truth is right before you! What are you waiting for?" This was followed by both the monitors surging like a tsunami and clobbering with kyosaku. Then a pregnant silence filled the zendo as everyone waited in anticipation for The Roshi to ring his teacher's hand bell. Hearing the distant tinkle of this tiny bell was like the firing of a starting pistol at the Olympics. The initial rush lifted everyone going to dokusan off their sitting cushions into a full-fledged gallop to get in line. Then, at the sound of the teacher's bell, each student would go into the private dokusan room and present the results of their practice to The Roshi.

I was always at the end of the dokusan rush because, unlike most, my legs would not allow me to get up quickly. Kneeling silently in front of the dokusan bell listening to somebody yelling "Mu!" and thrashing around inside a small closed room clears the mind. When the bell rang and the second last practitioner burst out of the dokusan room and headed to his seat, I entered, prostrated, and then plunked myself down eye to eye with The Roshi.

"What is your practice?" he asked.

"Mu!" I yelled.

He held his curved teachers stick in front of my face and said, "What is this?"

"Mu!" I bellowed form my guts.

"Good! Good! Just one more step and you'll be there Paul!" he said, and rang his bell.

Inspiration lifted me off the dokusan cushion and I raced back to my place in the Zendo with "Just one more step and I'll be there!"

I began to get clobbered harder and more frequently. In fact, I was getting clobbered more than anyone else in the Zendo and along with my legs and back, my shoulders were really aching.

During following dokusans, I was informed by The Roshi that it was now "just half a step" and I would be there.

Well, the sesshin ended and I had not gotten where I was supposed to be.

After the closing ceremony, one of the most senior sesshin participants said to me, "Boy, I'm glad I wasn't you!"

In the washroom, I took a look at my shoulders. Both were dark purple, and this was only a four day retreat.

The next morning I was informed that one of the monitors wanted to speak with me.

Taking me into an empty room, he took on an air of enthusiasm and said, "Well, I guess those training programs really worked!"

I thought it odd he would say such a thing. It wasn't the training programs that generated the dynamics of my practice, but my life in total. It seemed they were taking credit for something that was not theirs to take credit for.

In the months that followed The Doorchester Zen Center made a new rule that in order to become a member you had to go to at least 1 training program. I guess this was thought to be like a performance additive in gasoline to ensure high octane effects during sesshins.

I also got the nickname "Mad Dog".

The Roshi used to repeatedly point out that psychiatrists and psychologists had the highest suicide rate of any profession. I had also heard this from other sources. These days, it's supposed to be dentists. However, it is worth considering that those who are collecting and interpreting the statistics are now usually psychologists. This corresponded to my family experience with the trade, and underpinned the true worth of such an approach to the human condition.

Zen was the Way.

There was a great emphasis on commitment at The Doorchester Zen Center. It was repeatedly stated that it took great commitment to come to awakening and that this commitment was reflected in one's commitment to The Roshi and the teaching line... hopping from one teacher to the next, from one teaching line to the next as soon as difficulties were experienced was not the way of the masters of the past. I readily saw the truth of this attitude. It would be so easy to go off and look for greener pastures. A less severe teacher, one who gave approval easily seemed quite appealing. I felt that it was my own blindness that prevented me from seeing what I had vowed to realize, and that if anything else, a severe teacher was an invaluable tool.

The Roshi was fond of telling stories of Harada Roshi and his monastery, although he could only handle one year there. It made what we experienced during sesshins sound like a Girl Guide picnic. There were stories of sitting in "mosquito groves" at night in order not to fall asleep (many of us did this with mosquitoes, but only a few could stand sitting amongst some dwarf cedars located near the fence in the back yard of the Center property), sitting with a platform under your chin with a spike protruding from it so that the moment you nod off, you are brought back to Mu by getting the point, or being dragged and thrown into the dokusan room by a godo (monitor) when trying to avoid dokusan because you were terrified you couldn't show Roshi "Mu" to his satisfaction .

One of his favourite stories was of a student who, in order to not drop concentration of Mu on the last night of sesshin, somehow managed to anally impale himself on a tree branch. That night he had kensho and the next morning was certified by Harada Roshi. His underwear was "Caked in blood".

That story always struck me as not only being a little over the top, but quite weird as well.

These stories all had the ring of the more extreme cases in The Mumonkan. The Mumonkan is a set of recorded interactions that opened the Gateless Gate of Enlightenment between Chan Masters and disciples in Tang Era China. It was the basis of the Japanese koan system The Roshi inherited. First, you worked on Mu until you had "a breakthrough" after which The Roshi would assign you subsequent koans in the Mumonkan to work on. You would be passed on each koan when either your verbal answer or demonstration satisfied The Roshi. After the Mumonkan you went onto the Blue Rock Records, another Chinese compilation of Master-disciple interactions.

I did not know it at the time, but this was a relatively recent Japanese creation, implemented during the Meiji Restoration using the great work of the Chinese Chan Master Ummien. We were told that this was pure "Tang Era Zen". From the beginning I thought this statement a little peculiar considering that what we were doing were recorded cases of master-student incidents mostly from the Tang Era in China and nothing like the actual practice the original stories emerged from. It was like mistaking a butterfly collection for living butterflies.

The Roshi was unusual in that, unlike other teachers in Zen, he went to great pains to use the Chinese names of the Masters who were actually Chinese. The Japanese had given the masters that inhabited the Mumonkan and other works Japanized names to the extent you wouldn't know they were originally Chinese. In fact, at least 80 percent of Zen masters in Japanese Zen literature were actually Chinese masters. Lin Chi became Rinzai, Huang-po was Obaku, Ummien became Mummon.

The Roshi was also the first in the United States to publish a version of Charles Luk's Autobiography of Master Hsu-yun.

Every morning day and night when the Patriarchal Line was recited the Chinese Masters were always recited in their Chinese names.

The Patriarchal Line was an affirmation of the concept that transmission was something real, alive and well; a sort of verbal Shroud of Turin. It was a list beginning with Buddhas of previous world cycles transmitting transmission from Aryan Sanskrit, to Chinese, to Japanese. At that time, that's where it stopped.

At the Doorchester Zen Center there was great emphasis put on transmission. It was only those that had completed both books of koans that could qualify to get it. Of that exclusive group, I don't believe there was anyone who had been practicing less than 16 years with The Roshi. When I left the Doorchester Zen Center, there were only three or four students over a 25 year period who had received transmission. It was thought that this well groomed method of filtration produced real teachers. This proved to be a mistaken notion born of delusion.

For me, this form of practice was self-vindicating in that my afflicted mind disappeared in the living hell of sesshin. I did not need to receive recognition from The Roshi in any way except that I got clobbered on his recommendation in recognition that I could empty my mind of irrelevant thoughts. In this way I became a Zen mercenary. I was happiest living on the battlefield of sesshins. Over the years I got the feeling that although he seemed to admire and encourage me, he could not quite figure me out. I always had a sense of separation from him. It was not a lack of trust or faith in his teaching; it was as if we were quite different species of practitioner.

The palpable link between affliction and being free from it was those that dispensed the kyosaku during sesshin: the monitors. During my first ten years in that teaching line, the two advanced students that gave encouragement talks and wielded Manjusri's Sword in the form of the kyosaku usually boiled down to two people. One was a lay practitioner named Bob, the other became what was called "a monastic" and was given a Doorchester Hybrid Buddhist name, "Oneson".

In that teaching line, a "monastic" was someone who shaves his or her head, wears Japanese Buddhist monk robes, and still can have a wife or husband, house and family, … in other words they appear to be a monk while not being a monk, and not appearing to be a lay practitioner while being a lay practitioner.

Oneson was very perceptive in what encouraged practitioners during retreats. He was also very sharp in pinpointing people's weaknesses. This ability many wrongly attributed to insights acquired through Zen training giving him great opportunity for manipulation. This manipulation of course was limited by the constraints imposed upon him by The Roshi's wishes.

I was, even after years of not "getting through", one of The Roshi's "star students" on the level of do or die. If I didn't "get through", several people who sat beside me over the years did. I was beginning to think that The Roshi used me as some sort of kensho nest egg. Clobber me enough and the person sitting beside me would get enlightened. This was all right with me because it gave some meaning to what I went through. The hybrid Oneson treated me as a friend (albeit at a distance) and offered encouragement I rarely got in my life. Even though we were diametric opposites, him going from one woman to the next and being an athlete and loving the movie "Jaws" so much he saw it five times, I thought of him as a friend. Furthermore, he fitted the "Zen paradigm" The Roshi preached to an amazing closeness.

When I moved to the Toronto Affiliate Centre he was the resident leader there and was very popular having an "All American Athlete" charisma about him. He allowed me to bring my harpsichord and keep it in my room. This meant a great deal to me so that I could practice preludes and fugues. Unfortunately, the setting was not conducive to that sort of activity and I became aware that my practicing was getting irritating. To his great credit he didn't tell me to get rid of it. I even left it there while I finished up fourth year at Waterloo.

When I returned to live once again at The Toronto Affiliate of the Doorchester Zen Centre, another monastic leader was in charge. He was very different and being of German American descent, respected harpsichord music. There was something very natural, sensative and heart-felt about him. Furthermore, he, like me, also had a scientific background.

I decided that I couldn't play the harpsichord there, so I began to build a historically accurate fretted clavichord in my room. Along with the organ, the clavichord was Bach's favourite instrument because of its incredible range of nuance within very limited dynamic parameters. In other words, shut the door and you can't hear it. The pristine cleanliness and orderliness of the Zen Affiliate Centre stopped once my room was entered. Wood shavings, tools, music wire and tuning pins abounded.

The monastic leader had a sense of humour about it. Dharman, (his monastic name) was a wonderful friend with a heart-felt compassionate nature.

A Zen Pirate in training

It was at this time that my life began to take a big change. I met a Bodhisattva in the form of an attractive five foot two inch tall individual named Barbara.

The first time I met her was a couple of years before in the men's changing room of the Toronto Affiliate Centre. The men had a whole basement room to put on their meditation robes. The women had to change in a closet sized enclosure shared by a furnace. Being a "liberated woman", this simply was unacceptable for her, so she put on her robe in the men's changing room. This rebellion I thought was quite humorous. At that time she was married to a university English teacher and had a little daughter from a previous relationship. The daughter was a tough no nonsense four year old who had a habit of climbing all over anything and everything at the Centre. She and her little friend were, to my great delight, counterpoint to the austerity of The Toronto Affiliate Centre, and continuously rankled a couple of the "Zen People" who during meditation sat like incense pots. Dharman also thoroughly enjoyed their presence.

Unfortunately, Dharman did not fit into the Dorchester Zen Centre mold by not being austere or "GUNG HO" enough. He became the target of insidious criticism by some senior members, mostly behind his back. I certainly fit into the "GUNG HO" stereotype but that was the about the only component of my being that seemed to do so. I got the sense that I was becoming a koan for The Roshi. I was not a suckling politically correct individual nor socially slick. I experienced painful awkwardness in public that those near the apex of the pyramid did not seem to have. This I felt was due to my imperfections and that those individuals with charisma were leaders and future Zen teachers. All I had was an inexplicable drive to realize what I vowed to realize. As with my life in all other venues, I was a social outsider at the Dorchester Zen Centre. Dharman was like me, in a slightly different venue.

The young woman with the little girl suffered a second breakup and seemed painfully alone.

At that time women were once again beginning to come into my life.

This one was very different.

When she said she was moving to California to live with one of her sisters I felt a deep sense that I needed to take care of both her and her daughter. I had never felt that way about anyone before.

I decided to move out of the Toronto Affiliate Center and begin to form a family with both of them.

Barb and Angie

The combination of marriage and instant fatherhood was an unequalled opportunity for me to develop active compassion. The nature of compassion was always a deep question for me and it was because of this that I was fortunate enough not to be fooled into thinking it was always being nice, non-confrontational and a "buddy" to your child. This lead to a continuum of marital and paternal interactions that were not always pretty and many a time caused me to question whether what was experienced or inflicted was indeed compassionate. By not following forms of what was considered compassion such as "The One Hundred Ways to Praise a Child" I once saw posted in an Episcopal church basement for the spiritually dyslexic and disingenuous, but coming from a concern for those I lived with and the direction they tended toward, was not the easiest of paths.

Compassion is not something given from a state of perfection to those of inferior capability. It is inseparable from Enlightenment Practice. It is the life practice of awakening what is already there beyond self and other through the manifestation of self and other. Therefore, true compassion is not always pretty and open to criticism by those who do not understand. It must never be wasted on those of inferior ability because it will be misinterpreted.

Not Getting Through

Being a member of the Zen Center was being a member of a social hierarchy. This is true of any collection of human beings forming into a group. It is part of human nature.

At the top was The Roshi. Next were his advanced students, all of whom were given recognition of having realized kensho and were working on subsequent koans. By working on subsequent koans meant that you had an experience sanctioned by The Roshi. The nature of your practice was changed in that you were no longer seated in "kyosaku alley", the middle two rows of the Zendo and did not get clobbered with near the frequency or intensity of those who "had not gotten through yet".

The idea behind the clobbering was thought to induce the energy needed to punch through the Gateless Gate. But it wasn't all that simple. There were, as anywhere else, certain cliques of people, some cool, some not so cool, and, at the top of the pyramid's apex were those who were closest to The Roshi. All it took to fall to from the top of the Zen pyramid to the depths of hell was a critical statement made by The Roshi of "so and so" to others, with the target "so and so" not present.

Oneson was a perceptive student and heir to The Roshi's teaching in this regard.

There were those who "had gotten through" during their first sesshin. I guess I was a Zen Idiot because it took me eight years and around 30 seven day sesshins as well as roughly an equal number of shorter sittings following the sesshin schedule to have my seat in the zendo changed. The inevitable loud Muing, usually on the last night of a sesshin was always something to either look forward to, or dread if you were not fully immersed in Mu. This was because you bellowed Mu from your hara while your bruised or bleeding shoulders were getting clobbered with oak.

At times I started bellowing "Kannon!" the Japanized Chinese name for Kwan Yin, The Bodhisattva of Compassion.

I figured that since I hadn't gotten through Mu it must be due to some stupidity and blindness on my part and that I needed more help than the word Mu could offer. Also, being in kyosaku alley, a situation I found myself in time after time, it seemed appropriate to invoke powers of compassion because I needed them.

The most poignant memory of this predicament was the last evening dokusan of the December 1980 Rohatsu Sesshin. Of all sesshins, this was the big event, the big party. It always took place on or near the winter solstice and for that reason was charged with astrological significance as well as being a really great contrast to the notion of a Merry Christmas. It also took place during the purported date of Shakyamuni Buddha's Great Enlightenment.

It was announced that The Roshi was going to take a year off from leading sesshins. That last evening of the last night of what was billed as the last sesshin for the foreseeable future began following the evening meal with the usual silent round of meditation. As usual, ten minutes into the second round, one of the monitors quietly rose from his seat and, when the time was ripe, began the encouragement talk. In it was calmly stated that this was the last sesshin for the foreseeable future. Then the inevitable crescendo developed focusing on those who had not "gotten through".

"What are you waiting for?" the monitor pleaded, his voice reaching a new level of intensity. Hearing this, many people in kyosaku alley yelled "Mu!"

"This is the last opportunity you will have for a long time, perhaps even your last opportunity ever! It is right before your eyes! All you have to do is let go of the cliff!"

By this time there was an atonal symphony of primal sounds emanating from the aisle of the damned.

The monitor yelled, "This may be your last opportunity. WHAT ARE YOU WAITING FOR!"

At that both monitors burst upon us with fierce intensity.

After the shock wave of kyosakus fell upon the centre rows of meditators, then resurged and laid on me and a couple of others with very heavy blows, the intensity of the symphony of moans and wails of Mu subsided. The zendo was full to bursting with silent Chi energy. Its intensity glowed and permeated all things like electrified moonlight.

In the deafening silence before The Roshi rang his hand bell a peculiar thought came to me: "What am I supposed to do next? Explode?"

The rush to dokusan was particularly savage with people losing their balance and crashing to the floor, or being smashed into walls. As usual, after the carnage of the rush was over I hobbled over bodies still struggling to get to their feet and slipped out of the Zendo accelerating up the stairs. I could hear those who were close to "getting through" shouting and flailing about in the dokusan room. There were several of us in that condition, me being the most senior. This was not a comfortable distinction since it seemed to indicate a certain density. One by one their sound and fury was privately demonstrated to The Roshi. I hoped they would "get through" and, usually, if there was a pause after the commotion, it indicated that this is indeed what happened. One or two left the dokusan room with tears of joy.

I wasn't one of them.

In the incredible wind down that always accompanied the end of those sesshins, I congratulated a participant who was accepted by The Roshi.

He said to me, "Wow! This being the last sesshin for some time, I am so glad that I got through!"

I stood there in a gulf of separation generated by that statement.

"Is this the Buddha's Enlightenment?" I silently asked myself.

There was an intensifying question in my mind. I saw the behaviour of many who had "gotten through". Their actions were not always in accordance with The Precepts, sexual misconduct in the form of adultery being the most predominant. Some of it was blatant and indefensible. This was clearly not enlightened behaviour.

What was this "getting through"?

Thus, on my own, I got another koan or Hua-tou without asking for it.

Furthermore, the effects of an incident between me and The Roshi began to emerge.

I believe it was after the previous April sesshin, Dharman and I had been invited by The Roshi to have a private after-sesshin meeting in his apartment.

This was a first time honour for me.

Right from the beginning it seemed that The Roshi had it in for one of the monitors. He asked me what Bob's hitting was like, and I said it was heavier than Oneson's, and that I was having some difficulty with it. Dharman casually added another criticism that was more of an observation than anything of a complaint or maliciousness. We then left the meeting/social tea and I thought nothing more of it.

When I returned to Doorchester for the Vesak celebration, I noticed people staring at me. I had no idea why. Much later I found out that The Roshi had demoded Bob, telling him that I complained about his monitoring.

There was always great emphasis put on maintaining the secrecy of the answers to koans as well as anything else that went on between The Roshi and student.

Now people who were friends were behaving quite differently towards me. Given what I purportedly did to Bob, I couldn't blame them. By not knowing why this was happening caused my feelings of social awkwardness and being an outsider to intensify. I began to question why it was that people were down on me. Of course, nobody told me directly.

For a while I thought it was because I had left living at the Toronto Affiliate Centre and was now with Barb and Angie.

I also figured that was none of their business.

To Bob's very great credit, he treated me courteously. When he found out that Barb and I were now together he was happy, and told her that I was The Roshi's "star student", and a wonderful person. Tears come to my eyes as I recall this.

Although my lifestyle had changed completely with my new small family and place of residence, I maintained my sesshin attendance at four a year whenever possible. In order to maintain such a regimen, the only venue of income was self-employment. I joined a woodworker's co-op and worked with cabinet makers on various projects.

It was at this point that the Bodhisattva I was living with told me that she thought I should start building organs and harpsichords. I never had such encouragement to do so from anyone before in my entire life. However, given that Barb had a career in teaching with the Toronto District School Board and could not leave the Toronto area, me leaving Toronto and proximity to the Affiliate Centre to go off and apprentice (there were no real organ builders in Toronto) while maintaining a regimen of four sesshins a year was not an option.

While living at The Centre I had supported myself doing low wage jobs, usually operating metal lathes. I once had a position at an aerospace company that had all the possibilities of leading to a career, but found that asking for time off to go to seven day Zen retreats was not conducive to staying employed. I figured the same laws applied to being an organ building apprentice.

Therefore, I started studying in greater depth the scant literature on classic harpsichord building. From my experience with the particular kit and design from years before, I knew that I could design and build a better harpsichord blindfolded. And now I had reasonable woodworking facilities.

I designed and built a two manual French harpsichord closely resembling the drawing and scaling found in Frank Hubbard's "Three Centuries of Harpsichord Making". The drawing was of an instrument built by the German-French harpsichord maker Henri Hemsch in the 18th Century. I was unaware that I could buy an excellent full scale drawing of the same instrument from a printer in the U.S.

After this instrument was completed, I drew up a small business card and put it up in a sheet music store.

One evening while alone in the shop, the phone rang. It was an inquiry from the leader of an up and coming baroque music group. He asked if I would consider building them a continuo organ of three or four stops. I told him that I was very interested, but that I hadn't built an organ before. He then asked if he could see the harpsichord I had just completed. Upon seeing it, he was impressed, and told me that I could build them an organ if the price was low enough. Not being a businessman, I jumped at the offer.

In my youth I had done a significant amount of organ tuning and repair supervised by the local organ maintenance person in and around my home town (though we never worked on the mechanical action organ I later practiced on in the Anglican church). However, these were not instruments remotely suitable for Bach. If there was precious little literature on harpsichord making, there was even less on building classic mechanical action organs. At that point in time, the English translation of Dom Bedos' classic 18th Century text was not available. All I had to go on was George Ashdown Audsley's "The Art of Organ building" written from an Early 20th Century American/British perspective which was practically useless unless you were a Cavaillé-Coll fan, or worse.

The elegance, clarity and inherent simplicity of the organs of Bach's time had all but been lost with the introduction of modern engineering in the form of electro pneumatic and electrical actions, high wind pressure, nicked voicing and non key-channel wind chests. Pipe scaling was now logarithmic, conforming to mathematical laws. This "SCIENTIFIC" approach was thought to converge to musical truths unavailable to earlier master craftsmen. The only problem was that the instruments produced in this fashion were abject failures in the performance of Bach, Buxtehude, Sweelinck as well as a great many modern contrapuntal works. These new "modern" instruments were usually enormous in size, their speech flatulent, blurry and their actions sometimes slow and at best remote. Mechanically, they were more like pinball machines than something resembling a violin. Clearly the Northern German, Dutch and Danish organs of the 17th and 18th Centuries were far superior to what was built throughout the first half of the 20th Century. This was because the master organ builders used their sense of hearing instead of a book of logarithms. The emphasis on voicing was not some castrated laminar ideal but clarity, incisiveness and the flexible harmonic architecture peculiar to the organ. The organs of Bach's time were not an attempt to imitate the sounds of a symphony orchestra. They were not marble mouthed god boxes grunting out anthems of childish reassurance in an impermanent world. They were organs, sharp swords of the Northern European psyche, dragons of the sky and earth coming to meet through the hexagram of our sense of hearing.

But this was all forgotten. And it happened very quickly. The classic organ stopped being built. Only those old instruments in Northern German churches, the churches of Denmark and The Netherlands still existed. Where funds were available, many of them were ruined by electrification, or completely torn out and replaced. The harpsichord and clavichord ended up in museums or inside wood stoves and their design and methods of construction were completely forgotten, unjustly overshadowed and replaced by the piano. The music of Bach, Buxtehude and Vivaldi was also forgotten. It was termed "old fashioned" or "obsolete", only to experience a rebirth 200 years later.

This impermanence through ignorance made a very deep impression on me. Was this true about Western Religion of eons past? Shakyamuni Buddha spoke Sanskrit, a language that came from outside India and shares the same basis as Latin, German and most other European languages. Like the Northern Celts up until 900 years ago, the Aryan tribes of The Buddha's time who spoke Sanskrit did not always form their knowledge into written words but rather passed it down in spoken form. When they did write it was in the powerful magic of Runes and other symbols; the Swastika, the Siegel, the Celtic knot, Ygdrusil or The Tree of Life… Even today when words are put to letters, it is said that they are "spelled". That is because the Roman letters we use had their basis in Runes, and each letter was a certain spell.

Current accepted thought says that I have gotten this all backwards. Scholars these days think that Runes were copied imitations of pre-existing Roman and Greek written letters given magical meaning by the Celts in the temporal period after Julius Caesar. However, the forgotten proto Sanskrit speaking civilization that formed Indian, Ancient Greek and Roman languages, along with their written symbols, initially created these written symbols in their most fundamental direct meaning as spells.

The letters on this page are therefore a series of runic configurations forming interrelating spells, like a multiple part fugue.

In 1980 I had come up with a design for the 4 stop continuo organ I was to build. It was a simple key scale slider wind chest and would contain 216 pipes. It was at this point that an established organ builder who emigrated from Germany dropped by. He had just recently set up shop in a town outside of Toronto and was looking for people to work for him. His enthusiasm for me vanished when, in the course of conversation, I mentioned that I was building a continuo organ for a music group that he had also submitted an offer to. I had beat him in getting the contract because he was asking for over twice the money.

When I quietly mumbled the price I was committed to he said, "Oh mien Gott!"

He was right. I had no idea what I was getting into.

Pastoral Life

Shortly after that meeting, the beautiful old building housing my shop became slated for demolition. It was at this point that I began to weigh the financial possibilities of moving while my project was underway. Adding up what Barb and I were spending on rent for both apartment and shop led me to the conclusion that if we combined both expenses in owning a house with a room or two devoted to building small musical instruments, then not only would we save money while I maintained going to Zen retreats, we would have investment collateral as well. My machinery composing of a band saw, thickness planer/jointer and table saw were all quite small and of high quality, made from high impact aluminium castings. They were therefore very space effective and light. The only problem was the noise and any neighbour's perception of it. Given that it took over half an hour of travel time to get from our place of residence to either my shop, Barb's work or the Zen Affiliate, I came to the conclusion that the most expedient thing would be to buy an isolated farmhouse outside the city.

This idea was exciting for both of us. It was exciting for me because I had, discounting the time Mom was taken away, very fond memories of farm life at my grandmother's and grandfathers, and being from a small town, country life was more what I was drawn to. For Barb, the attraction was that she had never done it before, having grown up in the city. Furthermore, the deteriorating quality of the city neighbourhood Angie was going to school in concerned me. I knew from experience that these problems were far less intense in small towns. Also, farmhouse prices were then a fraction of the price of city houses.

With this attitude Barb and I piled into my heaterless pre-abused Volkswagen Van and drove North of Toronto in search of a house.

It was early December 1980.

After being guided by a real estate agent to a small house situated on the edge of what was referred to as Luther Marsh, it turned out there was nobody home to let us in, so we were taken to another house for sale in the little farming town of Shelburne. There we were introduced to the husband of the born again Christian family renting the facilities who was in the process of building a life-sized cross in the basement. Besides this activity, the place had a very weird feeling about it that culminated in an object inexplicably flying off a wall and hurtling cross the room as if thrown in anger. The landlord giving us the tour straightened and said nothing. I got the impression that this sort of thing happened quite frequently within those premises. That was more than enough and we decided we didn't want to see anything more.

We gave up and went to a restaurant for dinner.

Our table faced a large window. While eating, I noticed a real estate company cross the road. Although it was getting late we went over and checked it out. The agent said he might have what we were looking for, so once again we piled into the Volkswagen and followed his car deep into the countryside in failing light. The road became more and more remote in the surrounding darkness as the terrain became more and more a series of steep hills. I couldn't believe the pitch of the last hill we traveled down before the car ahead of us turned down a farm lane. It felt like I was driving a rollercoaster.

There was nothing else around. No Lights. Solid darkness, save for a full moon rising over the horizon.

Nobody was home. The lonely old brick farmhouse nestled in a deep valley was indeed isolated and, standing at its door, formed an ominous dark silhouette against the night sky. It was being used as a weekend cottage severed from the hundred acres its original inhabitants once farmed.

Shadowed from the full moon, the real estate agent fumbled for the keys, then let us in.

Upon turning on the lights a strong welcoming presence surrounded us. It seemed the house clearly liked us and an unmistakable feeling came over me that this would be a good place to practice. My first impression was the same feeling as Trivitt Memorial Church used to give me. It was certainly from the same era.

The dimmer switch in the kitchen was the same as the zendo at the Zen Affiliate in Toronto. Furthermore, the doors were very well made and were still fitted with the original 19th Century external cast iron latch mechanism I fondly remembered from my grandparent's farm house.

These were perhaps not the most logical and reasonable reasons to buy a house. However, Barb liked the place too, probably for different equally illogical reasons, so we decided to put in an offer that night.

Our offer was quickly accepted.

Since Barb's teaching career was quite tenuous because of funding cuts and a surplus of her colleagues and I had nothing much to show in the way of business profits or assets, we were directed by the real estate agent to a mortgage broker who had connections with bank workers. In this way we qualified to get a first and second mortgage while the owner of the house through desperation gave as a third.

In this way we qualified to buy the house.

After the purchase was made, the mortgage broker then revealed to us the wonderful possibilities of financial gain through membership under his guidance in Amway. He did this because he knew we needed to generate a lot of money that was not showing up on my side of the equation.

Before the deal closed I drove from my shop to the house to check everything out. The oil furnace was humming away and both its 200 hundred gallon fuel tanks were full.

Everything was fine.

Through strange coincidence, the deal closed on my birthday.

With the kind help from a Zen Affiliate friend, we rented a large panel van, loaded up all of our belongings, and headed north. The pitch of the hills once again impressed me. It had now snowed considerably and things were a little slippery. Upon arriving at the top of the lane to the house, it struck me how steep its downhill gradient was.

The van shot down the lane as if it were on rails. After an uneventful unloading, I fired it up, turned it around and headed nose first back up the lane to the road.

It didn't make it.

The rear drive wheels began to slip and forward progress diminished, even though I knew enough to reduce throttle setting so that traction was maximized. This resulted in slowly backing down the lane and having another go at it. After three or four attempts including putting everyone in the back over the drive wheels, the lane had gotten very icy. It was during the backing up phase that traction disappeared enough and the van slid off the lane and into a deep depression, leaving the vehicle precariously tilted with no hope of emerging under its own power.

I got out, walked to the top of the lane and surveyed the situation in the failing light. Out in the middle of nowhere the van was tilted at a thirty degree angle beside a laneway that had no way out except up.

A ball of fear rose inside me. Written cross the cargo box in elegant script was the slogan, "An adventure in moving!"

It was quite cold, so, with nothing else to do, I returned to the warmth of the house. Before getting in my sleeping bag situated on the floor, and turning down the thermostat from the 72 degree Fahrenheit setting it was at when we arrived, something told me to go down into the basement and once again check the level of the furnace oil tanks.

To my horror both were practically empty. A wave of panic washed over me. Four hundred gallons in less than four weeks! This furnace had the fuel consumption of a 747!

Fortunately, there was a wood stove. However, there was no wood.

After the local towing service extracted the moving van from the side of our lane, the final bits of moving were done with my Volkswagen van. We didn't dare drive it down the icy lane, so I bought a toboggan and put our cargo on it. To my surprise, I found that I could get on the toboggan too and the complete package of me and cargo kept on moving down the lane right to the house.

One of the last things out of the van was Barb's bicycle. I told her that the lane was very slippery and to walk it down. Instead she jumped on the bike, yelled "Ya Hooooo!" and shot downhill over ice and snow through the barnyard gate, almost hitting the barn door. At least one of us was enjoying themselves.

Not knowing what Amway was, but fully knowing I needed a second source of income, I went to one of their meetings. For me it was like being abducted into a U.F.O. full of aliens, coming from a universe of dimensional paradigms I didn't share, so I left the mother ship without going for the ride.

I would have to make my money building organs, although any sane look at our financial situation indicated we wouldn't last six months.

After everything had settled it seemed to me that I had bit off a way more than I could chew. Yes, theoretically Barb's commute wasn't temporally any longer than before but it was on open highway and over a far greater distance. Very few people were doing that daily commute in those days. The cost of heating was far greater than I had anticipated and there was the desperate pre-dawn exercise of repeatedly putting steel ice grab devices under the rear tires of the van so that it could inch up and out of the lane and onto the road.

With three mortgages, one at twenty percent interest and a bottomless heating bill, I faced building a portable pipe organ in what was a farm house living room decorated with wall paper depicting 18th Century ladies, gentlemen, and carriages. I was now considerably behind schedule and running out of money to buy materials. What bothered me the most was letting down my client by going bankrupt.

To make things worse the musical group I was building the organ for had scheduled an inaugural concert for the instrument. It was going be a series of organ concertos featuring the famous harpsichord/organist Colin Tilney.

The pressure I was under was enormous. With Barb teaching in Toronto and frequently staying overnight at her sister's and Angie away all day at school and quite often staying at her little friends' homes, I was operating woodworking machinery in isolation. One slip at the jointer could mean immediate amputation in a setting that was not conducive for things like ambulances getting to or leaving. The only transportation I had to get to the nearest hospital approximately twelve miles away was three bicycles.

This situation fueled a grim Zen attitude within me. Each moment was on the edge and there was no place to find comfort. When we sat in meditation each morning before Barb bravely drove off to work, it was like we were both mediating on the precipice of disaster.

Sesshins were now like heaven to me.

The prevailing wind was cross the road. I had never before lived in a place with such strong and frequent wind. Sometimes in January it would take only fifteen minutes for the road to totally disappear under six foot deep drifts forming off the growing mountain of snow piled at roadside by the grader. The grader itself got stuck on several occasions, not being able to climb the hill in front of our house while pushing a wall of snow even though all its drive wheels were fitted with serious chains. Because of this they stopped plowing beyond the entrance to our lane leaving what appeared to be a glacial cliff, at times more than seven feet high over the road. By law they had to keep access open to our house. However, little Angie had to walk half a mile to catch the school bus. Many times our road was totally "socked in" causing Angie to stay at her friend's home and Barb to stay in Toronto. During those weeks we had to leave our car half a mile from the house and toboggan in supplies.

Despite all this the old house felt friendly, and the natural surroundings it was nestled in were incredibly beautiful. Barb thoroughly loved it.

Many a time I turned on the tap in the kitchen and lifted a glass of clear water to the light.

"Look at that!" I would say, "Pure water with no fluoride or chlorine!"

I would then drink it down.

This took a sudden turn one evening that first spring after a warm spell lasted long enough for snow in the barnyard where the well happened to be to turn to slush.

After making it home from work, Barb was relaxing in the bathtub while it filled. Suddenly, the water turned a putrid brownish red. This was too much for her and she began to cry. Up until that point she was very happy with her new surroundings and, once being a university cheer leader, was giving me team support.

Now, in less than an instant, the table was turned.

I grabbed a flashlight, put on my rubber boots and strode out into pitch darkness. The well, nestled under a large maple tree in the barnyard, had the hood off a 1967 Chevy Impala covering it. For the first time I slid it off the well's mouth and shone the flashlight down its depths.

What I saw almost caused me to throw up into it. Cow manure, leaves and what might have been a dead ground hog floated on its surface. I drew back in revulsion.

We had been drinking out of that. To this day I can't explain why we didn't get cholera and die. If we had, nobody would have found us for a month or two at least.

When spring finally came and one could get down the lane and out again safely, the old farmer who had cattle on the land surrounding us and apparently once owned a 1967 Chevy Impala entered the house without knocking.

"Like it up here?" he asked, then without waiting for an answer added, "Wouldn't be so bad if it weren't for the goddamned hills. Nobody lives in this house for very long, you know."

For my entertainment he left a pile of yellowed legal documents comprising of all the former deeds of the 100 acre farm and house since the day it was built. It seemed that nobody lasted there much longer than ten or fifteen years, same as little as one or two. There was even a long period in the early 1960's when the house was left abandoned.

That first winter the plumbing froze and burst in the crawlspace under the kitchen floor. I spent a couple of days wedged on my back between mud and floor rafters fighting off claustrophobia while armed with a flashlight, blow torch and a coil of solder.

The 19th Century doorknobs I found so charming had an uncanny habit of pulling off in my hand no matter how diligently I tightened the setscrew. This made me figure that they had been all been taken out of a box and put in place in order to sell the house. To this day few of the doors have knobs.

The old Volkswagen van finally managed to make it to a place near the front door of the house and had a mechanical stroke. There it stayed for 13 years becoming a lumber storage container holding quarter sawn white oak boards of 8 foot length protruding over the driver and passenger seats for wooden organ pipes and case work. These would be wrestled out of the van and through the front door of the house into my 16 foot long living room shop, cut down to a little over required length with a hand saw then jointed and planed.

One day during a January blizzard I was out getting a couple of boards from the van. Despite the conditions, I had to leave the house door wide open so that I could easily get inside while carrying the long boards.

Just as I had both boards in hand, the gale force wind slammed the house door shut. This door was fitted with a heavy-duty automatic locking bolt. Unfortunately it was set in locked mode and I found myself dressed in only a work shirt, jeans and running shoes holding two eight foot boards of rough oak while standing in a forty knot white out. Not having functional latches of a conventional sort, all the other doors were bolted shut from inside. There was no choice but to go into the shed, get the axe, and hack out the lower panels of a leeward kitchen door, then crawl head first through the hole.

Within my living room workspace space was a woodstove with a large top loading door. This proved to be the greatest of convenience since I could help heat the house with scrap. A great deal of this scrap took the form of planer chips. With no dust collection system, the oak planer chips would blow out the top of my combination jointer/ planer and rain down onto the floor like snow. Once the pile got deep enough I would put on a welding glove, open the top of the wood stove and dump a couple of shovels full of chips over glowing embers. Thick gray smoke filled the combustion chamber and was drawn up the chimney. Quite a bit escaped into the room. I would then slam the lid shut, stand back and wait for the inevitable explosion to lift the cast iron lid a couple of inches and blow smoke out the stove's intake. Then the shop turned into a sauna in January. It was an insurance company's nightmare that fortunately they didn't know about.

We had adopted a little barn cat who had full run of the house including my shop. One morning after rapidly shovelling the combustion chamber full of chips and the resultant explosion and cloud of smoke, the room filled with an aroma emanating from the bowels of hell. I looked over to the little fellow standing in the corner. He returned my glance with an expression of disbelief as if to say, "I didn't think you'd burn it!"

I left the shop slamming the door behind me. This happened quite frequently until it stopped bothering me. It's surprising what you get used to, especially when you have guests.

Hard at work meditation

Voicing a wood pipe

Operating a shop in rural isolation is the antithesis of convenience.

If you were using a number drill and it broke near its shank so it couldn't be re-sharpened, the closest place you could get one was about an hour's round trip drive in a car I didn't have. The same applied for drive belts, wood screws and a wide variety of other things. To have such things delivered usually meant a fee that was an order of magnitude greater than the price of the object of desire with the added winter and spring bonus of the delivery van getting stuck trying to get up the lane and me spending an afternoon helping it onto the road.

Spring eventually arrived and after the frost left the road, the whole thing turned to a bottomless pit of mud. Mud was worse than snow because there was an unending supply of it beneath the wheels. Digging it away was therefore not much of an option. Of course, the road being such a challenge attracted the four wheel drive off-roading fanatics who would chew it up into a soup of deep ruts. These ruts would then freeze overnight creating rock hard sharp serrated edges that made short work of CV boots and other expensive components found under most vehicles. Even the road grader stopped coming to the top of the lane. The road would wash out every spring as torrents of newly released water gushed cross it. There was a wonderful background roar accompanying this.

Such a spring was a powerful experience. I loved the isolation and the challenges that the road, land and house provided. It was quite remarkable in that only a mile away, things were very much easier and civilized. Farms were easily accessed and business activities as well as school bus services were about the same as anywhere else. We had situated ourselves in hell's little valley on a section of road that was legendary amongst the locals.

Hearing the first redwing blackbird of spring was a powerful experience.

Robins!

Despite a seasonal improvement in conditions, there was no getting away from work because it was very unmistakably in our living room. The project was extremely behind schedule and the only way it would move forward was through my efforts. I had to personally make 108 oak organ pipes of 8' and 4' pitch, and along with another 108 metal pipes of 2 foot and 1 1/3 foot pitch made in Europe, fit them into a case 4 feet high, 3 feet wide and 28" deep that would sit on a 3 foot high base containing the wind system. Unlike most organ builders, I also made the keyboard, wind chest, stop action and wind reservoir instead of ordering them from a supplier. Furthermore, unlike many other continuo organs, I designed mine chromatic down to low C. This meant more long bass pipes had to be mitred and fit into the case. However, the instrument was more versatile by not needing to be tuned each time a work in a different key was chosen. Das Woltemperierte Klavier could be played without interruption.

The whole thing had to be portable. I designed the metal pipe's scale and display configuration, chose their alloy content and had them made in Holland by Jaques Stinkens, a famous organ pipe making shop.

Finished 4 Stop Positif Organ with Pedal Board ready to deliver

Positif Organ with case doors open and panels removed.

Progress for the organ was not in any way close to what I had projected. I told them I couldn't meet the deadline for the concert. This caused a very understandable degree of concern on their end.

Although only the pipes I had made were voiced and fitted, they sent Colin Tilney out to see what was going on. As he played, a ray of light emerged from my troubled heart. The music flowing from him was the voice of compassion itself.

When he stopped he smiled to his friend who accompanied him.

"I like this little organ," he said.

At those words I experienced heaven.

"I'll talk to the orchestra and have them change their concert plans," he said.

This forced change did not endear me to my clients.

Every time I looked out my shop window I saw our closest neighbour standing a quarter mile distant on the large hill to the west. This neighbour stared back with the empty eye sockets of glassless windows consuming light within a farmhouse abandoned for over thirty years. It was still covered in cedar shakes and faint remnants of what was once a tasteful earth red window trim. Derelict, the spine of its roofline had long been broken. It loomed prominent on the Western horizon coming in and out of vision like a mirage during January whiteouts. What was once a pretty little house was now an eerie monument of dreams crushed by back breaking farm work and the violence of wind in an open field.

Twice a year the full moon would set behind it. There was nothing more haunting yet beautiful.

The demon fear of failure was my constant companion. It played on me every moment I worked and strengthened with every difficult situation. My only recourse was the sesshin practice I had found refuge in. In Dhyana or Zen practice, work meditation is fundamental. For those not beyond easy and difficult, work meditation practice is the most difficult. The energy of staying focused on work so easily diverts to other things not work related.

The greater the power of one's practice the greater the power of demons attracted and generated when the slightest separation is allowed.

The sesshin practice I had made my refuge was relatively severe. The daily life situation I found myself in was also severe and surreal as well. However, in isolation there are no external forms to guide one through each moment. I would like to say that each day was a day with The Buddha. However, for me each day seemed to be a day locked up with Mara.

I had no choice but to continuously enter Zen practice, fail, fall down, get up and begin again as if nothing had happened. Buddhist Dhyana retreat training in this situation is invaluable because it is this very thing.

I naturally began some unusual practices like walking up our icy 300 foot snow covered lane and back in my bare feet dressed in nothing but a kimono style bathrobe in January. I also went out to the well at the barn for drinkable water in blizzards wearing open sandals and the same bath robe. In fact, my favorite attire while not operating machinery was either my meditation robe, or bathrobe. Both were of similar design. The Japanese warrior art of bushido felt familiar and fitted with my intense sense of impermanence and fear of shame associated with failure.

Periods of sitting meditation over 2 days in length were very rarely done outside of sesshins because I was always behind in work.

Barb would come home after over an hour's drive from work and the kitchen would be a mess. I had usually not got done what I set out to do that day and was reeling in frustration. This was the perfect conditions for marital fights. Barb was an excellent marital artist in this regard; something I learned to respect. I would never live with someone with weak convictions.

I was equally as good at fighting. All hell would break out further upsetting both of us, and making my situation feel all the more hopeless. Angie would go upstairs and either watch T.V. or talk on the phone for long periods with her little friends. Unfortunately, all her little friends were in what was then a separate phone jurisdiction so that the rate for her doing so was twenty cents a minute.

In this isolation punctuated with fights as well as moments of great appreciation, the beauty of the land sometimes turbulent and sometimes glisteningly serene with boundless unpolluted night skies naturally honed my sensitivity to unseen things. I took responsibility for the demonic lusts of thought that came and went by accompanying them with a natural sense of shame and a vow to do better. In this way they had less power over me, even if I could not rid myself of them. I also became aware of benevolent presences and an abyss of historical experiences and truths opened to me. Some of these presences were ancestral beings inseparable from Bodhisattvas. Many of the historical experiences and truths were not the same as taught by conventional wisdom or found in history text books used in school. At the time I wrote many of these things off as delusions stemming from an overactive imagination until much later they began to emerge as historically correct through modern empirical historical examination outside of established controlled thought.

A Little Portatif Organ with classic winding.

Another little instrument.

Furry Teachers

It was at this point that we brought into our lives a female Siberian Husky pup. Angie gave her the name "Misty" because of the foggy spring day when we first brought her home from the kennel.

Siberian Huskies do not consider themselves dogs. Furthermore, this domineering pup considered herself far above the pinnacle of being a Husky. Since she was much faster than me on foot and could catch a running jack rabbit in her teeth (something I never tried, but probably would have trouble doing), she privately considered herself to be superior to human beings too. She was a true little bitch in every way.

A year later, after a brief but romantic affair with "Nanook", she had a litter of five surprisingly large chipmunk sized purebred puppies.

Siberian Huskys share the same code of ethics as wolves. This we found to be a combination of canine Bushido that included on the male side macho refined intelligence that could in a moment write the book on violence, and an appreciation of the female principal, while on the other side, female grace, intelligence and appreciation of the male principal while also being an excellent co-author of the book on violence.

Our family was now both human and other-than-human. I saw that many of the great character strengths embodied in these beings shone far brighter than in many beings of human form. Their ability to bear and endure while following simple convictions was an enormous and profound inspiration. In mornings following a heavy snowfall they were nowhere to be seen, save for the presence of snow covered Tao Symbols. Then one by one, each husky would emerge up out of the snow, shake themselves off, and then casually stretch. On sunny days in deep sub-zero weather they would lay out on the snow as if on a Caribbean beach.

There were two male pups. One was larger and heavier set than the other and I assumed he would be the leader. The other was a peculiar little fellow of a more wiry nature, having one blue eye and the other brown.

I named him Fenner. Fenner did not look at you, he looked through you. This had a certain disquieting effect on both dogs and people.

One day after turning off the thickness planer I heard a series of unearthly shrieks coming from the kennel. Upon racing outside I was greeted with a visage of Misty standing over her half full grown pup Fenner as he lay on his back screaming for mercy. Her jaws were firmly clamped on his neck while she emanated a low pitched growl. After he stopped shrieking, she snapped her head powerfully from side to side in a neck-breaking technique that caused another round of shrieks.

Knowing well enough to never get my hand inserted into a husky fight, I grabbed a 2 x 4 and levered them apart. As soon as Misty was away from Fenner and could clearly see me, I let go a couple of heavy hand slaps on her hind quarters.

"What are you trying to do! Kill him?" I yelled.

Misty sat down and looked at me as Fenner managed to get back on all fours and bolt away.

As soon as I left the kennel and returned to the house the shrieking began again.

As I emerged once again with the 2 x 4 in hand something came over me and I stopped.

Fenner was on his back, once again in his mother's jaws. I watched Misty apply pressure while growling and snap her head from side to side as if to break the terrified pup's neck and realized that if that was her intention, it would have been all over in less than a second. Something else was at work here that I didn't understand. Why was she picking on him and not the others? About all I could figure was that she thought a near death experience would look good on his resume.

It became obvious in the months that followed that Fenner's bigger and heavier brother was not the leader of the pack. He did not have the incisive power Fenner had. Misty saw this when I couldn't and her over-the-top severe treatment was necessary for his development.

She never attacked him again after that. In fact, she made a point of having little to do with any of the now mature pups, focusing instead on a position closer to the privileged human side of things. Thus by severe teaching, she guarded the strength and survival of the pack. This display of natural, non-politically correct wisdom made a deep impression on me. I would recall this teaching in later years.

Living in isolation with these intense beings developed a bond beyond form. I realized the Germanic name Wolfgang did not come from shallow roots.

I bought a beautiful mortise, tenoned and lashed dog sled and spent countless hours yelling "GEE" and "HAW" at my lead dog Fenner who knew that it was he who was actually in control of sled and team. They naturally followed paths and when we were on one, I could shut up. Then we sped in dynamic silence cross open fields and dodged trees looming in perilous forest turns. Once again in the open and off a path, Fenner knew I was standing on the back of the sled yelling at him to go either right or left because that's what I did, and therefore chose to ignore me. As a team they also came to the realization that they could go much faster without me standing on the runners, so each time I fell off or was otherwise dumped, they took off and left me to walk for miles following their tracks.

A Change in Practice

I DID JOIN THE RANKS OF THOSE WHO HAD "GOTTEN THROUGH MU". IT came unannounced and without drama during a spring sesshin in 1983.

During the morning service, I was calmly chanting The Heart Sutra along with everybody else. Suddenly I felt a sensation of clarity and certain meanings in the Sutra opened to me. I did not mention this to anyone and passed it off as something far short of the enlightenment I had vowed to realize. Nevertheless, the moment I entered the dokusan room, The Roshi saw that something was different. He asked me several questions and was pleased with the answers.

Then he told me something I have ever since been grateful for.

He said, "Paul, I want to show you something".

He drew a circle with his teacher's stick on the mat in front of him.

"This is enlightenment," he said.

He then placed the tip of the stick on the imaginary line forming the circle.

"This is you", he stated, then added, "Actually, all this doesn't exist."

Without any pause for reflection his face became aglow.

"I am going to change your practice to the koan, "What is the root of Mu?" he said.

"When working on subsequent koans, there need not be any forceful striving. At first this will seem easy."

His expression then became grim as he added, "But that sensation won't last."

I returned to my seat not knowing what happened. I continued working in my normal way knowing that something in the form of realization had come to me, but that it was far short of what I had set out to do. Therefore, what happened didn't matter much. It wasn't good enough.

Had The Roshi said, "Yes, this is Mu! You have gotten through…" as he apparently had told others, I would have got up and left. Why? I still realized I was consumed by affliction. I did not want an Oscar for a dokusan room performance. He was sharp enough to see this.

Working on subsequent koans had its perks. Outside of leg pain, Sesshin practice became much more pleasant because I wasn't getting clobbered so much.

After eight years of getting clobbered, I was finally given a rokusus. A rokusus is an intricately stitched cloth square worn around the neck as a Japanese abbreviated form of the Buddha's robe. Right up to that point, wearing a rokusus at the Doorchester Zen Center meant that its wearer had "gotten through". Therefore, the prestige associated with this piece of attire was quite high for some. For others, not having one caused a great deal of anguish. Therefore, in the spirit of equality, the rule was changed so that instead of "getting through", a rokusus was given after being a full Doorchester Zen Center member for a two year period. I can't remember if I got it before or after this change in qualifications.

What meant a great deal to me was that my Buddhist name given to me by The Roshi was inscribed on its back. It read, "Given to Laughing Cloud by Roshi, November, 1983." I removed the plastic circle ring that linked the neck piece replacing it with one I turned out of Lignum Vitae, a dark brownish-green rare wood of the greatest hardness.

I had been given the same form of name as The Roshi's two teachers, Daiun (Great Cloud) Sogaku and Hakuin (White Cloud) Ryoko, as well as Hakuin Zenji and most importantly, Xu-yun (Empty Cloud) whose autobiography, published by The Roshi, I had read three times. I was very honoured by this name and vowed to make a sincere attempt to live up to the tradition of those great masters.

It was shortly after receiving my rokusus that the former Toronto Zen Affiliate Centre leader and sesshin monitor was now back in Toronto.

I was overjoyed.

He had been in Poland leading the Center there for a year or two and had not yet received transmission from The Roshi. There seemed to be some sort of problem and he was not in position to take over the Doorchester Zen Center when The Roshi retired.

This seemed strange.

His style was very similar to the traditional Zen attitude of The Roshi, being heavily into the Japanese paradigm of hard practice without watering it down with psychology. The monastic, whose hybrid name was Baldone, was now in favour of taking over. Having a degree in psychology, he was heavily into its practice and thought it to be an integral part of the Western psyche rather than the result of controlled media marketing.

I knew that this Western media/educational system promotion of psychology was a recently invented fallacy. In Western thought, physics, engineering and mathematics go back over five thousand years to what was the basis of The Hermetica and beyond. Psychology was created within the last 120 years.

I had always marvelled at the depravity of the many "scientific" animal-as-machine experiments conducted in the name of psychology to define the parameters of what they called "mind". I knew that the attitude in physics towards many of these experiments was that of shaking one's head in marvel of their callous nature.

"This is an experiment?" was a common question emerging from many trained in physics, chemistry or engineering after becoming aware of certain examples of psychological methodology. I loved animals, as did many of my colleagues in the real sciences.

Of course, I also knew that there were compassionate people in psychology that did try to help others. I had met some. I had also met some who were better described as demons feeding off human misery both by paycheck and position.

There are certain things in the way of classification of action/reaction associations and perceptual forms people take that can be good to know, but these classifications in practice are more often than not quite naïve and useless. Psychological diagnosis is like referring to a book full of two dimensional pictures of birds and giving them Greek names. Then the pictures and Greek names are taken as the reality of birds. This is once again the question of observer–phenomenon separation. Years later I began to classify psychologists and psychiatrists as entertainment for psychopaths. I arrived at this from direct experience. Besides instances reported by the media, at least two bona fide psychopaths I had dealings with were married to psychologists and a third was a psychologist.

What was shaping up in the way of teaching inheritance in Doorchester I put down to Zen Center politics. Oneson was a person who had given me so much encouragement over the years and I looked forward to working with him. However, he could also be incredibly cold and able to hit you at your weakest.

When this happened, I would say to myself, "What do you want, a friend or a teacher?"

I did everything I could to get Oneson in position in Toronto as resident teacher. Part of this was in gratitude for the encouragement and help he provided during sesshins.

He had returned with a new woman interest from Poland. Doorchester was still dragging its feet about giving him permission to teach so he quickly went to a Japanese Buddhist Church in Toronto and married her. This seemed to do the trick and he received the teaching title "Sensei" from The Roshi in a special ceremony.

Of all the members at the Toronto Affiliate Centre, I was the most senior in number of sesshins participated in. There were others who were more senior in years, but rarely took the time and sacrifice to attend sesshins.

I had never been rejected to attend a sesshin with Roshi. I was part of the inner core of his arduous practitioners that formed the heart of Zen Centre practice. However, I also believed that practice should be for its own sake and not for gain of status within social systems. This was not a common attitude amongst the demonstrated arduous and many made the socio-political move of being a celebrity in the form of what was considered Zen spontaneity, popularity at social events and the resultant ability of getting elected to the directing committee. From this perspective it could be clearly seen that practice was not the only motivation for these denizens. I had meditated with them over the years in intense sesshins and knew that they began practice very seriously. They had very strong issues that needed to be resolved. But, when they were given recognition and acceptance by The Roshi and entered social cliques that were close to him, status and the resultant power over others became their driving force. Their practice was all but dead. When they did go to sesshins, they went as subsequent koan practitioners and the whole form of their practice was different than those who had not yet "gotten through" thus adding to the temptation of falling into the pit of Zen elitism. The most glaring thing about this was that they were unaware of their selling out. Seeing this, I made it my personal practice of staying away from these pitfalls. When I went to sesshin I went as if I hadn't realized much of anything because my own personal introspection told me I really hadn't. Looking in the mirror was for me seeing the face of Yama Raja.

It became painfully obvious that people in general were fooled by these popularity climbers by thinking that they were true practitioners. I realized how easy it would be to trick others into thinking one is enlightened by hanging around a Zen centre and picking up the mannerisms of senior practitioners. And even worse I realized how easy it was to fool oneself into thinking that by passing some hurdle with a teacher, one has the Buddha's Enlightenment. This is making the practice of not mistaking the finger for the moon into mistaking the finger for the moon. Without knowing it they traded their precious jewel of practice for a dumpster filled to bursting with raw sewage.

By working on a documented case of a famous Chan Master, demonstrating it before your teacher and then receiving acceptance of your understanding to move onto the next case incites one to think that you are the equal of that particular Master. Thus, Koan system practice becomes something little different than the Pavlovian control system of formal education. However, it is thought that since it is called "Zen" and by definition Zen is the heart of Mahayana Buddhism, then the results of such a practice, along with the numerous teacher sanctions should be the Buddha's Enlightenment. Therefore, such a form of teaching should be The Buddha's Teaching.

Seeing how many people who had this sanctioning behaved, as well as some saying statements such as "This is the form aspect of such and such and this is the emptiness aspect of such and such," when from my experience I could not separate by distinction either, lead me to question the validity of their realization. Furthermore what we were practicing was not the practice of those masters but something more akin to literary criticism of miniature plays of great profundity.

I was most fortunate. I had an impetus for true realization that most people didn't because my life was a nightmare of constant inner stress in isolation surrounded by a beautiful natural setting.

A Great Responsibilty

With a new teacher, membership at the Toronto Affiliate Centre grew. I drove to Toronto twice and sometimes three times a week to take part in evening sittings and weekend Teishos (Zen lectures). Furthermore, we started to have sesshins and I was asked by Oneson Sensei to be the monitor. This was a very great honour and responsibility. I was now helping lead sesshins in the style and form of classic Roshi sesshins and quickly became a skilled monitor. This was because I had so much experience on the receiving end of the art. All the sesshins I helped lead and later led on my own were very precious opportunities for all involved to transcend human suffering by immersing in it. I truly felt that sitting through a week long pressure cooker of leg pain with competent, carefully applied encouragement from the kyosaku was an experience unequalled in possibilities for realization. On my own part, I was passing koans at a very fast rate.

Even though I had private misgivings about the koan system's validity, I was seduced by the feeling of progress towards an end.

I rarely went to Doorchester anymore. My sesshin practice was now in Toronto.

The Centre needed an altar for the beautiful gold Chinese Buddha figure given to us as a gift from Doorchester. It was the original figure that sat through so many sesshins there in the past. It was an honour for me to make this altar.

I designed and built it for free. The only payment received was my material costs.

I did get help.

Many people from the Polish Zen Centre Affiliate had come to live in Toronto and practice with Oneson Sensei. One of the first came out to work with me. He could speak very little English but that didn't stop us from having great fun. We became good friends.

By this time I had practiced in isolation for about six years and was beginning to get orders for small organs. Things were looking like they would work out. Financially, we were still very deep in debt, and I was spending an inordinate amount of time and money helping with sesshins, going twice a week to Toronto for evening sittings then once again for the weekend Teisho, paying for the gasoline to do so, and building projects for the Centre.

There was a growing consciousness of the beauty of the hills where we lived and people started buying up old farms and other property causing our own property's value to go up. At the same time, interest rates were going down. On several occasions I had reached a point of desperation where we didn't have enough to carry on. However, we found we could increase the size of our mortgage and turn it into cash. This is how we survived.

Getting What I Wished

Two things kept me going in organ building. The first was the potential of getting a steady stream of orders. At that time there were several organ builders who had a ten year waiting list. All that was needed for me was that one instrument in a church to act as a show piece. The other was that the size of my shop did not permit cabinet making. It was living hell to work with a 4 x 8 sheet of plywood in there, and furniture making with its steady influx of materials and output of product was not possible in a small space situated in an area that had very limited access four months of the year. Oddly enough, organ building was well suited for our situation in that materials need only be shipped and stored once or twice a year, and I would be really productive if I could build two small organs a year. Therefore, all I needed to do was get them ready for shipment when the lane and road were passable.

On paper, everything was within the realm of success and wonderful possibility. One larger organ of say 12 to 16 stops built within a year and a half at a very competitive price would not only pay the bills, but leave us with a little extra. A couple more of these and our debts would be paid off.

I was spending a great deal of time answering inquiries from churches concerning organs. This was on the eve of computer word processor printed letters. If letters were run off a copier, the inquiry was probably not that serious. If it was typed (you could tell by the indentations left by the typing head), then it was serious because of the effort involved in making an individual letter.

One particular inquiry was typed, and supplied with photos of the inside of the church, as well as measurements where they would like the instrument to be placed.

I felt that this would be the pivotal instrument of my career. I sent along a quote for a two manual and pedal 14 stop organ ideal for Bach and priced it very competitively.

They informed me that their organ consultant was impressed with my offer and would be interested in seeing my shop, and one of my instruments. I picked him up at the airport and drove him to Mansfield.

It was refreshing to hear someone besides myself play the small 4 stop organ in our living room. He fell in love with the little instrument, commenting on its liberal scaling, clear but gentle voicing, slightly unstable and therefore alive winding with responsive clavichord-like touch and subtly of attack. After he finished playing he told me that he was going to recommend me to build the larger organ.

I was elated.

It now looked like I would be able to go to sesshins and meditation sittings while not descending further into debt. Furthermore, with the projected profits, I could build a small shop separate from the house. This was the instrument that would launch my work into a steady stream of profitability, and Barb could retire from teaching.

I considered renting a more suitable shop space in town, but nobody would be home for Angie since Barb left for work long before she got on the bus and returned long after she got off the bus. There would be no dinner ready and the house would be frigid, unless we heated completely with oil, which would from all previous experience triple our heating bill. Working off our property was not an option.

I got a quote from a local contractor to build a small shop with enough ceiling height to assemble the instrument which was going to be 14 feet high. Then I arranged a loan with the bank in order to finance its construction. All that was needed was the contract to be signed.

The actual signing of the contract was not that easy. After the consultant gave his wholehearted recommendation there developed the standard church committee nonsense. They kept changing the terms of the contract and wanted what was called a performance bond included in it. Not knowing what a performance bond was, I went to a lawyer. After he read what they had added into the contract he burst out laughing.

"Do they want your first born too?'" he asked.

The consultant wrote me a letter.

It began "I can't tell you how badly I feel. The whole price of the instrument you propose to build is pizza money for at least three of the millionaires sitting on the organ committee. I apologise for their ignorance."

Enough was enough. I decided I would personally drive down there and give them a take-it or leave-it ultimatum.

The meeting occurred in the church basement. All of the members were very polite and well-meaning save for one retired executive who was flexing his corporate feeding habits, perhaps to impress other church members, but definitely to impress God Himself. I focused on this corporate T-Rex as the problem and flat out said that if no agreement was signed that night, the deal was off.

It was at that point when the church warden who happened to be sitting next to me exuding the unmistakable scent of whiskey addressed the committee with good natured, yet oddly powerful words.

"I think what Mr. Martin is saying is that we should get on with it and build an organ!"

Even the corporate T–Rex listened.

I returned home the next day with a signed contract.

In order to get construction started on my new shop, I submitted the signed contract to the bank. A couple of days went by and I didn't hear from them. Wondering why there was a delay I phoned the manager and was told that the organ was going to the United States and therefore they had no way of seizing it as an asset. The loan was off.

I sat dumbfounded holding the phone. I was now under contract to build a 14 foot high organ containing over 800 pipes in a thirteen by sixteen foot room with a 9 foot ceiling.

It was one thing just building the instrument. But to build it in a farm house living room was a far bigger trick than building a ship in a bottle because the bottle containing the ship is usually bigger than the actual model ship.

Fortunately I had designed the instrument along a classic configuration of two 7 foot high modules stacked one on top of the other and a third 10 foot high module sitting behind. I preferred the German terms Hauptwerk and Brustwerk of these modules or divisions over the more retentive and churchy English terms of Great and Swell. The lower module contained the keyboards, pedal board, stop action and action harness as well as a small wind chest of 5 stops and 280 pipes. The upper module contained the main wind chest of 7 stops and 435 pipes. The pedal division was to be ten feet high and located behind the main case. It consisted of sixty pipes, the lowest at 16 foot pitch. These lower frequencies would diffract easily from behind the instrument's case thereby offering good dynamic egress.

Thus each module could be built in our facilities. However, actual final assembly and complete voicing would have to be done on location.

To those filled with romantic thoughts about the practice of Chan or Zen, it may seem that all this engineering is something very much apart from Zen or Chan practice. This perception is also common amongst many practitioners as well.

The truth is, it is romantic ideas that are apart from Chan or Zen practice and not technology and engineering.

What use to humanity is the Dhyana Practice called Chan or Zen if it remains outside of engineering and art?

Early on I made it a vow to make technical work /art a method of Dhyana practice.

Why?

Without technology we are not fulfilling our inherent nature dividing us from the animal realm. This puts us in a state of being lower (more vulnerable) than the animal realm.

I once saw a cartoon wherein two alligators were spread out on their backs on the bank of a river, their tummies obviously full. Beside them were remnants of a surf board and shards of clothing. With a look of satisfaction, one of the alligators is turned to his friend saying, "That went down really nicely. No antlers, fangs, hoofs or claws."

I organized the construction so that the modules of the organ would go together in the most space efficient way. However, final assembly including not only voicing, but fitting the pipes on their windchests would have to be done on location.

As part of the deal I had agreed that the church could use my 4 stop continuo (positif) organ until the larger instrument was finished. This had the advantage of getting the little organ out of the house/shop so that all available workspace could be utilized.

After delivering and installing the little instrument in the organ loft of the church, I proceeded to tune it. As I began, the church warden that had such on influence on the committee appeared and asked if he could help.

I told him that it was a matter of carefully listening to the "beats" that occur between pipes off unison or some harmonic multiple. He said he had a bit of experience doing just that by synchronizing the two engines in his F4.

I was amazed.

"You flew F4's?" I asked.

"Yes," he replied. "I was in the navy for 27 years before I realized I didn't like it."

We became immediate friends. I much later found out that not only was he a navy fighter pilot, he had reached the rank of captain and was the commander of the air component of an aircraft carrier strike force. Stationed in the Atlantic during the 1960's, he sat on the carrier deck strapped in the cockpit of his fully armed F4 Phantom ready to go during the nightmare called "The Cuban Missile Crisis".

Opening a Portal to The Flower Ornament Sutra

After installing the little organ in the church and returning home to my shop in Mansfield, work on the larger instrument proceeded well. It was a very good time. There were several serious Zen practitioners from Poland who came to stay at The Toronto Zen Affiliate Centre, and I hired them as part time help, paying them a good hourly rate. Only one of them spoke English and so not only did they learn fundamental woodworking skills, they got free English lessons, breakfast lunch and supper, a place to sleep and stayed in a beautiful country setting. Since I was head of the Zendo and lead the Chanting for the teacher's weekend dharma talks, they also got free transportation to the Centre, then back to work. They were a very big help and we had a great deal of fun both in working and sitting in meditation.

I greatly loved and valued their friendship along with other practitioners who came to visit.

Sesshins became very powerful, and now there was another person to help take care of the Zendo and monitor during extended sittings or to help when I couldn't make it to Toronto. He had been given recognition by Roshi as having "passed Mu" after a couple of years as a member and was a salesman of building supplies as well as a 5th degree black belt in Karate.

I was very good as a koan jockey and went quickly through each case of the Mumonkan. This took about four years and probably over 300 dokusans. Of course one's progression in such matters is relative to the understanding of the teacher. Since the answers and demonstrations of koans are all kept secret under the threat of Zen excommunication or worse, the whole thing is a closed system giving the teacher an unprecedented potential for manipulation. In fact, once you start working on subsequent koans you become a member of a secret society. Therefore, this form of enlightenment is a function of grooming.

Once completing the Mumonkan you went on to the Blue Rock or Blue Cliff Records.

I didn't.

I was told by Oneson Sensei to do all 48 koans, commentaries and verses in the Mumonkan again with the words "Do not Pass Go, Do not collect 200 dollars!", a statement out of the board game "Monopoly". I left the dokusan room and entered the Buddha Hall. I looked at The Buddha. Bowing deeply I returned to my seat in the Zendo.

I later found out that none of my colleagues were given such treatment.

My popularity as a sesshin monitor and senior practitioner began to grow. I loved to give encouragement talks during sesshin, and offered further help with a broad range of use of the kyosaku. To me nothing could be more important than encouraging people to deeply immerse themselves in their koan. That was really all I thought I could do, and to that end was very effective. On many occasions I was privately told to hit harder by Oneson. He would tell me behind closed doors that certain individuals needed "A hammer blow to the back of the head". I found this statement obnoxious but nonetheless had faith in the teaching and "the teacher that was teaching the teaching".

The Roshi had now retired and a less traditional more psychologically based form of practice was taking place at the Doorchester Zen Center under the guidance of Baldone, the teacher there who had also received transmission. Because of this change to a less traditional form of practice, several senior Doorchester practitioners came to Toronto for sesshin.

One of these senior practitioners was a staff member of over 10 years' experience who was working on subsequent koans. Being a very close friend to Oneson Sensei, he was given my job of head monitor during a sesshin. I remember Oneson telling me of this decision, then inferring that I had difficulty being "deposed". I felt perplexed at his addition to my character of feelings and thoughts I did not harbour but gave it no attention.

Half way through the sesshin, the guest monitor gave a talk. In it he said that in all the years before he had a realization vindicated by The Roshi he could not find the "doubt mass" associated with the Koan Mu. It was only when he found that all the emphasis on doubt and questioning unnecessary that he "got through".

The Roshi had always used the Western philosophical term "doubt mass". To be honest I could not find it either, although while trying I became a ball of doubt and questioning without knowing it. Even though the landscape had changed in that I was assigned to go from one koan to the next, I still was a ball of questioning, dissatisfaction and shame associated with my shortcomings. This was the unavoidable and primal drive that kept me going. I had not reached a state where I could say I had realized something that allayed all doubt or that I honestly had a sense of self satisfaction.

I began to wonder if this guest and I were sharing the same practice. He certainly was of long standing rank and position. Clearly given recognition that he had realized something, he was surfing on the high crest of that recognition.

Family Practice

After returning to home and shop, work progressed well on the organ. Very close friendships were made between me and the Polish, Swedish as well as Canadian practitioners I hired as part time help on the project or who came to our house/shop for weekends just to relax and meditate.

Along with me, both Barb and Angie attended sesshins. This was something unheard of in Doorchester; a whole family attending sesshins. Even the Zen practicing wife of Oneson Sensei stopped going to sesshins. Eventually, she even stopped going to the weekend teishos given by her husband.

While all this was evolving there was a disturbing competitive element emanating from the karate trained monitor and friend, Punch. What was even more interesting was that during the frequent meetings between the monitors and Sensei, Sensei would speak to Punch and not to me. Considering my seniority I thought this odd and somewhat ignorant. I weighed my actions, my practice and whatever else I was aware of then came to the conclusion that the other monitor was receiving privileged attention because he needed it.

Punch's not so subtitle sleights towards me increased in frequency. I did nothing in my own defense because I viewed his behaviour as some sort of delusion experienced in practice that would vanish on its own. I assumed that Oneson Sensei had the same love of practice as me and I trusted that he was my friend because we both went back years in intense practice.

If all these articles of faith were true, then I had nothing to be concerned about.

It was at this point that a staff member very close to the new teacher in Doorchester, inexplicably moved to the Toronto Affiliate Centre. By association that he had been on staff in Doorchester for years and had "gotten through Mu" as well as exuding a patronizing thick syrupy niceness, people automatically thought that these characteristics were the product of a wonderful human being. Punch and he became very close friends.

Both seemed to have a problem with me.

Around this point in time, the Toronto Affiliate Centre received a beautifully carved Manjusri figure from Japan. In the thick of building the organ in very limited space I was asked to build a free standing altar out of solid cherry. I would be paid for the materials only and would get free assistance from one of my Polish friends who worked with me, so long as I fed him, gave him a place to sleep, and provided all transportation. In spite of the mounting tensions of reaching a state of completion on the organ in order to get the next payment instalment, my friend and I spent over two weeks building the altar.

When it was completed, I had no vehicle large enough to carry it. After asking Sensei how we would get it to Toronto, he said he would send somebody with a truck.

The truck that arrived was a large open boxed affair full of Zen Affiliate garbage. I told the Polish driver that there was no way the altar was going to Toronto on top of that. He readily agreed and said that it was Sensei who told him to pick up the altar and throw it on a truck load of garbage despite his own protest.

I got on the phone and told Sensei the truck was unacceptable. He expressed an air of disappointment giving me the impression he thought I was on some sort of ego trip and that putting my work on a heap of garbage was his rarefied form of teaching. This was at odds with the fact that we had built this altar for Manjusri. Despite whatever motives Oneson Sensei thought was fueling me, I was not going to have Manjusri's altar delivered upon a load of garbage. Besides I couldn't take more time fixing the inevitable scratches, dents and other potential damage done by such a delivery.

After the altar was properly delivered and installed, the sickening sensation of running out of money while under contract to build an organ in unfavourable circumstances started to emerge once again.

It is difficult to express the feeling of fear rising from one's gut after writing cheques to fully cover the hired help, then seeing on the balance sheet that there is little money left to continue. Of course, the hired help had no idea of the stresses involved, thinking I was the beneficiary of all the wonderful profit within a capitalistic system.

Oneson Sensei, never having maintained a position in the real world, was of the same mind

A Hint of Something Rotten

The accumulation of completed components was making mobility within the work space more and more difficult further slowing progress.

I bought a used motorcycle in order to reduce the costs of driving back and forth to Toronto to lead evening meditation.

One evening a female practitioner asked if I would give her a ride home. I got the feeling she wasn't just asking for transportation and explained that I only had one helmet and it was therefore illegal to take her along.

She said, "Oh come on! You're a practicing hypocrite too aren't you?" and burst into a fiendish laugh.

I had no idea what she was talking about.

Another evening after sitting meditation another young woman asked me what she should do if she did not like her teacher and if I knew of any other good teachers. She was from Poland and her English was not very fluent.

In naiveté, I told her that sometimes practice is not easy and that, up to a point of her discretion, she should bear and endure the difficulties. She politely thanked me in a way that acknowledged what I said was totally useless.

She said nothing more to me about the matter. This rested in my mind in a strange and haunting way, but I did not ask anything further.

ANGIE

My daughter Angie had just turned 16.

She was remarkable in that she, with my encouragement, started to go to sesshins. To my knowledge, she was the youngest person to have ever done so at either the Toronto Affiliate or Doorchester Zen Center.

Of all the things I had ever done as a father, despite all the disagreements and fights between us we had, because of this, I thought I must have done something right.

I was very proud of her.

For somebody that young and within the high school social paradigm she lived, what she did was truly remarkable.

Angie had a definite will of her own and was not doing this just to please me. In fact, like most young people relating to their parents, she made a point of not doing what I wanted. After all, I was the same with my parents.

Yet, she still went to sesshins.

Barb also went to sesshins in Toronto, and there were some sesshins where all three of us attended.

Again, no other family did this.

I had no idea that this situation was being interpreted by Oneson Sensei and conveyed privately to other senior people that I was forcing my daughter to go to sesshins against her will. After all, in his "All American Athlete" mind, she was just a very pretty 16 year old blonde. What would she know or care about freeing herself from the endless cycle of rebirth?

The truth was I could never get Angie to do anything against her will.

She was like her mother.

If I ever appeared as a family tyrant, I felt it was for good reason and would do my best to sail the heading I felt was correct. This did not always fit the two dimensional paradigms of what many feel a nice enlightened "Zeny" Dad should be.

There were many people who were now living on and off with us in our own house and would unintentionally report to a very curious Oneson Sensei on how I was relating to my family. None of these people were married, much less raising an adolescent.

I had no idea how I was being made to appear to others in secret. Lack of concern for appearances was one of my weaknesses. It was also one of my greatest strengths.

In the fall of that year I was invited to go on a canoe trip into Algonquin Park with the core senior students of Oneson Sensei. I found it odd that Oneson Sensei told them he didn't want me to accompany them, but they invited me anyway. I always felt like an outsider to these Zen Center cliques and this was no exception. I attributed it to my drive to build, master and love things that others thought strange. This also applied to my exact same approach to Buddhadharma. I was also aware of the envy others had of the position I had at the Centre, but I made a point of ignoring my feelings. After all, I was close to Oneson Sensei. He was my older Dharma Brother.

One of these core persons, Tibs, had been a member two years longer than me and was considered a senior practitioner even though he went to few sesshins. Another was Doctor Proctor, a psychologist just finishing his PhD thesis, and the third was Punch the salesman, karate black belt and monitor who had been passed on Mu, and was second in command so to speak, to me.

We all had a great time. For me it was a wonderful release after living and practicing in isolation for eight years under considerable stress. I felt I was part of a group of wonderful friends.

We paddled and portaged to a somewhat remote lake. Punch was well into the business of patronizing me because he initially thought I didn't have a clue about canoes, the wild, navigation and whatever else awaited us. However I couldn't hide the fact that as a kid I had spent a great deal of time in a kayak on rivers as well as the open water of Lake Huron, and knew how to handle myself.

After staying a night we began heading back. Upon reaching the entry to a portage we met a group of four young women. The others in my party stopped and stared at them. The predatory energy directed toward the women also washed into me. In disbelief I stood there feeling both perspectives at once, and wondering what kind of companions I was with that would project such a raw frightening potential. There was nobody else in that area for miles and in the tense silence and isolation the women became visibly afraid.

Not letting this linger any longer, I smiled and asked them what lake they were headed to and if they needed any assistance. Relieved, the leader told me that they were just fine and wished us a good trip back.

The trip back was quite a test. It was late October and a strong icy wind was on our nose. This made forward progress difficult, but conversely, the work heated us up.

I returned home half frozen and elated. I felt a deep bonding with my friends and looked forward to the trip we already planned for next year.

Snow

Late fall turned into early winter.

One morning I awoke, went downstairs, stoked the woodstove, then threw open the drapes.

Overnight the abandoned farm house on the hill cross the road had suddenly been covered in snow.

Upon this unexpected visage, profound Emptiness engulfed everything.

This was a realization much deeper than I had during sesshin in Doorchester. As remarkable and wonderful as it was, I immediately put it down and did not mention it to anyone except Barb.

I also made a point of not mentioning it to Oneson Sensei in dokusan.

However, my responses and demonstrations of koans changed causing The Sensei to cautiously say, "This is interesting."

Winter set in and I started making the smallest of the wooden organ pipes. This was an activity suited for a single person. Since it was now impossible to increase productivity by using our outdoor picnic table as a work bench on nice days, it was not productive to have anyone else in the shop. The organ had reached a stage where the windchests were built with the smallest chest mounted in place within the lower case. Also completed and taking up space was the wind system that would house the blower, 456 oak action squares with bushings, and case framework made in the summer.

Unlike many other organ builders, I made my own action parts and keyboards. This gave me more control of the instrument and, in the unlikely case of something actually needing replacement, I could make the original component instead of ordering it. Of course, since my action squares were all mortise and tenoned together in solid oak, the chances of failure were small. In the tradition of classic organs the keyboards were non-bushed like a harpsichord's and covered in wood instead of plastic or ivory. The edges of the keys were slightly bevelled giving a warm natural appearance and a superior sense of control and touch. The delicate job of bevelling the keyboards I assigned to Angie. She did excellent work.

There isn't much scrap left over when building an organ if you make all your own wooden pipes and action components. You start with the large pipes and work down to the smallest. Since practically everything was made of quarter sawn white oak, save for the windchests and wind system, pieces of scrap could be machined into action part components or turned into pipe feet and stopper handles. Save for planer chips and board ends, there was very little waste.

This meant that heating wood still had to be bought. When the weather was warm, planer chips could not be burnt in the wood stove and did not do well in a pile outside because they absorbed water. The mountains of these chips were only good for garden mulch. I never did find out if oak being full of tannin was good for gardening because we had no time to garden in a serious way.

Somehow, after paying everyone, we had enough money to make it through the winter without losing house, machinery, the car and anything else bank usury could grab.

Spring arrived and the organ was coming together as best it could in a 19th Century farm house. The upper case was made and I had finished hand carving the vine-like pipe shades that filled the space over the glistening 70% tin principal display pipes.

The action harness was installed in the lower case, and the stop action and sliders fitted. The instrument now took up the two main rooms in the house's lower floor.

One of the most interesting things would be building the oak 16' Subbass pipes for the pedal. These were stopped pipes that therefore had a wavelength four times their physical length and because of this spoke at a frequency equal to open pipes twice their length. Thus low C in a stopped 16 foot rank was approximately 8 feet long.

Pipes speaking at 8 foot pitch are erroneously said to speak at "piano" pitch. This is an error of convenience since most people are familiar with the frequency range produced by a piano and are ignorant of the fact that, in unison with the human voice, it was the organ that first created a physical length associated with that range. Making a pipe speaking at 8 foot pitch, then another slightly shorter and of slightly less cross section, then another slightly shorter and of less cross section than the one before is one thing when the rank of stopped pipes ends at 8 foot pitch. In this case, low C is only 4 feet long. This I had done many times before in my tiny shop. The longest pipe for this stopped 16 foot rank was over 8 feet long.

This 16 foot rank of pipes could only be mounted and voiced on location in the church for a good reason. I remember fitting the stopper in 16 foot low C on the workbench, then taking the pipe horizontally into the assembly room and without thinking raising it vertically thereby putting the stopper handle through the ceiling causing a rain of debris to fall on my head.

The Crushing of Dreams

With the arrival of spring my friend/employees could be hired once again.

The pressure of completion was on a crescendo. The smallest wood pipes of the Brustwerk division were now planted on their wind chest within the lower case frame. Directly below that were the two finished keyboards with turned stop knobs on both sides in the traditional Northern German and Dutch tradition. Although on an absolute basis a classic organ of 14 stops is still relatively small, this lower half of the instrument looked colossal in what was supposed to be our dining room. It almost touched the ceiling.

The removable case paneling was not installed for ease of access to the action harness and windchest. In this way the beautiful symmetries of ranks of action squares, pulldown wires and coupler dogs were visible.

I would look at this object of complexity and wonder who or what created it.

It wasn't me.

It was a mystery of the deepest order. It condensed in time and space despite seemingly impervious obstacles through love, faith, team work and great effort. It came together against all odds through practice of the indescribable.

It was Dhyana itself.

Summer flowed by and the projected delivery date of early August neared.

Oneson Sensei had not been to our house since work began on the organ. He only offered half joking observations about what he heard from his sources. One of those criticisms was that while people were working in the thirteen by sixteen foot shop room or outside, I was upstairs spending time on a newly acquired computer. It seemed that my employees thought I was goofing off on the job.

Of course, what I was doing upstairs on the computer that they didn't have a clue about was making the necessary scale drawings of components so that they could continue working. These drawings could then be used for future instruments and could be printed at the computer and taken into the shop. If glue was spilt on them they could be easily reprinted. Before this capability, all my drawings were done in pencil on a drafting engine, and if anything happened to them that was the end. In order to make reproductions of a drawing I had to drive over fifteen miles to the closest town.

I invited Oneson Sensei to offer his blessings on the success of the instrument. Included with this was a decent monetary offering that I could scarcely afford. Not only did I lead most of the sesshins I attended, I had to pay the full fee of participation. I later found out that other monitors went to sesshin for free.

When he entered the dining-room-turned-assembly- room in our house he was wearing his black robe, purple rokusus and freshly shaved head.

The purple rokusus was a thing of strange fascination with me. Around ten years earlier during a sesshin teisho that Oneson was present at, The Roshi spoke of a great Japanese Zen master who refused a purple rokusus given to him by the emperor because at that point in time it was the rokusus only worn by masters of the highest attainment.

The Sensei looked over the lower assembly of the organ and began to laugh.

"I can't do this," he kept repeating as he laughed.

I was puzzled.

Why was it an issue that he couldn't do this? Did he think I was doing this to show off? I had watched him show off with a basketball doing things I couldn't do. Why was there such an emphasis on self and other in his observations?

It was after this point that things began to get very strange and frightening.

I had been asked by Oneson Sensei to monitor a sesshin that would be attended by one of my Polish friends and employees. From the outset it was indicated to me by The Sensei that this friend needed extra pressure to get through a certain problem he had.

Now, it was clear to me that this person did have "certain problems" in the form of a sort of precognitive know-it-all attitude wherein he would interrupt what you were saying with the statement, "Ya, Ya," indicating that he knew what you were talking about when in fact he was clueless.

This was an expensive problem when building something complex and intricate.

The Sensei found it annoying. Although I didn't realize it at the time, he also had an unspoken vendetta against my friend.

Right from the beginning of the retreat both Punch and I were told to put extra pressure on the object of The Sensei's teaching.

In other words, "Hit him harder. Much harder"

From my own considerable experience at getting severely clobbered, I had come to the conclusion within the paradigm I was working within that such a sesshin event is an open doorway to removing karmic obstructions. However, this can only happen when the physical encouragement is linked by the recipient to whatever form of blindness they have that causes far greater life-long suffering than any short term sesshin event could possibly generate. It is a rare person who can use this form of true compassion, and I knew it. I also had faith that this person was of such high calibre. I was proven correct in this faith.

However, the one who failed this test was Oneson Sensei. Without my knowing, I was being set up to imbed in people's minds my "brutish nature" as it was described to others behind my back by The Sensei.

It was past the halfway point in the sesshin when Oneson Sensei, behind the closed "sanctified" doors of the dokusan room told me that my friend had once again interrupted him in dokusan with, "Ya, Ya" when being instructed on some pivotal truth. He told me that the most compassionate thing to do was to really let him have it with all that I could give.

There are innumerable stories in the history of Zen and Chan of masters hitting students, slamming a door on a disciple's foot thereby breaking it, having a finger severed by the master when a student feigned a gesture of enlightenment with it and so on. These events preceded enlightenment realization and were the stuff of the Mumonkan. I knew it was no accident that these stories existed and took this form. This interactive affliction is the highest compassion dispensed freely to liberate the disciple from infinite endless suffering that would remain their legacy were the teacher incapable of administering such severe treatment, and the student incapable of realizing through this treatment what lies beyond the veil of rebirth suffering and death. These stories engendered a "do or die" attitude in practitioners.

Certain teachers now ascribe the nature of these stories to "Poetic licence," and in political correctness say that they were metaphors for what really happened. Their implication is that we, as "Sophisticated Westerners" armed with the Western "miracle" of psychology can take a far kinder, gentler approach and be all the wiser. In doing so, such teachers disarm Manjusri of his delusion cutting sword, replacing it with a paint ball gun so that everyone can have their blinding delusions shot and marked, yet survive intact because the rounds fired were not penetrating and the whole game is make believe to preserve appearances and student numbers. Thus such an attitude, if taken as a teaching, makes spiritual eunuchs of us all.

However, although guided discipline and a diligent attitude within the meditation hall is absolutely vital, it is a very great mistake to operate under the assumption that all people are of equal ability and temperament, and can be brought to realization through severe means.

Some thrive under this pressure, some do not.

The energy building use of the kyosaku had results for some. Others could not use it. It was becoming quite clear to me that although collective energy could be very strongly aroused with its skilled use to a point where you could almost "cut it with a knife", it did not necessarily radiate from or develop out of a Buddhist Samadhi. It was a battlefield warrior samadhi that some of us excelled in while others found it to be a useless hurdle.

It is obvious that the potential of abuse of power under such a paradigm of administered affliction is enormous. This was certainly the case in the situation I found myself in, but not in the way one would normally consider. The person who got repeatedly struck did very well in using what befell him to his advantage and to the advantage of others. Here it was me acting in the spirit of direct compassion that was made victim by The Sensei who had received transmission.

This was Upia inverted.

When the time came, I did lay onto my friend as if a cyclone hit him. Being skilled in the use of the kyosaku, I knew not to hit causing single blow physical damage. Rather, multiple blow cumulative pressure, something I was very familiar with on the receiving end, was a great catalyst in the use of this form of karma cleansing compassion.

Most important to understand in all this is that there must be purity of mind and heart for both the giver and the receiver. There can be no separation.

Of greatest consideration is the nature of the infliction offered.

Injuring is not remotely desired. Power, shaking up and an experience of extremity that could not be safely experienced anywhere else in the light of Buddhadharma is this manifestation of the Sword of Compassion.

What is most powerful is sound. Each shoulder was always hit twice. The last stroke on the right shoulder, although heavy, would be accompanied with a full force down stomp onto the wood floor accompanied by an explosive exhalation. This was far more powerful and effective than putting all the energy into the physical strike. However, it sounded like all of hell's creation was descending upon the recipient. Others in the Zendo upon hearing this power amplified it through their senses and oneness with the focal point.

As I struck my friend I yelled from my guts, "Only The koan Mu! Put your life into it!"

He was crying.

So was I.

I too was putting my life into it with no thought of how this might appear to others.

Punch also came along and hit him as best he could, but lacked the drama and ability to release Chi.

With the front of my robe and rokusus wet with tears I passed The Sensei's seat.

He was watching the proceedings.

What I saw hit me harder than anything in the preceding moments.

He radiated an open mouthed grin of enjoyment.

It made no sense to me. What I saw was far different than the purging hell my friend and I were experiencing.

It took me a long time to realize that what I saw sitting on the teacher's tan was the betrayal of the teaching in the Mumonkan as well as the basis of the exquisitely powerful history of Dhyana, Chan and Zen Buddhism.

The Sensei empowered by transmission was enjoying his own cunning. I had been set up to be perceived by others in the Zendo as being a monster, and I did it flawlessly.

It was so easy.

Just have somebody "stupid" enough to believe in The Teaching of Buddhadharma and how The Masters Taught it. Then all you have to do is appeal to the sophisticated politically correct masses living in fear, and you have an instant public hanging and removal of what was perceived as competition. Now all those old stories could be seen as lies or actions of the unsophisticated ancients far less smart than modern psychologically inclined "Westerners". All these recorded tales of extremity are unnecessary to actually live.

"There is an easier way," is the voice of such people, their words right out of a pharmaceutical commercial.

This was just the beginning.

A week or two later there was a weeklong work retreat at the Centre where participants would work eat and sleep there. Remembering my experience in training programs, I encouraged Angie to take part in it.

When she returned home she was deeply troubled. She told her mother that The Sensei would take her for long private walks after work and meditation was done for the day without the knowledge of his wife. She thought that it was a little weird. Since she was familiar with male tendencies, she knew what he had in mind and found the whole thing very upsetting.

Barb immediately told me what was going on.

The next weekend after the customary Teisho, I asked to talk with Oneson Sensei alone. In the most polite terms I could muster I told him that his attentions bestowed upon my daughter were upsetting her and that I would like him to stop.

"That's none of your business," he shot back.

"I believe it is," I replied.

He laughed off my words. I sat in silence, then got up and left.

I had noticed my non-Polish friends Punch, Tibs, Cottonmouth and Doctor Proctor who had positioned themselves as a sort of gnostic elite, developed a patronizing dislike for me that I didn't understand, other than the fact that they were perhaps competing with me for position. I thought that this was all their delusion and that in time things would right themselves if I gave it no attention. I had great respect for all of them.

As the summer weather evolved, The Sensei would drive up to our house and take Angie to the beach.

Knowing what any idiot could see made it very stressful for both Barb and me. He would not visit us but was more concerned about being alone with Angie.

It was very weird, strange and predatory.

The priorities of my life at the time were to maintain my help to those practicing The Way by leading sesshins and meditation, and deliver an organ that was not nearly finished and while doing so not go bankrupt. I did not separate practice work and commitment. Despite a growing body of evidence, I had faith that The Sensei was like me and although he had a weakness for women, would leave it at that. After all, I too had an appreciation for women that could very well lead to a weakness and therefore thought he would temper this part of the male condition with Buddhadharma.

However, as events unfolded it became obvious that something was dreadfully wrong with my model of his thinking.

The power of enlightenment is proportional to the power derived from cutting through seemingly impervious affliction with the infinitely sharp sword of Buddhadharma. In this way the objects of sexual polarity are great Bodhisattvas in all aspects. However, if you want to fall into endless demonhood, then indulge in sex using the power derived from practice as a tool. This attracts the objects of desire as a focal point and the energy channeled by the engine of Zen sitting meditation supercharges the combustion.

Dhyana practice is not found in a lack of appreciation for the opposite sex. It is found in a love of the opposite sex that is at heart the transcendence of affliction. Here self and other fall away while not changing nor negating their nature. Liberation is found not in the negation of sex but rather in not practicing gratuitous sex, or even not practicing it at all.

In terms of poetry and music, it is not getting that produces longing at the heart of noble art. This art is noble because it links with the ethereal and is a portal to entering the Mind That Seeks The Way. If you are not clear on this or doubt it, read Shakespeare's Sonnets or listen to Beethoven.

It is a fundamental fact of Buddhist Monastic life that is lost when monastics are allowed to marry.

And with all this, it is a fact that marriage in itself does not stop this boundless sexual craving for the other. Once a decision is made to enter this realm of seeking sex and calling it a method of Buddhist practice, all is lost to hell. Tantric or not, it is mistaking orgasm for enlightenment. There is no greater stupidity.

My belief that The Sensei was a practitioner of Buddhism began to evaporate.

Almost all of my active concepts about practice were formed by the teaching line I was in. If the teaching line did not consider me a teacher, then I was not a teacher. However, what I had realized was self-vindicating. I had the ability to walk on my own, more so than I realized at that time. Therefore I was very slow to pass a comprehensive judgement on somebody considered to be a teacher, much less a friend.

The trust in one's teacher is not an exercise in stupidity but the functioning of a proper attitude towards self and other. It is the functioning of empiricism based on self-honesty rather than the delusion of thinking oneself enlightened. This must be embodied in faith in one's teacher, but most importantly, this faith is not a blind faith. Because of this, you may be fooled for some time, but will mysteriously and automatically find a true teacher worthy of you.

This is because The Buddha transcends self and other.

If honesty dictates that you consider yourself not enlightened, then you must activate and practice a great deal of forbearance in working with a teacher. This is called "bear and endure". It takes a very big event coupled with lack of attachment (true results of practice) to break trust in a teacher.

Moving Into Church

Due to the lack of space in my miniature shop, much of the final work needed to be done on location in the organ loft of the church. This meant that not only would I be taking the disassembled organ on an eight hour drive cross the border, I would also be taking my jointer/planer, bandsaw, drill press and hand tools as well. I would set up shop in the organ loft. This was traditional in the old days, but in modern times the idea is to get in and get out as fast as possible. There are good reasons for this.

Once we had arrived and set up shop in the organ loft as planned, it was of the utmost importance to keep my concentration focused on finishing the organ. The minister had scheduled an inaugural concert for late November.

This is something to avoid.

A new instrument needs to settle in so that any mechanical glitches are worked out. This was his way of hurrying me along, not realizing that he didn't need to. For me to take a day longer than was necessary was decimating my bank account with usury and that this alone was incentive enough to get the job done.

He also made a point of making it living hell to work on the instrument in the organ loft, perhaps so that I wouldn't linger there. The church had just been fitted with a brand new state-of-the-art air conditioning system. Since it was late August, on certain days the temperature in the organ loft was well over 90 degrees Fahrenheit, leaving me dripping sweat. I took to wearing a black headband to keep the sweat out of my eyes giving me the appearance of a pirate, or an outlaw biker.

One day I asked the minister if I could switch on the air conditioner. He replied that if any of the church elders found out he was spending money on air conditioning on any day except Sunday, they would nail him to the cross at the front of the church.

A couple of days later, a church elder climbed the stairs to the organ loft to see how the project was going.

He took one look at me and said, "Why don't you turn on the air conditioning?"

After delivering the organ, my father came to help me out. This proved to be a disaster. For the first time he had to be under my direction and the tension built, becoming unbearable.

Our place of residence was in the church office/house's basement. I made sure he stayed in the room with the good bed and ventilation. I slept in the actual basement part very close to the active air conditioning unit since it was important to run the church house's air conditioning 24/7 to keep the minister's office cool.

Because I was sleeping in a cold, dank draft, I became very sick with pneumonia. The unusual thing about this was that I could still work.

It was at that point that Dad had enough of me giving him orders and after offering several observations of my shortcomings and character, told me he was going home. Nothing I could say would dissuade him so I offered to do the eight hour drive and deliver him back. Even this would not do. I told him that the least I could do was drive him to the bus depot, an offer he accepted.

After stopping in front of the bus depot and helping him with his luggage, I doubled over in a coughing fit and wretched blood and green phlegm onto the sidewalk. When I straightened up and faced him, he made no sign of noticing. He simply opened the door and entered the terminal. That was it.

He had left me alone single handed.

I had no idea how I was going to finish the instrument by myself. There were so many things that had to be handed up to me as I stood on a ladder, parts that had to be held in place while they were being fitted, and any one or a combination of 112 keys and 32 pedals that had to be held down for voicing and tuning. However, I was so sick that this problem was the least of my worries.

That day, after delivering Dad to the bus terminal, I just went to bed.

Later in the evening, I phoned Barb and told her what had happened. After offering some well needed words of comfort she paused, then told me that Sensei was coming up and seeing Angie in my absence and it was obvious that he was not responding to the talk I had with him.

She kept saying, "This isn't right, Paul. This isn't right!"

I agreed with her.

The next evening I was up on a ladder working on the upper division of the organ while incessantly coughing.

A voice came from the base of the ladder.

"Do you need a doctor?"

It was the minister.

I felt like Christ crucified.

Quickly figuring that this was not an offer of charity, I politely declined. If I went to a physician I'd be paying the full shot plus medication. This was something I could not afford.

Later that week a Bodhisattva appeared.

Like the navy aviator he was, Captain Tully came out of the sun unannounced and offered to take the place of my father. He said that he wasn't as technically versed, but since he was retired and had some spare time, would do his best to help.

Now I had all the help I needed.

Work progressed well, albeit slowly. The careful design back home in the shop paid off and everything went together as intended. What took extra time was the fitting that could not be done in the shop.

I took to working through the night in order to avoid excessive daytime heat and people dropping by to watch. The pivotal inspiration for this change of work hours was a daytime occasion when I was trying to install a difficult fitting in a cramped space while in sauna-like surroundings. As usual, I was dripping sweat and wearing a black headband. While over-reaching, I slipped and dropped the fitting eight feet down into the base of the organ case. In a lapse of mindful practice, I allowed a colourful word or two to leave my lips. As I turned to descend the ladder, I found myself looking straight into the lens of a shoulder-mounted video camera. A church member had quietly entered the organ loft and was videotaping me working!

The inevitable series of questions and suggestions flowing from daytime guests was more than distracting, especially during the voicing process. Claude was kind enough to drop by after dinner to hold keys and draw stop knobs. I would then continue through the night.

The Universe Aflame

It was at a point after the pipes had been installed and initial voicing was completed that I decided, at about 3 A.M., to hear the tonal egress of the instrument in the church sanctuary below. I wedged down low C in the pedal with the 16' Subbass and 8' Octav drawn, then wedged C, E, middle C, E, G and the same triad an octave higher on the Hauptwerk keyboard with the full Principal Chorus including the Mixture drawn. Low C thundered in the bass forming the foundation of a harmonic spectrum that reached up to little pipes in the Mixture a fraction of an inch long. They glistened in the treble forming the tonal sword edge of the instrument.

I went downstairs into the darkened sanctuary, walked to its front and turned around. Up in the loft the organ case was lit by spotlights, its principal façade pipes glimmering. In perfect stillness a spectrum of sound based in thunder reached the heavens filling all time and space.

This sound did not appear to come from the organ but seemed to emerge from the space surrounding it. It was not unbearably loud but full and natural. Since the instrument was only rough tuned, the different frequencies heterodyned producing slow waves that beat in steady periodicity underpinned by the thundering of low C in the earth spirit pedal.

I stood transfixed.

Here was the focus of my great vexation, trouble, and doubts about the future speaking. Its sound was wonderful and profound.

Did I make this? All I could take credit in making was personal anxiety about all that could go wrong. Along with this vexing creation were the numerous troubling thoughts about what was going on at home between The Sensei and my family.

But what now filled my senses was something beyond all this.

The motionless instrument illuminated in darkness slowly cycling thunder and tonal light encompassed all of mind's creation and beyond. How could blurry, troubled and muddled me take credit for this?

I don't know how long I stood there filled with this flaming chorus in a burning universe. It was a living primordial question wherein I could find no place to stand apart.

This question had no answer, its answer being the question.

The fall weather had turned from warm and pleasant to cold and bitter. Light dustings of snow began to cover the lawns and roofs around the church. I had been living in an organ loft and church basement for over three months now.

Kind church members asked me if I was homesick being away so long. The truth was I wasn't homesick at all, but would very much like to be done with this whole ordeal, get paid and go home. However, there was no great longing to be somewhere else even though I would appreciate Barb's presence.

Console of 14 stop organ

14 stop organ installed in loft

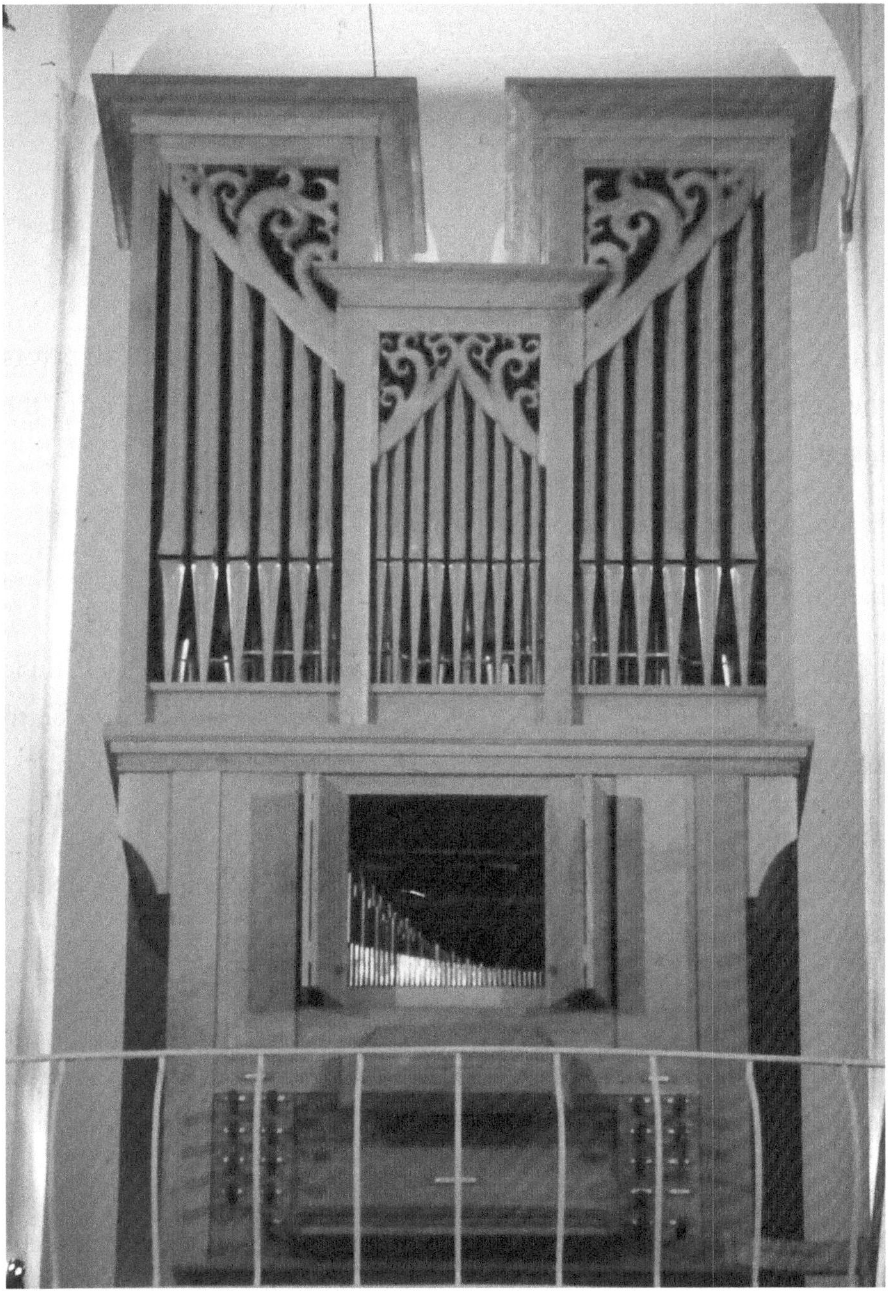

Home to Trouble

The night of the concert arrived. The musician featured was the organ consultant that had suggested I build the instrument in the first place.

It was good to see him.

Barb and Angie came too. I hadn't seen them in three months.

I sat in the church while the guest organist practiced Buxtehude's Prelude and Fugue in G minor and was overcome with tears. He then went on to Bach's Prelude and Fugue in C, and the Toccata and Fugue in D minor.

The instrument behaved very well. Considering that the furnace was now turned on causing the relative humidity to plummet, no squeaks or ciphers materialized.

The concert was a great success.

Afterwards, in the church basement there was a reception. Claude offered a toast to the organ, then another one to me. This was especially moving since I could not have done it without him.

The next day I was given the final check and returned home with my machinery.

A couple of days after arriving home I phoned The Sensei and told him that we needed to talk. He told me to come to the Teisho and we would talk afterward.

During the private talk after Teisho behind closed doors, I once again expressed my concerns about what was going on between him and my daughter. I also added that it was upsetting Barb a great deal and that for both these reasons he should change his behaviour.

He told me he was unaware his actions were so troubling, and then added, "The monitoring talent here isn't that good without you. I missed your experience and help, and I'm glad you're back. We need you to be in the Zendo when Punch does that dharma talk I had to reschedule twice because you weren't here."

The Sensei had been pressuring me for some time to attend a Dharma talk to be given by the other monitor.

Many years before, I had attended a few of these events in Doorchester under The Roshi's guidance. Unless the person giving the talk was within the clique at the apex of the pyramid, they were usually pretty rough affairs that even went as far as the reptilian act of spitting at the individual giving the talk. The Sensei himself tore up a copy of the book "Zen and Creative Management" in the face of the senior practitioner who wrote it, and threw it on the floor in front of him.

Since I thought the other monitor was a serious practitioner as well as accomplished in the martial arts, he would be able to use a hard knock if necessary. Because of my implicit trust and respect for people I considered to be my friends, I didn't know that I was continually being set up by using my faith in the teaching and ability to live it.

On the night of the talk, Punch sat before the full Buddha Hall on a platform. From the beginning his manner and words indicated he was full of wonderful attainment. He held up a book about Hakuin Zenji telling everyone of the great wisdom it contained. Through association we were to think that some of it rubbed off on him.

When he was done his talk I was the first to ask him a question.

"Why don't you just burn that book and burn with it?" I forcefully asked, then added, "All of this is attachment. It is nothing but a sack of trouble, pain and suffering. Burn with it and be released from it!"

A deep silence consumed the hall. Then, one by one, other people, some with very little experience, began asking him questions he couldn't answer. The intensity and cruelty of the questions increased. Punch was beginning to be disemboweled by the assembly and didn't have a hope in hell of defending himself. It quickly went past getting out of hand, and as things escalated, I wondered why The Sensei let this pathetic situation go on.

I had no intention of it becoming a public stoning.

Then the sugary sweet voice of the Doorchester ex-staff member Cottonmouth moistened the air.

"Punchy, can you show me what you would do if you had to die?"

Upon hearing this standard dokusan question given to everyone by The Roshi, Punch finally had something to grab onto and faked falling over dead.

"Well that would certainly get Cottonmouth brownie points for taking over the Centre should The Sensei be deposed for some reason," I thought.

After the talk ended and people had left, I knew I had better say something to Punch. Even though I had seen much worse in Doorchester with little or no bad side effects, something told me to find out for myself if everything was O.K. Furthermore, I really was offering true help in the best, most honest and direct way I could.

However, I had a feeling all was not well.

I met Punch leaving the Buddha Hall.

Making sure we were alone, I gently asked him how he was doing. Without acknowledging my presence he brushed past leaving me standing alone.

With this I knew I had overestimated his ability to practice. Was it a mistake thinking that a sanctioned-by-The Roshi person with a practice based on the events of the Mumonkan could not see the unsugared help I offered? Did he not understand the nature of these recorded cases?

Apparently not.

His practice was, just as I had pointed out earlier that evening, a shallow display of attachment to position and image. Take this away and you become a target for hatred.

I knew I was in for trouble.

At that point I was still too trusting to realize that this was all part of a set-up formulated by The Sensei. The Sensei was using practice as a cover and image to hide under. It was for him a means of getting power and the things that are gotten with power. The only difference was that Punch was more honest.

Not long after this circus event, I too was scheduled to give a talk.

Now it was me sitting on the platform in front of everyone.

I thought it rather strange that The Sensei slid the lectern in front of me in exactly the same way he had done for The Roshi in years past. This was something that would not go unnoticed by Punch and Cottonmouth. I also noticed his hands were visibly shaking as he did so.

Why?

Was it stimulation, fear or both? He was obviously aroused.

My talk centred on the urgency of not settling for the trappings of image, position and thoughts of attainment. I said that to do otherwise was like nailing one foot to the wheel of Samsara and walking in circles.

My words were well received by the assembly, even if they were perhaps not fully understood.

Punch asked the first question.

His voice and mannerisms took on the form of what a television fed couch potato would interpret as an ancient Zen Master. Gumming his mouth as if he had no teeth, he spoke in a feeble voice that we were to interpret as being old and wise.

I was so amazed at the strangeness of this display I still can't remember what his question was. Here was Hiram Abif at a Shriner's Convention being older and wiser through the consumption of 26 ounces of vodka. This was dokusan room style demonstration at its worst.

Then Cottonmouth asked me a question, his voice self-righteousness and heavy.

"How do you know these things, Paul? HOW DO YOU KNOW?"

His divergent squint glared at me.

"How does one know anything, Cottonmouth?" I replied.

He had no answer, but sat glaring at me despite the fact that it was now apparent he was only capable of firing blanks.

The evening ended with people receiving my talk and not being swayed by attempts to derail it.

There were open comments from several that I should be a teacher.

However, all this would be derailed if The Sensei talked to Punch, Cottonmouth and Doctor Proctor telling them that I was full of ego and needed "a hammer blow to the back of the head."

Apparently he wasted no time in doing so.

Once this was done I had more secret enemies than Julius Caesar in March. This was orchestrated with full knowledge that the plebs really had no say and no power. When the inevitable time came when they were asked to vote on what they thought, they would be convinced of an artificial hybrid of the facts through disinformation enforced by "nice guy" political correct spin and lies that, like sheep, would herd them to "vote the right way". Thus they would have little or no problem with how reality was manufactured for them.

This was, is and always will be the true workings of democracy.

Building a Timber Frame

Unlike The Sensei, I had to make a living.

I needed a shop building outside the house with adequate ceiling height for larger organs as well as more space for machinery and work benches. Since I had very little in the way of profits following the installation of my latest instrument, I decided that I would build the shop myself.

I fell in love with timber framing.

With timber framing, a house, barn or shop building is held together with classic joinery such as mortise and tenon or dovetail joints. In effect, the building is like a piece of fine furniture. It is extremely strong yet flexible. The wood ceilings of European churches and cathedrals employed this marvelous form of construction as did the Buddhist temples of China and Japan.

After reading a couple of books on the subject written by practicing timber framers in the U.S., I drew up a set of plans for a 32 by 40 foot shop with a poured concrete floor and a 23 foot height to the apex of its ceiling. The poured concrete floor would act as a platform to assemble the joints into units called bents. These bents would be quite massive and lifted into place by a crane, a practice much safer than the historic use of muscle power and gin poles.

The design was pretty standard and straight forward, being based on Germanic or Dutch barn design popular in the State of Pennsylvania. A 45 degree pitch angle on the roof offered great snow load removal, strength and excellent ceiling height.

I bought a timber framing slick and a set of heavy framing chisels and set to work hand sawing and mortising out joints. What heavy timbers I couldn't lift myself, I moved about on the concrete floor with rollers and a rented hydraulic hand truck. This was a nice change from making intricate organ action parts and pipes, and since it was done outside and not in a small living room, had an expansive quality to it.

Even though I took my time, the work on the components went surprisingly quickly, and the frame was ready for assembly within a month.

I arranged to have my friends from the centre come up for a couple of days and help with the raising. I would supply food and refreshments.

Two of them, Punch and Tibs, were in the building trade.

They arrived after the Saturday morning meditation and teisho at the Centre in Toronto. I was surprised how many people came to help. Apparently my monitor friend and building tradesman Punch had told everyone that I didn't know what I was doing and had got myself into trouble. Any help offered would be appreciated.

The crane arrived, and the building went up with no problems.

As with others in the trade, I called it a timber frame. Cottonmouth my friend and spy for Baldone Sensei, who also came out kept correcting me, calling it "a barn".

"It's a barn, Paul. It's just a barn," he kept reiterating.

The building trade friends had never seen a building that wasn't fastened together with nails. Both were consternated by the four tapered and wedged interlocking scarf joints forming the 40 foot sills, and expressed overly charged admiration.

I didn't give it much thought. After all, those joints were classic timber framing joints and although I found them difficult to make, were nothing new.

I was too busy to get suspicious.

If one is actively doing such a project there is no room for the separation of constantly being aware of the political correctness of how one should appear to others. This activity is only reserved for those of a less than honest nature.

Consumed in the work of the moment, I guess I appeared as a show off to those who wanted to see me that way. Of course, to these denizens of moldy fart-filled meditation cushions, this meant I had an enormous ego, and ego is the antitheses of enlightened "Zen-like" practice. Anything unusual in their molded mouldy perception is looked upon as being some sort of showing off.

The highest level of education of these senior denizens was grade 12, save for the Doorchester spy who had a general arts degree, and the rapidly advancing Sensei approved koan jockey psychologist Doctor Proctor. His rapid advancement was despite the fact that he clearly demonstrated no hint of Zen Buddhist understanding during a dharma talk he had given earlier.

Like Tibs, he was "passed on Mu" by The Sensei.

Again, I had no idea that The Sensei was telling my friends behind my back that I had a real problem with ego and showing off.

Of course he knew that this is what they wanted to hear.

That is the art of lying: tell people what they want to hear and they will believe it.

At the day's end, the elderly crane owner and operator said to me, "This was the easiest timber frame I ever put together. All the angle braces fit."

That statement meant a great deal to me.

Now I had a frame that needed to be closed in. Although a matter of simply nailing materials onto the frame, the closing in did not go as quickly and winter was setting in.

The Beginning of the End

At that point in time I had several promising prospects for building organs and it seemed that things would be falling into place and Barb could retire from teaching. With this new shop things would be incredibly easy.

But that was all to change.

The Sensei did not stop dropping by and taking Angie out on dates.

While we were coming back from a weekend meditation retreat at The Centre, Angie was driving and I was in the front seat. As we rounded a turn on the highway, I reached down to the floor for something.

As I did so, a shadow flashed in front of the windshield.

There was a violent impact. I bolted upright not knowing what we hit.

"What was that!" I exclaimed.

Angie calmly slowed the car to a stop on the shoulder of the highway.

We had hit a five point buck. It had passed in front of the car, impacting its hind quarters and causing its antlered head to crash through the driver's side window. Its body landed in the ditch on the opposite side of the road.

"Are you O.K.?" I asked Angie.

She sat petrified, turned white as a glacier, and began to cry.

The window on her side of the car was shattered and a trickle of blood ran down her white knuckles still clenching the steering wheel.

I examined her hand.

Miraculously, it wasn't broken and the cut, although deep and requiring stitches, was not nearly as bad as it could have been.

Barb was sitting in the back seat.

After she made sure her daughter was not seriously injured, she went looking for the deer. She found it flung in the ditch dead and offered a prayer.

I got out of the car and inspected the damage.

The front end including the radiator was crushed, the driver's side window completely shattered.

A tractor trailer pulled over. Its driver came over to the car.

He congratulated Angie on her professional driving skills saying that over the years he had once seen someone hit a deer and panic, causing a fatal accident.

I was very proud of Angie.

This was in the days before cell phones. The driver went back to his truck and radioed for an ambulance.

Then things began to get really weird.

A couple of cars stopped. At least two people approached me asking if they could have the deer. I asked them why they wanted a dead deer and found out they were going to eat it! One actually offered to pay me.

It was as if we went hunting and bagged and tenderized a five point buck with our Toyota.

Returning to our car, the trucker mentioned that the buck was a fine specimen and that his hobby happened to be taxidermy. Apparently he made it a practice to stuff and mount all the creatures he hit with his truck. Politely he asked if he could throw the body in the back of his unit.

Of all the people there, he was most certainly deserving and I told him he could have it.

It didn't take long for the police to arrive and take Angie to the hospital to get her hand stitched up.

The next day we found out that while I was away installing the organ the insurance for the car had lapsed because Barb, stretched thin between holding a teaching job, driving three hours a day, and hearing the details of how The Sensei was relating to her daughter in my absence, had forgot to send the company a check.

The news was devastating.

The estimate on repairing the car was far more than what was in our bank account.

The Sensei didn't have time to come out to our place to see us as a family.

He did however have time to do the hour and a half drive to pick Angie up as if they were going on another date, coming the very next day after we hit the deer with a big bouquet of flowers for her.

Then he topped it off when Barb told him that the car wasn't insured by saying to her, "With Paul around, you're lucky I came!"

The obvious insinuation was that I would have beat the daylights out of my wife for having caused such an omission save for the fact that the hero teacher Sensei was going to arrive.

Barb had been warning me that The Sensei was far sicker than I realized, and to be careful.

Here was a Zen teacher and my "best friend" showing all the signs of a psychopath. I felt it important to get him to stop stalking our daughter and he showed no desire or indication of doing so.

Both Barb and I felt a deep responsibility to the teaching of Zen.

For this reason alone we said nothing about what was going on because we didn't want to give Zen a bad name.

Apparently, we were the only ones with that concern.

When I was not absorbed in building something or sitting in meditation, I was internally being torn with emotional pain.

I had spent 18 years in arduous practice with faith in the teaching line I *was* in.

Now, having just turned 40, my world was falling apart.

Once again I phoned Oneson and asked to speak with him.

Once again he told me that we could talk after his teisho.

This particular Teisho comprised of thinly veiled criticisms of me controlling the lives of the people in my family and that the lives of people in my family were none of my business.

As I sat listening to this my anger began to grow.

This was blatant abuse of transmission and the position of being a teacher.

A ball of power rose from my solar plexus into my hands and heart. Although I sat in horrified disbelief at what he was doing, I contained this power, not letting it rise further.

This caused me to start to shake involuntarily.

Anger and horror mixed with disbelief strained my voice when I talked to him after the Teisho. Although I had never had this intense mixture of sensations before, I maintained a calm, mannerly discourse.

This was because, unlike the one sitting before me who had received transmission, I had gone beyond these things in a very real way.

His manner was trite and he openly laughed at me.

I realized he was trying to get me to explode within the hearing range of other Centre members inside the Centre building. This would confirm to them what he was saying about me behind my back.

The worst part of all this was that he actually thought he was performing Upia.

When I had enough, I said to him, "Look! You're tripping over your dick!"

The only other people that knew what was going on outside of that room was my wife and daughter.

Once again he laughed it off in "Zen-like" fashion.

A couple of weeks after that meeting, a strange thing happened.

The beautiful wooden Avalokitesvara figure in one of the meditation rooms at the Zen Affiliate Centre mysteriously crashed to the floor, shattering the intricate carved nimbus mounted behind her.

The Sensei asked me to repair it since I was the only one capable.

It was a special non-paying trip to Toronto and a day-long job very similar to assembling a jigsaw puzzle.

I was honoured to heal Kwan-yin (Avalokitesvara) because I treated all the Bodhisattva and Buddha figures as being alive and intelligent.

They reciprocated the thought.

Angie was now telling her mother that despite my talk with Sensei, his attentions to her were really heating up.

On one such trip he casually left a kyosaku with an inscription on it for me to refinish (for free). It was given to him by a Roshi during one of his paid-for visits to Japan.

Hell's Portal Opened

Things were getting more and more intense around our house.

Barb was becoming very disturbed about The Sensei and his pursuit of her daughter.

One weekend I had to go to my parents, a two hour drive, and stay overnight. When I returned Barb was gone. A heavy premonition swept over me.

I ascended the stairs to find the inscribed kyosaku smashed to splinters and strewn across the floor. Racing back downstairs I checked the phone answering machine and saw its light flashing rapidly, indicating several messages. The messages were left by The Sensei, his voice strained and shaken. I immediately contacted The Zen Affiliate and got the source of the messages.

I was told by a still very shaken Oneson Sensei that Barb had personally tried to kick him and got him in the shin. The Sensei then told me that "I had to phone the police!" and that she was in the emergency psych ward at the nearest hospital.

"You need to go see her immediately!" "She went crazy and kicked me very hard!" he said, his voice charged with fearful excitement.

Being the great purple rokusus Zen Master he was, he phoned the police and had her arrested and taken away in hand cuffs.

I later found out what triggered her rage.

While I was away, she decided to take the day off and drive to Toronto to have a meeting with him. When she told him to stop what he was doing, he told her that she was overprotective of her daughter and, as he said to me earlier, that all of this was none of her business. Barb is only five feet two inches tall and barely 120 pounds. Had she been a little taller she could have properly planted her boot in a far better place than his shin. That would have done justice to the evil he was playing with. Here was a 45 year old man clearly trying to seduce a 16 year old girl and it was none of her mother's business? And all this told by the perpetrator?

He had no intention of stopping.

The worst part was THIS CLOWN HAD TRANSMISSION.

Automatically, the veracity of The Roshi's perceptions and therefore enlightenment in general came into question. The veracity of the teaching line and what was taught was now highly questionable.

What this Clown was doing wasn't Barb's Zen, nor was it mine.

It also wasn't the Buddha's Zen.

The pressure was just too much for her and she did something about it when words had no effect.

There were a couple of male witnesses present at the Centre when this happened. Being opportunists, they would later remain silent and follow what they were told to say and do.

I drove to the hospital and was directed to the psych ward. As I passed a padded cell, Barb's voice cut into me.

"Paul!" she cried out, as if drowning.

A little body crashed against the inside of the cell door, her face pressed to the window. Seeing my sweetheart in such a condition was the most horrid and painful moment of my life.

My first thought was to get her out. In order to do so I had to be accompanied into the cell by two psychiatric nurses, one a male and the other a female. The male nurse began assaulting her with questions in a thick Pakistani accent.

I looked at him. His eyes were goat-like.

"Do you hear voices, Barbara?" he asked without empathy, then quickly added, "Do you want to kill yourself, Barbara?"

I told him to lay off and gave him a look to assure that I meant it.

The woman nurse sat silently, her head lowered in sadness.

This is how I got my sweetheart home.

But things were not well in the least. Barb was in an altered state of consciousness and would collapse at the top of stairs or in other dangerous places. The whole situation was a nightmare independent of sleep or wakefulness. I functioned on automatic, drawing on my years of sesshin retreat practice, even though it was my "Zen Teacher" that had triggered this. I had realized that Oneson Sensei, the fool, had tapped into a horrid interpersonal trauma that Barb had carried with her since childhood and beyond. This hidden burden was something I had suspected long before.

The Sensei was infinitely out of his league beyond the videogame called "the koan system" within the gaming arcade called "the dokusan room." This had both made him a teacher and also made him stupid enough to think he was in any way qualified, although to be fair, he was fatally predisposed to be a fraud from the beginning. It was all a game to him. However, he was playing with other people's lives; our lives. The fact that we did not know this gave him a sense of empowerment which, to him, was very much like sexual gratification. He was using the teaching of Buddhadharma as a sports stadium to enforce the illusion that he was enlightened.

This enlightenment is of the same perceptual essence as thinking that a talking mouse cartoon character is an entity met in daily life. It was like mistaking a video game or some other shallow entertainment-based virtual reality for the actual experience. It is evidence of a person and personality type that lives, draws power and thrives in the shallowest of contrived universes most like the format of a sport rather than the infinite complexities, nuances and karmic responsibilities paid out in the pain and suffering of daily life.

This is why predators seek out positions of religious holiness and externally enforced positions of wisdom and salvation of the human soul to hide within.

From this cover they seek out their victims.

Despite what many psychologists were saying at the time, that repressed memories did not exist because concentration camp inmates could recall without question (or being questioned) the most horrid of personal events of the human imagination, I knew from my own experience as a three year old locked in a basement that repressed memory did in fact exist.

Furthermore, given the Buddhist law of rebirth, is it not the common every day way we all function that we cannot remember the traumas of our past lives and deaths not to mention the undeniable existing trauma of our birth into this life?

Barb's collapsing and dissociative behaviour did not show any signs of abating.

I stupidly decided that Barb needed some "professional help" and phoned my psychologist Zen Affiliate friend Doctor Proctor, who was working at Sunnybrook Mental Health Centre. He referred me to a psychiatrist who got Barb admitted to another hospital close by.

In hindsight, I would not have done this but rather taken the risk of keeping her at home. However, I also did not know how far this horrid affliction would consume her, and drawing on my childhood experiences, went "on automatic".

Later, when I phoned Barb's father and told him that his daughter had a "nervous breakdown" and was in a psych ward, his first words were, "What did she say?"

This stunned me.

The way it was said sent a sharp chill up my spine.

I remember saying to myself, "Oh, my prophetic soul!"

Later on, the hospital phoned. They told me that a male family member was there trying to get Barb removed from care. I don't remember how many times in the following weeks I drove to Toronto to prevent him from offering to help her sign out of the hospital without my consent. She was definitely in no shape to be out and about. I was very grateful that her three sisters were in agreement with me.

Also, I became aware of another disturbing thing.

After some time, the psychiatrist seemed to have come to the conclusion that I was the cause of my wife's troubles. Because we both did not want to give Zen a bad name, we kept the real reason of Oneson's psychopathic predation to ourselves and dared not mention it.

In addition, I was still struggling to come to terms with what was actually going on. It wasn't an easy thing that now, in hindsight I could say that I had it all figured out given the evidence. I wasn't that smart. I believe few are in the midst of such powerful confusing forces.

Punch came and visited Barb in the psyche ward. I attributed this visit to his compassionate concern over our wellbeing and we both appreciated it very much.

Neither Barb nor I spoke a word to them about what triggered her painful emersion into hell.

However, on the other end, Oneson Sensei was speaking volumes in private. Out of his "compassion-filled" observations and insights, there were reasons why this had happened to Barb, and of course none of it had to do with him.

Like the conclusion the psychiatrist seemed to form, it had to do with me. It seemed I was a brute prone to slapping my wife and daughter around, forcing them to go to sesshins.

Of course, this was caviar to the ambitious ears of his minions, and it fitted what they considered their deep insights into my personality.

More often than not, insight is the product of desired reality.

I was unaware this was going on. Only much later did I piece it together that I was being set up by The Sensei's "Foxy Zen". This must have been quite stimulating for Oneson Sensei. I guess I looked really stupid and properly put in my place after showing off building things he could barely spell.

For those good friends in high places who made it their business to analyse me and my family, I came across as an unrepentant male.

This paradigm had become politically incorrect.

They based what they wanted to believe of me on their collective observations that when I talked to Barb in front of others, as usual, I had no concern for political correctness. Since most, if not all of the guests that stayed at our house had never experienced marriage, they could be easily guided to embrace the idea that I was an inferior testosterone filled tyrant because I was not always sugary and nice.

Of course they didn't see that Barb was also very direct with me and that this was something I had developed a respect for.

However, even if they witnessed her directness, they would interpret it as the behaviour of a wonderfully liberated and modern woman faced with an abusive male.

Please keep in mind that none of these ambitious denizens had a spouse, son, daughter or other family member attending meditation retreats.

To complete the picture, the wife of The Sensei stopped making the arduous trip down the flight of stairs from their upstairs apartment to listen to her husband's teishos.

In addition to all of this, there was an unmistakable paradigm within Zen Circles that the ability to practice technology is not part of Zen.

Just sweep floors and clean toilets.

Since I had long before realized that a practice at odds with technology or in ignorance of it was a useless false practice indifferent to the fabric of our society and psyche, I was thought of as being "Un-Zen-Like".

This attitude was evident at The Doorchester Zen Center.

The Roshi was remarkably incompetent with anything mechanical, including dialing telephones and the ability to open a typewriter case without destroying expensive pottery situated nearby.

From the very beginning I found the romantic view that a master sits in a cave and comes to the true meaning of things crippling to those who don't live in caves.

Being part of the only family in both The Toronto Affiliate and The Doorchester Zen Center that participated in meditation, not to mention intensive sesshins was unheard of, so something had to be done about me.

After things had settled down a little, I told The Sensei that I needed time off from the Centre and didn't want to monitor any more sesshins for the foreseeable future.

Following my decision, Oneson Sensei secretly told my monitor friend Punch and others that I had to be told to stop monitoring and that I resisted.

According to Oneson Sensei, I had a real problem letting go of my "position".

After a period in the hospital, Barb had settled down and could come home.

To this day, she has never since had an episode like that.

This is proof that there was a peculiar triggering effect coming from outside our relationship and not because of it, as The Sensei led people to believe what they liked to believe.

Because of the nightmare we were living, I had neglected my business and the all-important correspondence with the several good leads I had.

Now they had evaporated and I had no committed clients.

I invited one of my Polish friends out to our place for a weekend.

Although I had given him the extra attention demanded by The Sensei during that previous retreat, he seemed to be functioning as if nothing had happened.

He brought with him a book called "Getting Buddha Mind" by Chan Master Sheng-yen and suggested I read it.

I was too preoccupied with what was going on to look at it, and besides, no one in Zen these days called themselves "Master".

Needing to share my feelings I confided in him what was going on between Angie and The Sensei.

To my utter amazement, he told me that this same thing happened with Oneson Sensei when he ran the centre in Poland.

"He was doing this in Poland? This isn't the first time?" I asked.

"He caused a lot of trouble there with practitioner's wives and other female students," he said, then added, "He didn't go after anyone as young as Angie though."

Why didn't he tell me this earlier?

That was the reason Doorchester had called him back and explained their reluctance to give him transmission.

Why didn't someone there tell us in Toronto what we were dealing with?

I had been too busy practicing Zen the way The Roshi had taught to see what was secretly known to others including The Roshi and his minion Baldone.

Others in Doorchester who knew things I was blind to were too busy doing and saying the right things in an attempt to get something out of their practice in the form of being a "Dharma Heir".

Anything that would smash their glass menagerie would thereby smash what they clung to as real.

They would stop being enlightened.

What fueled their practice was *not* the need to transcend birth, suffering and death, but to get a reward for making an appearance of doing so.

Inseparable from this set of mental operators was that there was a concerted rivalry between Oneson and Baldone as to who should ultimately take over The Doorchester Center when The Roshi retired.

Oneson was very popular when he went to Japan because, being a chameleon, he easily fit the paradigm of a traditional Zen practitioner.

He also had friends (including me) in Doorchester and elsewhere who thought he should inherent The Roshi's vacant throne.

Baldone, on the other hand, thought it was his destiny to make Zen "Western" by infusing it with psychological perspectives.

This was at odds to what The Roshi had sold for nearly thirty years, and the Japanese masters of that lineage before him.

The advantage Baldone had over Oneson was university training that entailed writing essays and papers. In other words, Baldone could write and Oneson couldn't.

It turned out that apparently The Roshi needed a lot of help in the field of writing.

The Roshi's first and most famous book that apparently sold over a million copies was later revealed to largely be the work of an unaccredited Japanese practitioner who meticulously translated into English the student-teacher interactions that occurred in "authentic Japanese Zen", and gave the book its unusual edge of being a journalistic first-time revelation of the true hidden realities of mysterious Zen Practice.

The contents of this book were naturally construed by naïve Western practitioners as a means of ending the sea of affliction they experienced.

All this wrapped into one book was a pretty powerful marketing angle.

Baldone helped The Roshi a great deal in the writing of his last book.

What the Doorchester Zen Center had done in moving Oneson around was no different than what Christian Churches had done with their pedophile priests and ministers; knowingly move sexual predators from one unsuspecting congregation to the next.

This cemented my conclusion that Oneson Sensei was not merely suffering some infatuation of a middle aged man with a 16 year old girl, but a case of sexual predation.

Since this had gone beyond my family, I decided to tell my friends in the higher echelons of the Toronto Zen Affiliate.

As fall was deepening, I was once again invited to take part in a trip to Algonquin Park.

This time it was not a canoe trip.

Instead we rented a cottage in the town of Huntsville and drove in early morning into the park.

The first day I remembered going for a long hike.

As we were heading back to the van my four friends went ahead of me, joking and behaving like kids.

I found myself left far behind.

A sad familiar thought came to me.

I could never be like everyone else. I could never be part of a clique.

Then a gentle inner voice said, "It will get much worse for you."

When I arrived at the van only Punch realized I was left behind.

As our eyes met I could see that he was momentarily aware of the situation and felt empathy.

That evening I sat alone outside the cottage.

Night had fallen.

Cottonmouth came out and sat beside me.

"I've noticed that there's something bothering you, Paul," he stated.

"Would you like to talk about it?"

Although I had my suspicions about him, I still valued the paradigm of friendship and the trust that goes with it and desperately needed a friend to talk to.

I told him what The Sensei had been doing and how my family was paying the price of keeping it secret.

He said, "Let's go inside and share it with the rest of the guys. They're a great bunch of guys."

I was used to this observation of his.

Punch said the same statement with great frequency.

Of course, by implication, each one that said it was a part of that exclusive group that I was invited to be with.

After I had told my story; it was apparent that Punch could not grasp what was happening.

The denial was enormous.

Once he finally got the facts under his black belt, he said, "I can't blame Sensei for doing what he's doing if a young girl comes up and rubs her tits against him."

Was this something a friend would say?

I sat speechless.

Then the others chimed in that out of compassion, they needed to take matters into their own hands and out of mine.

This ordeal was a secret Barb and I had kept for over a year and by finally letting it out, a great sense of personal relief set in.

The relief was one thing, but something new had just been born. I could sense it immediately.

Yes, the weight of the world was off my shoulders, but so was the nature of how this thing would be manipulated.

I immediately felt that any power I had was stripped away.

The "Great Bunch of Guys" decided that I should phone Baldone Sensei in Doorchester and tell him what had happened.

It was not compassion, I sensed that night.

It was, however, the initial stages of slick serpentine political manoeuvring.

I had an immediate sense of being discarded and this was where they wanted me.

Talking to Head Office

The morning after I got back, I phoned Doorchester and asked to speak with Baldone Sensei.

I had been to many seven day sesshins with him and it was he who monitored the sesshin in which The Roshi changed my practice to subsequent koans.

He was an old friend.

Once again, the last thing I wanted to do was make this whole thing public.

The practice of Zen was precisely my life, and my life was precisely Zen practice. It had brought me together with my wife and daughter, and carried me through very difficult times simply by sincerely looking into the nature of mind and phenomena illuminated by the most fundamental empiricism of Buddhadharma.

To make this whole horrid thing public would dissuade those afflicted by the nature of life from entering a path I knew for myself was the unending way of liberation.

However, what I didn't realize was that those I was practicing with had abandoned this path and were seeking the rewards of membership in a cult.

They dressed the same as me in the Zendo, chanted the same words, but were of a divergent path.

The distilled essence of this is deeds, not words.

This whole experience was the Great Bodhisattva of Compassion showing me this truth.

If I did not speak up but keep what was going on secret, then this path would be hidden and lost. Thus my life, and the Buddha's teaching would be betrayed.

However, at the time this clarity was not part of my awareness. I felt that the walls were closing in and therefore wanted to retreat from any attempts of public exposure.

After leaving a message with the secretary in Doorchester that I needed to speak with Baldone Sensei, I was told that he would return the call.

After the call was returned and Baldone had dispensed with the common platitudes of phone conversation, I began by quoting The Roshi's frequently used statement; "In Zen there are no secrets."

There was an awkward silence on the other end as if those words had a jarring effect.

This struck me as strange.

I then told Baldone that Oneson was attempting to seduce my 16 year old daughter, that I had talked to him several times about this with no effect and that this was the first time I had made our horrible secret public.

I remember feeling my voice full of pain and it was difficult to talk.

Baldone Sensei replied, "How do you know they haven't already *done it?*"

This struck me far harder than his previous awkward silence.

It was a very peculiar thing to say, as if he was hoping they had "done it".

Wouldn't a friend and spiritual advisor allow the small solace that the possibility of the act most hurtful to consider did not occur, even if it might have?

Why throw it in my face?

Was it that he too was impatient with me not losing to uncontrolled anger and going ballistic?

It seemed he was prodding me.

Perhaps he wanted me to go public and put the actions of his competition for job security in the public eye.

This would be the end of Oneson Sensei and would put Baldone in a superior position proving that his psychologically assisted "Zen" was superior to the more classic form The Roshi taught and Oneson feigned to teach.

Of course I was viewed as a disposable catalyst in this reaction.

As the conversation went on I began to get the feeling that he knew far more about the situation than he was letting on.

This I attributed to ambitious Cottonmouth who had stayed in my home and with my family getting free meals and board while being paid for the work he did, all the while reporting back to Baldone as a spy.

I had long since figured that this was the real reason Cottonmouth came to Toronto in the first place.

Baldone Sensei's "Foxy Zen" had planted a spy on his adversary Oneson.

Once Oneson was removed as a potential heir to the Doorchester throne and my family was sacrificed as a catalyst for this to happen, Cottonmouth would be the default teacher of the Toronto Affiliate Centre.

Thus Baldone was using as a spy a person with a divergent nature harboring something to gain.

One of the great results of sincere Dhyana (Zen) practice is that you get an unexplainable sense of what people are thinking and doing without knowing through the channels of the senses.

It is not something that is practiced or has a set of practices to experience, but comes naturally as attachment to the senses vanishes.

In the beginning it is most easily seen while people are sitting in meditation.

Their delusions, resolve and potential are all at once known, though not necessarily in a form associated with normal consciousness.

For those who have not truly experienced formlessness, the interpretation of these perceptions can be unreliable.

There is no specific posture, no specific facial expression - nothing that the senses can say is theirs from which these things can be seen.

This knowing is not as defined in the way of knowing through the six senses, and can operate on the level of not coming totally into focus, thereby imparting a feeling of great intrigue of that person, or a disturbance and unease.

A sense of disturbance and unease about Baldone Sensei was growing within me exponentially.

Was he at heart any different than Oneson?

The famous Sun Tsu statement, "Keep your friends close, and your enemies closer," are very wise words for those in anything political.

My problem was that I implicitly trusted that those surrounding me were not in nature political.

This could be said to be stupid.

However, to be fair, the beginning of wisdom is the realization of one's stupidity.

Zen practice has nothing to do with politics.

However, I had no idea that just by my being in the situation I was in was an extreme political situation.

This wasn't Dhyana practice, but the parameters of political manoeuvring that is a necessary for it to appear in this world of affliction.

It is the same root phenomenon that causes us to appear in this world with an affliction body subject to birth, suffering and death in order to practice Dhyana and the realization of Buddhadharma.

Any intellectual thought of past traumas like one's birth, or future concerns about one's inevitable demise are not Dhyana practice, although they fuel it.

However, living a life without impermanence written upon one's forehead is to live a life devoid of what *fuels* enlightenment.

Baldone told me to "keep a low profile" and that we should not tell anyone else about what was going on until he had looked into the matter more fully.

Over that winter I had absolutely no income or prospects.

In order to try and make ends meet, I took on a job as a car salesman.

This was out of naiveté based on a printed promise in the career section of a newspaper that anyone can make a very decent take-home pay without previous experience.

I thought that if I could do this I could pay our mounting bills.

Selling cars was something I had never done before and found that there was a very steep learning curve.

Furthermore, the dealership was in North Toronto requiring a long commute.

I was the only new salesman out of six at that dealership who actually sold a car in a two month period.

I was also the first to quit.

Over that winter I privately told The Sensei that I needed to have even less to do with the Centre.

On the night I drove to Toronto to tell him that, I entered the Buddha hall to pay my respects to the Buddha. As I picked up a square cushion full of wheat husks as I had done countless times before, it burst open, the husks spilling onto the floor.

In that moment I had an uneasy premonition of things to come.

Then a realization flowed into me.

The Buddha Hall imbued me with great warmth and love.

I knew from that point onward that whatever will happen, I would not be alone.

A Gun to His Head

Baldone arranged that my four friends as well as Barb and I should come to Doorchester for the Vesak celebration in early spring.

When I asked Punch where we should meet to drive to Doorchester, he told me that it would look like the four senior directors were supporting my family over Oneson Sensei and that we should go in separate vehicles.

This was very hurtful after what my family had been through.

It was also very intentional.

Barb and I drove down to Doorchester by ourselves.

There I was warmly greeted by friends I had gone to sesshin with over the years and it felt very good and healing. Of course they had no idea what was going on in Toronto and even less about what was going to happen.

After it did happen, they still really didn't know the truth.

The Doorchester Vesak celebration was always great fun with colourful costumes, balloons and little dramas for the children.

I waited until Baldone was finished playing his part as a monk showing people the way to the Buddha while wearing his usual monk's robe as well as a white rubber swimming cap to tell people he wasn't a real monk, an exercise in political correctness I found extremely interesting.

When it was my turn to enter his office, I sat down in a chair in front of him.

I believe that he had removed the rubber swimming cap.

What struck me was that as I began to speak, his face became serious and pained as if in empathy.

This was the expression I had seen worn by numerous psychologists over the years when relating to my family members.

There is a passage in the Vimalakirti Sutra where Vimalakirti tells Manjusri not to appear to those afflicted in such a way because Manjusri too manifests his teaching through an affliction body not outside of being engulfed by suffering.

Therefore, there is no need to look pained and concerned.

To do so is to step outside the situation and appear as the compassionate one empathising with the afflicted one. Thus one has transfixed oneself in the duality of subject and object.

This is the heart of duplicity.

I began by telling him that this whole thing was breaking my heart. I had talked with Oneson Sensei as a friend and had kept the whole thing secret, yet my talks had no results.

He said, "I know Oneson. We are Dharma Brothers. You must keep a low profile in this affair and how it will be handled."

I asked how it was going to be handled.

He said that Oneson needs psychological help and has already agreed to undergo treatment.

"He has also agreed to make the situation known to the Sangha," Baldone added.

I looked at him and simply said, "What if he doesn't stop?"

Baldone Sensei replied laughing, "He has to stop because he has a gun to his head! He has no choice!"

I thought this to be a strange choice of words.

"How can any repentance be sincere when one has a gun to one's head?" I asked.

To this he replied, "I know Oneson!"

I left the office with those words ringing in my ears.

It was clear to me he didn't have a clue what he was dealing with. He was blinded by his own ambitions and manipulative nature.

After my interview, he met privately with my friends Punch, Tibs and Doctor Proctor.

Having talked with me first enabled him to know what to say to my friends on how to deal with me.

The trip home with Barb was a lonely affair for both of us.

Gone were the days when we would stop for ice cream with friends. We had been spiritually quarantined under the direction of Baldone Sensei.

A general notification was sent out to the Toronto Affiliate membership by my friends who had been told how to deal with the situation. It announced that an important meeting concerning the improprieties of Oneson Sensei was going to take place.

This was done by phone on short notice.

Strangely, Barb, Angie and I were not notified. I found out about the meeting through other member friends. Upon hearing what had been set up without our knowledge I was both angered and very suspicious.

Even more angered was Angie, and she made it a point to go to that meeting.

When I phoned and asked what was going on behind our backs I was told that Sensei thought, out of compassion, that my daughter was too young and delicate to withstand what was to be revealed, and it was better to not have her present.

This was horse shit at best. In the twisted set of values of The Sensei, it was O.K. for her to be sexually stalked by him.

After hanging up I made it a point for us all to show up at the meeting.

The packed-to-capacity meeting in the Centre basement began with Punch sanctimoniously intoning that Oneson Sensei and wife needed all the help they could get and that we should all recite the Dharani of the Bodhisattva of Compassion.

After this was finished, Punch then quoted the Bible saying, "Let ye who is without sin cast the first stone."

Then my friend Doctor Proctor, PhD. in psychology, started the meeting by saying that Oneson Sensei has had inappropriate relations with some of his mature students, plus one other "insignificant" case that need not be discussed.

I spoke out. "Is it insignificant that one of these people was a 16 year old?"

Doctor Proctor seemed at a loss for words.

Tibs tried to shut me up by stating that it was not my turn to speak. I was unaware I even had a turn considering I wasn't invited to the meeting.

Then a letter scripted from Baldone Sensei was distributed to everyone in the room. Tibs read it aloud as if it was from Mount Olympus or perhaps even the Vatican.

It stated first of all that Zen came from Japanese culture which looked at sexual relationships in a different way than we do in North America. He then went on to state that a Zen teacher can be enlightened and still have problems and that these problems need psychological treatment to which Oneson Sensei has agreed to undergo.

Therefore he could still remain a Transmitted Zen teacher and have students.

The letter continued saying that the statements of the great Chan Masters speaking of all one's doubts and confusions vanishing upon True Enlightenment were simply poetic license. According to Baldone Sensei, things were really not like that after enlightenment, *or at least his*. According to Baldone Sensei, you could still have Zen Enlightenment and be a psychopathic sexual predator.

This was outrageous.

What kind of enlightenment was Baldone Sensei talking about?

It certainly wasn't Buddhist.

Was it a little fart or two of insight someone called kensho? In Japan, attachment to realization is called "Zen Stink".

I had long realized that even at best, kensho was a tiny glimpse of the light reflected off the Sword of Wisdom rather than *being* The Sword of Wisdom.

In physics there is the fundamental tool of empiricism called "Occam's Razor".

It is the principle that, "from among competing hypotheses, selecting the one that makes the fewest new assumptions usually provides the correct one, and that the simplest explanation will be the most plausible until evidence is presented to prove it false".

I had already come to the conclusion that the behavior of Oneson Sensei was not Buddhist Enlightenment, nor should it be considered Zen Enlightenment.

What Baldone said was certainly not what I had lived and breathed for 18 years of my life.

I didn't consider myself to have attained the Buddha's Enlightenment and that's why I very much needed to continue practicing.

I also intuitively knew I still needed a teacher.

It was becoming clear to me that Baldone Sensei had not realized anything like what the Great Masters of the past had realized, but having spent serious time in a Zendo and making a living doing so, would sacrifice true practice to preserve his position as teacher, and the paradigm that there is something to transmit and cling to called "Wisdom".

It was also imperative that anyone who received transmission from The Roshi should be protected at all costs because the paradigm of Doorchester Zen Enlightenment had to be preserved at all costs. Otherwise the denizens now promoting it would stop being Enlightened.

Now I had a greater problem than before.

I too had spent serious time in a Zendo, had sacrificed a career in physics to do sesshin practice outside the unreal insulated cocoon of being on Center Staff and threw myself into a now failing business that helped finance practitioners who came from as far away as Eastern Europe.

Unlike anybody else in either Toronto or Doorchester, I was leading sesshins and my wife and daughter were attending those sesshins.

Yet, because of the nightmare created by evil hiding within The Three Refuges, my family was being destroyed, and my business had fallen into neglect.

By making Zen "Japanese" with an angle on sexual impropriety, Baldone Sensei also made it *not* fit the Western values of integrity, honesty and decency.

This was at odds to my view of the Japanese spirit.

As this orchestrated meeting came to a close, Oneson Sensei told everyone how sorry he was about his actions.

It was at that point that Angie spoke out, her voice strong and clear.

"That's easy for you to say", she said, "but I have to live with what you've done."

Oneson Sensei broke into sobbing. I watched with a critical eye. The sobbing was contrived. It wasn't even good acting.

A senior psychiatrist who had begun to practice Zen at the Toronto Zen Affiliate also had his attention riveted on this display.

His expression was stone cold. What he was seeing he had seen before. Perhaps he had been fooled by it many times.

After that night I never saw him again. This whole thing was the end of the road for him, as it was for many others.

I felt a very great sense of responsibility for the practice of the Centre Members.

What was being pushed that night was an insidious dismantling of the Buddhist architecture of concept by a secret society of dokusan denizens and koan jockeys.

Because of the effect Angie's words had, the dokusan denizens leading the circus began to realize the whole thing was getting out of their control, so they abruptly called the meeting closed, curtailing further discussion.

They did however announce that there would be another meeting the following week.

What transpired that night left us stunned.

The horrible conflict of feelings generated by those purporting to be friends while clearly supporting and enforcing a predator who had stalked my family was nothing other than a deep betrayal.

It was thought that I would have too much to lose by bringing the true nature of what had happened to light. Eighteen years of intense training and results recognized by The Roshi.

It was unthinkable for those now formulating Center policy that anyone could throw it all away by not agreeing with the way things were being manipulated. They didn't have the intestinal fortitude to do so and assumed I'd "keep a low profile".

This observation applied right to the top.

The thought of going to my old teacher, The Roshi, and telling him my side of the story was for me was very strong.

However, the incident years ago involving Bob and me, as well as other observations including the contradiction of handing power over to someone who was pushing a psychological approach to Zen at odds with what he had repeatedly said in the past did not settle well within me.

Furthermore, The Roshi was 80 years old and had formally retired from teaching at the Doorchester Center. Was I to expect him to say that he was wrong about two of his most senior transmitted teachers with the undeniable implication that he had been fooled and was therefore incompetent?

We were told over the years that Japanese Zen as practiced at the Doorchester Zen Centre was authentic Zen training. Although I had internal misgivings about this, I believed there was nothing better. We were lead to believe that Chinese Chan had collapsed, Master Xu-yun being the last great Chinese master.

This attitude was inherited from a certain predominate Japanese view.

I tried to rationalize my friends' actions.

They seemed to think I had a problem.

I was the first to admit I had many problems.

Did I having problems deserve this kind of treatment?

Did I having problems deserve the predation of my daughter, the arrest and breakdown of my wife, as well as the subsequent loss of my business?

Very strong feelings of isolation, heartbreak and confusion spawned a very powerful desire to retreat from the world. However, Dhyana practice would not abandon me and was fueled so much by what was happening that it was now a flaming conflagration.

The Last Indignation

The next staged meeting the following week took place with The Sensei absent.

There had been time for my friends to consult with Baldone Sensei about the unexpected turn of events during the first meeting his "Foxy Zen" did not foresee.

This Centre meeting started with one of the inner circle giving a talk on how we can all help Oneson.

Surprisingly, a couple of women offered their service. I began to wonder at their innate intelligence given the fact that what was being displayed openly was evidence of psychopathic predation. Despite New Age "liberation", sometimes nothing seems to change.

The new angle now being spun through Doorchester was to make the predator the victim. Even though I did not confuse Zen with psychology nor had any faith in psychology's healing powers, I did study and learn what was useful in it.

This new move conformed to another common trait of psychopathy, the amplification and manipulation of cognitive dissonance to confuse the defining parameters of transgression in order to protect the guilty. Now it was the institution that was emitting psychopathic behaviour.

A senior member who was part of the audience and had gone to many sesshins suggested that, in the future, a Centre bylaw be made that anyone undertaking sexual misconduct be barred from teaching.

Once again I spoke out.

"Isn't there something already written long ago called 'The Precepts'?"

There was no answer to that one.

A rank beginner who had perhaps been to a one or two day sitting at the most addressed me. "There are people here putting in a lot of effort to get through this thing and make it work. You should cooperate with them!"

When I tried to speak again, Tibs cut me off.

A Jamaican member yelled out, "Why don't you let Paul speak?"

A refreshment break was declared.

I cornered my friend Doctor Proctor at the juice table and asked him what it was he and his cabal of friends were doing.

He told me that I was displaying anger. I said that it was natural for me to do so given the circumstances.

In a haughty voice he replied, "I expected you to say that!" and walked away.

Then Cottonmouth came out of the woodwork and asked to speak with me in private. After leading me to the men's changing room and closing the door behind him, he turned and started with, "Paul, I think when you monitor you try to beat the living shit out of people."

And here I thought I was going to get words of friendship and support.

Hurt and in disbelief I said, "I didn't try to beat people as you say. The Gateless Gate needs guardian figures and it was my job to be one."

His expression shone with the radiance of a spent nuclear fuel rod. A wave of skin rippled across his face forming a sugary smile.

"But then there are Buddhas," he said, doing the best he could to smile like one.

This made me sick.

"Look you little shit!" I yelled.

"If you want to cross swords with me I'm all for it right here and now!"

The radiant smile vanished as his face turned clammy white with fear.

He fled the changing room.

In his flight one of my Polish friends stopped him, told him that he was not liked, and had no idea of what he was talking about.

After everyone had settled for the second half of the meeting, the four knights in shining armour there to save the Centre addressed the throng. They began by announcing that there were problems with my monitoring and that I would have no such position in the future.

My only thought was, "This is the first time I heard of this."

I looked about the audience. Several people were deeply upset and nauseated by what was said.

Then Angie yelled out, "THIS STINKS!"

I had thought to say something more, but in seeing what I was up against and how emotionally charged I was, realized it would be pointless. They really would like me to fly off the handle in public. I got the feeling Cottonmouth having a talk with me prior to this announcement was designed to trigger me to do so. That would make their evening.

The familiar sensation that the walls were closing in intensified. I had given my life to Zen and had no friends outside of the Centre. While experiencing the sensation of being buried alive, I could clearly see what was going to happen.

This whole ordeal had now taken two years out of our lives.

Angie had to go back to University that night so Barb and I drove home alone. When we parked the car in our driveway and turned off the headlights it was midnight. We sat in disbelief, looking through the windshield to the stars burning within the Milky Way.

We were both numb and speechless, yet comforted by the vastness of what lay beyond.

I don't know how long we sat in silence.

A thought of making a heroic stance and fighting to the bitter end for justice rose within me, and was gently answered with a calm inward voice. It was the voice I heard at the van near the end of my last camping trip with my friends.

"No," it said. "You have far more important things to do with your life than expending it on this."

I ended the silence by saying to Barb, "Well, I guess this is it."

"Yes," she said, and we hugged.

SAYONARA

The following week I got a phone call from Punch. He told me that they would like me to attend a meeting regarding my place in things. Since they didn't want to appear in any way to be on my side of the chasm they created, we would meet "half way" at a restaurant he was familiar with.

I told him that I didn't like the way this whole thing was being handled by being constantly silenced by those who were supposed to be my friends.

"Well," he said, "we don't want to let you to tell everyone that you have a wart on your dick!"

"Clean it up!" I yelled over the phone.

I could feel those words had an effect on him as his voice became withdrawn. He repeated the directions on how to get to the restaurant.

"Why did he say that?" I asked myself after our conversation.

Of course it was salesman talk, but why the malevolence?

The following evening I phoned Doctor Proctor to get more of a navigational bearing on what was going on. I asked him if in his extensive studies of psychology he had ever run across a category of people who are amoral, deceiving and predatory while appearing perfectly sane and charismatic, and whether this category might pertain to the case we are dealing with.

His response was like a decree.

"I am not prepared to believe that," he responded.

"See you tomorrow," was all I finished the conversation with.

After driving for the better part of an hour trying to find the restaurant, I found a hamburger joint on the edge of Toronto fitting the address.

I entered and realized it was the right place. At a table were my three friends showing obvious discomfort at having to wait for me.

Cottonmouth was conspicuously absent. After all, being an American Doorchester x-staff member, he wanted to make it appear he had no stake in what was to take place.

The waitress came to take our order of four coffees. I remember that she only spoke to me. It was like that moment with the female canoeists in Algonquin Park.

Doctor Proctor looked at his watch. He clearly had no time for this. I should have thanked him for showing up.

Punch started the conversation.

"Look at that hamburger being served over there," he said. "Wouldn't you like to take a big bite of it?"

Considering we were supposed to be vegetarians, I found his observation a leap in honesty.

Then Tibs with eyes overflowing in compassion said, "Paul, there isn't a place for you at the Centre. You are too much involved with what has gone on. You need to go your separate way. Phone me if you need help. I get so busy I tend to forget these things."

This came to me as no surprise. I had already long before made the decision to leave The Centre. However, that fact didn't reduce the pain I felt.

"Tibs," I replied, "After all these years it's come to this? I find it very difficult. You guys are my friends."

To this came the statement, "If you truly had any realization, you wouldn't feel this way. This shouldn't bother you."

I simply said, "Well, I guess this is Sayonara," a Japanese word I picked up from an old movie.

I couldn't help the fact I was in tears.

Doctor Proctor, showing agitation, was the first to get up and leave.

Punch was a quick second, catching up with Doctor Proctor and striking up a conversation as they left the building.

Tibs seemed to linger to inhale further the meaningfulness of his compassion.

Instead, I got up and said "Goodbye."

As I did so, I made a wise and silent vow never to phone Tibs.

If this was a game of Chess, I was more than a game's length ahead of all of them. Knowing this, I wondered if it was an advantage or a curse. Part of me really did want to be "One of those great guys".

After getting home I got a phone call from Oneson Sensei telling me that what had taken place in the burger joint was the right thing to do.

He then said that he would come out and talk with me, but was too busy.

A Dizzying Spin

The next series of meetings that took place at the Toronto Affiliate Centre did not include me or any member of my family. However they were attended by several people who were very supportive of us.

We were informed that now when I wasn't present the public assassination of my character was in full swing. This came as no surprise.

There is a Precept recited at the Doorchester Zen Center of not speaking of the misdeeds of others. This is one of the Ten Precepts traditionally recited by Buddhist monks and not traditionally included in the Precepts followed by lay practitioners.

I learned I was in violation of that Precept by making public what Oneson Sensei had done. Of course this Precept did not apply to Oneson Sensei who had filled ambitions ears with all my purported misdeeds in the first place. Apparently this precept didn't apply to his minions either.

I also got a letter from Baldone Sensei telling me that Oneson Sensei "was showing great integrity and courage in undergoing psychological treatment."

He then went on to say that I had anger issues and would do well to follow his example.

After reading this gem of insight I wondered what the point of Baldone's Zen practice was.

If the human reaction of anger cannot find resolution within the scope of Zen practice but must seek help within psychology's two dimensional optics of taking the images produced by mind's mirrors as reality, then one does not have a viable Zen practice.

Through my sources I heard that one of Punch's brothers, also a member and highly accomplished in karate attended one of the meetings. He too had a young daughter.

When he found out what had gone on with Oneson and Angie, he yelled, "I'D KILL THE SON-OF-A-BITCH!"

Nobody suggested he go seek psychological counselling for his outburst. Instead there was a cadre of members who immediately thought that Sensei needed protection from *me* even though I never uttered him a threat.

Maybe I was missing something. I was and still am the first to admit I'm not perfect, but given what had happened, my behaviour and anger control were exemplary. Wouldn't this be used as evidence of the usefulness of Zen practice in living through a horrid circumstance?

Something was very wrong with the whole picture. If I tried to defend myself I would be labeled as full of ego and the antithesis of enlightenment. If I got angry, I would be denigrated to something evil. The portrait that was being crafted of me was a person full of himself.

I came to the conclusion that I really did have a problem. It was my association with the teaching line I had believed so strongly in. It was betraying me for its own sake.

Within its abberated optics I had to be wrong and its "enlightened" teachers had to be right. I was expected to shut up and disappear by committing spiritual seppuku so that the "enlightened" could remain "enlightened".

What was most painful as well as frightening was the realization that I was wrong about the majority of practitioners. Except for a couple of very dear friends who were not part of the ruling elite, the general membership did not behave like the lions I thought they were, but rather more like sheep following their leader. They could be told anything and if it came from The Vatican in Doorchester it was to be believed on face value. People who before these series of meetings showed a great deal of respect towards me were now showing disdain.

An old member who was a medical doctor and a good friend of mine had lost his addiction to alcohol through Zen practice. The last meeting I attended at the Zen Affiliate Centre he critically addressed Oneson Sensei heavily drunk and slurring his words.

I later phoned him up to see how he was doing.

He wouldn't talk to me.

There were others who did not go along with what was happening. However, apart from one young friend and resident practitioner heroically ripping into Oneson Sensei in private, most merely remained silent and watched things unfold.

Nobody stood up in my defence.

Of course nobody knew what was being done to me and my family. Seeing how those in control were functioning, it was impossible for me to come forward with what was really going on.

In fact what was happening to me wasn't really an issue, it seemed.

Lots of concern was focused on Angie, including the offer of free psychological treatment at the Zen Centre's expense. And even more to Oneson Sensei.

This institution was now a shrink referral service.

It was functioning as a cult.

Burying The Three Jewels

As the nature of what had transpired at the Toronto Affiliate Centre became apparent many people became despondent. They blamed Practice for what had happened and quit.

There were some that appeared quite eager to do so as if they were looking for an excuse or a ticket for freedom from the exertion of practice they found difficult. They did not care to realize that this outcome was *not* the results of practice but rather the results of *not practicing* Buddhism while doing a great deal of "Zen-like" sitting meditation.

The subsequent results of *not practicing* Buddhism supercharged by the energy of sitting meditation transformed The Way into demonhood evidenced by a pathological lack of honesty, reliance on image and position, and self-delusion of attainment. All the precepts save for the actual killing of a human being had been broken in secret by a person who had received transmission. And even this last precept had all the foundation work of being broken.

In other words, were it not for *my* Dhyana Buddhist Practice, what the Doorchester Center did would have killed me.

I was a living realization that Dhyana Practice has the unequalled ability to carry one through hell to the other shore without regression. This is the jewel of true, honest Chan or Zen practice as best as I could do.

Word was now being spread by the denizens leading the Toronto Affiliate Zen Centre that I left because I wasn't going to be allowed to be a teacher.

Actually, I suppose part of that was true in that under directions from Baldone's "Foxy Zen" they weren't letting me talk and therefore teach.

However, the fact was that I did not want to be teacher at that point in time. I wasn't ready. I knew and realized I still needed a Master and that Doorchester had proven itself worse than deficient.

So, in that way I really was a teacher but didn't know it. I was the only one teaching Buddhadharma, and had a meditation cushion shoved in my mouth for doing so.

My problem was that I really knew Dhyana Buddhist practice was the Way of Liberation and that it was my destined job to teach others. However, given the assassination of my character by the teaching line I was associated with now going in full swing, any attempt by me to stand up for The Three Jewels was seen as an act of naïve stupidity as well as a pitiable clinging to the last shards of establishing myself as a teacher.

The realization of how stupid I must have looked having trusted, supported and worked within that teaching line was a bonus torment.

Despite all the wonderful talk about how compassionate Zen Buddhism was, nobody within the Doorchester Teaching Line was offering anything in the way of support for me and my family, save for the offer of psychological counselling.

Their Zen was a referral service for psychologists. Again, this naturally leads to the question, "What use is this form of Zen?"

Since nobody was taking up my defence, I quickly realized that there was no way I could defended myself within the arena they owned.

My whole validity as a human being capable of helping others was being sacrificed on the altar of defending a psychopathic predator.

This is how evil functions.

It needs what is commonly referred to as a scapegoat to deflect and absorb the karma evil acts generate so that the actual cause or causes can remain hidden, functional and profitable. It is within the theatre of people's minds that the cure of what afflicts them is framed. If what afflicts them stages the show, then it in turn owns the theatre and therefore people's minds.

The friends that appeared at my side began to quickly fall off. One told me he met a psychologist who was "a very nice man". In fact he was "nicer" that any Zen teacher he had met.

I wondered how niceness was a measure of one's ability to offer freedom from the savage clutches of Samsara.

One person, at a Centre meeting in my absence told people I was not nice to her, even when my recollection of the interaction in question was that I was polite and, well, "nice".

Some said I was ambitious.

Some thought I was O.K. but because I kept going in practice, too stupid to see that I had been had by all this Zen stuff.

Some thought I was a brute.

Some were eager to think I was false like the teachers in the teaching line I had left.

Many thought I had been kicked out, when in fact I had left of my own volition.

The truth was there were as many versions of me as there were people who said they knew me.

If there was any effort on my part to dispel any of these "me's" floating around out there I would be laughed at and told that I am clinging to the past and, as usual, overstating my importance in the grand scheme of things.

And yet, if anyone sincerely asked what happened to me, these critics would over-ride any alternative version and rabidly project their clung to version of "me" as the truth. This is supposed to be fine for them to do because their definition of enlightenment or holiness depends on hiding within an institution that found it useful and convenient to make me into a demon in order to protect an inside evil.

This is how an institution can infect The Way of Liberation.

It is nothing new.

As for my own version of me, I had none that I constantly carried around, but was still not clear about it.

If one version came to my mind, I became tangled in painful confusion, and my heart became muddled.

I was happy only when I was an embodiment of a resolve to offer The Gateless Gate of Dhyana Practice. It was like a holiday from my own living hell.

With the Centre removed from my life, I had only private home life to live this embodiment. This was very difficult with bills piling up and having once again to take on minimum wage jobs.

The context of living Buddhadharma sometimes became obscure in practice while easy in theory.

My being was so wracked in vexing pain I actually thought I was going to die.

I had to go somewhere else.

I had to find a Master.

The problem was that after spending almost 20 years within a certain teaching line I could not expect to be welcomed with open arms in another.

In fact, in modern Japanese and American Zen Circles, it was unheard of.

There were good reasons why this is so.

First, you will be arriving out of the blue with experience and baggage that will have the potential to disrupt the status quo of the next institution. Everybody has something they got and cling to from practice, be it status, image, power of position or whatever else. This is receiving from Buddhadharma something that is not Buddhadharma. Anyone or anything outside this fishbowl is seen as a threat. It doesn't matter if those concerned are monks or lay practitioners. The parameters are the same.

I knew from the outset that this was a very big problem, having already been on the receiving end of institution politics.

So did my adversaries in the teaching line I left.

However their model of "me" was as incorrect as their model of Buddhadharma.

Furthermore, this clinging to one teaching line after spending decades within it was at odds with the practice I had read about in Tang Era China, or in pre Meiji Restoration Japan for that matter.

However, the obvious question coming from any new teacher would be, "What was wrong with where you were?"

The obvious answer was that you were a trouble maker, a fallen unworthy creature in search of vindication elsewhere when vindication was not given. There could be nothing wrong with Zen as it is taught.

I desperately needed vindication. Although my actions, words and deeds were in line with what I had awakened to know was true, I still very much needed to be told I was right and have someone of authority tell the world that I could be a help to others.

Although I deeply wanted someone to tell the world I had upheld the teaching, more than anything else, I wanted to come to a realization that was self-vindicating beyond all doubt.

Master Sheng-yen

Late one August afternoon I was unable to find a caulking tool to seal around a window frame in our old house. The only place it could be was down in the mud floor basement, within a bin relegated to a diverse number of things including tools and old magazines.

One of the magazines caught my eye. It was an edition of the news publication of the Doorchester Zen Centre.

It was strange that it was down in the basement in this bin. I obviously never read it. It got stashed there with all manner of other printed literature that had arrived by mail that I had not sorted through, or arrived while I was away installing an organ over the strained past four years. Out of curiosity I began thumbing through its pages.

Suddenly, a picture of a Chinese monk wearing dominant dark rimmed glasses appeared with the name "Sheng-yen" in bold print.

On seeing this picture a bolt of sharp energy shot up my spine.

This was the Master in my dream 20 years before.

This was also the Master who had written the book my friend wanted me to read.

The article was about this Chinese monk who was one of the few teachers to have been invited by The Roshi to give a talk at the Doorchester Zen Centre.

Conspicuously absent in the writing was the title, "Master".

The article was written by Baldone who had not yet received transmission at the time. Although it was fine to call someone Roshi, it was not politically correct to call someone a Master within the abberated optics of the Doorchester Zen Center. They had such high standards they became dizzy with them.

The picture had far greater effect on me than the article.

I ran up the basement stairs with a resolve that I needed to get a copy of one of this Master's books.

In the early 1990's there was no online book buying. In fact, there was no online much of anything. I decided that Barb and I would go to Toronto and see what we could get in what was then Canada's largest book store.

We parked our car in front of old Varsity Stadium and walked.

Entering the store, I directly went to the religion section and there, in prominent display, was a black and white bound book entitled, "The Sword of Wisdom", (not to be confused with a later book by Master Sheng-yen of the same title).

The whole trip including the buying of the book was strangely easy and fluid.

The young man at the store's cash register obviously had a hard previous night and was in a state of semi slumber. I put the book down on the counter in front of him. Without looking at the title, he dimly opened his eyes, and said, "Could you enlighten me?"

I laughed.

He had no idea why I was laughing until he saw the subject matter of the book, frowned, and also burst out laughing.

Upon reaching our car, we found a folded sheet of paper wedged under the driver's side wiper. Upon opening it I was astonished to see a print of a crudely drawn Bodhisattva surrounded by flames. An inscription read something like, "Life is short. Take advantage of The Teaching of The Buddha while you can!"

This was most strange. Even stranger was when I looked down the bumper-to-bumper row of parked cars, ours was the only one that had this printed matter under its windshield wiper.

A soon as I got home I consumed the book. I found within it a writing style, series of concepts and sense of humour that resonated deeply within me, as if I already had known its author.

What was also very odd was that while studying for his doctorate, Master Sheng-yen stayed at a Japanese Zen monastery where Bantetsugu Roshi was the Master. Bantetsugu was a direct Dharma heir of Daiun Sogaku (Harada Roshi). Although in North America the teaching line founded by Harada Roshi is prevalent within Zen lineages, in Japan it is extremely small. Therefore the probability of a link in such a way through a Taiwanese Master was significantly small enough to indicate something else at work.

Here was a living Master who was very familiar with the lineage and severe "kensho factory" training methods I had undergone, yet I saw from his writing a far greater scope and perspective than I had seen within that framework.

I wrote the Chan Center in Queens New York and received more information.

One of the peculiar things that came about when the transgressions of the teacher at the Toronto Affiliate Centre were brought into public awareness was that several practitioners who were quite peripheral to Centre social life and practice suddenly became charged with energy and strange enthusiasm.

One such person was named Brian. After hearing my enthusiasm about Master Sheng-yen, he had written and told the master what was going on at the Toronto Affiliate Centre, and had been accepted for a seven day retreat (sesshin) there.

Before the public revelations about the nature of Oneson Sensei, Brian had very little to do with me. Now he was one of my friends and in my situation, I valued all the friends I could get. Furthermore, he was an engineer/physicist and therefore had a similar technical background, although he worked for The Nuclear Power industry, something I was and still am completely averse to.

His mental approach to things was very "scientific", a mindset I had avoided over twenty years earlier. However, I still felt comfortable with such a way of thinking, and respected its result driven professional integrity.

Since he had already been accepted to a retreat at The Chan Center, I decided to offer my application, along with a somewhat detailed letter of what happened at the Toronto Affiliate Centre so that Master Sheng-yen knew what he was encountering in all honesty.

I briefly recounted the history of what happened in Toronto, what happened to my family and how things began to be manipulated, saying that I did not want any break in practice. I just wanted to continue on because this whole thing was so deeply troubling for me, and I was clearly not free from affliction.

A couple of weeks later I got a letter from the head monk that I had been accepted to the retreat.

Queens

I had never been to New York City.

This in itself was not something I had ever yearned for. I figured it was like Toronto, but more so.

No concept could ever prepare me for arriving at LaGuardia in the falling light of a late November afternoon.

During the flight from Toronto, Brian had filled me with stories of how he was a world traveller from an early age, going from airport to airport in his British boy's school beanie and uniform and that this was a familiar experience for him.

He then went on to say that he had heard in the news of some place in New York where a person with a personality issue walked into a crowded building and emptied the full clip of an Uzi sub machine gun set on full automatic. He was concerned that this might happen to us.

I gleefully comforted him by saying, "Well, if it does, we would be splattered with 9 mm rounds while practicing the Buddha's Way. All things considered, there's no better way to go out of this realm!"

This did little to console him.

We got in a taxi at the airport. Everything was darkening into night. I could feel the presence of the city. It breathed thickening darkness.

This was *not* "like Toronto but more so".

It felt like this place could eat you alive.

I also felt a compassionate heart that, although business like and matter of fact, was the very essence of the human condition. It could be easily overlooked if stuck in the superficial.

As we passed the graffiti painted buildings of Queens and dark figures standing around for unseen reasons, I could make out that our Sikh driver was a pretty tough customer.

It was directly after that observation that Brian asked, "Is this a rather tough area of the city?"

This was like asking a fish, "Is water wet?"

The driver offered no response. He simply flashed a look in his rear view mirror.

We were dropped off in front of an unremarkable storefront. The only reassurance was a sign saying "Chan Meditation Center".

As my foot lowered out of the cab, I felt I was stepping onto the surface of the moon, or some other alien planet.

"One small step for a man…" I said under my breath as festive Mexican music from cross the street assaulted the ear over the enormous city's hum.

My friend asked how much the cab fare was. He received the news as if it was a Punjabi death sentence, and paid it on the spot. After the cab left, he commented about the high cost of cabs in New York. I told him I'd pay for the trip back to the airport (I later found that the trip back to LaGuardia cost half as much. Perhaps LaGuardia was downhill from Queens, requiring less fuel).

Queens itself was like a guardian figure at the temple gate. Having confronted its presence, it let me pass to the sidewalk's other shore and open the door to the Chan Meditation Center.

I entered into a space filled with bright florescent light.

Before me was a large painted Kwan Yin figure encased behind glass offering the drink of Amrita. To my right was a reception desk behind which a very warm and animated Chinese woman graciously greeted us.

After removing my boots I immediately entered the Chan Hall.

At the front of the hall, a life sized painted Buddha was seated on a red Formica covered altar, fluorescently lit. Blue indoor/outdoor carpet ran up the centre of the hall and on either side of the carpet where the familiar round sitting cushions facing a faux wood grain paneled wall.

A rectangular array of electric votive lights hung on the back wall.

For 18 years I had sat in Zendos with the most delicately balanced lighting, wood floors and the most tasteful Zen motif décor with a heavy accent on brown. Here that was all thrown out the window. And yet, standing alone in the empty Chan Hall, I felt an unmistakable presence of Compassion I did not feel as strongly elsewhere.

Downstairs was very busy with a remarkable kitchen in the height of food preparation. Voices in Mandarin filled the air. It was all strange yet strangely familiar and I began to feel very much at home.

About 80 percent of the retreat participants were Chinese. Unlike so many Western Zen places I had been to, there was no pretense to their practice. It was natural. It was what they did. And they were more than happy to show me around.

I climbed the stairs to my room. The building was very old, and went up three floors. The stairs were on something of an angle reminding me of a woodcut by M.C. Escher. I entered a room designated as the library and was astonished at its modern computer equipment and the number of books. This was really a serious library. What consisted of a library in the places I had formerly practiced went little more than one small cabinet of selected books, and absolutely no visual presence of computers. Here learning was valued and aesthetics were not an issue.

Bedding was about the same as I was used to in my Zen training. You brought a sleeping bag and thin foam mat, and slept on the floor. My room was at the front of the building over the street below. The Mexican music went non-stop into the night.

Before dinner I met two of the resident monks. As my friend and I were speaking with them, I happened to notice a senior monk silently looking at me from a distance in the dimly lit hall. There was nothing remarkable about his appearance. He seemed to condense in time and space with no air of specialness.

As he walked past us, my friend said, "I guess that was Master Sheng-yen." I instinctively bowed.

You could always tell who the teacher was in the tradition I had spent 18 years in. It was unmistakable. Here an old monk appeared as if he had always been standing there, gently registering in my mind.

He carried nothing with him.

After unpacking, I went downstairs for dinner. In the foyer Master Sheng-yen was talking to folks. What struck me was his natural manner. It was clear he knew these people for years and spoke with them as friends. There was no student-teacher air of specialness.

The dinner was spectacular. I never had such exquisite Chinese food in all my life, far better than any restaurant I had ever been to. I could live on this stuff!

At the head of the table, Shifu sat and ate with all of us.

There was then a break followed by the first round of evening sitting meditation.

During the break I put on my brown Zen robe and rokusus, then went downstairs into the Chan Hall and took my seat. While doing so I realized everyone except the ordained monks simply wore their normal clothing. One woman actually had a sweater sporting hundreds of little yellow smiling happy faces.

The meditation schedule was pretty much the same as the schedule at the Doorchester and Toronto Affiliate Centres. The first round of meditation went by very quickly.

At the beginning of the second round we were told to re-arrange our cushions on the floor in front of Shifu's cushion.

Shifu took his seat with his young translator/monk at his side. The monk handed him a list of the retreat participants and he began to read each name, politely welcoming each person. This was quite time consuming considering there were about fifty participants.

"Brain. Where is Brain?" asked Shifu, as he looked over the heads of the participants.

The monk interpreter interjected saying, "No Shifu. It's BRIAN. His name is B-R-I-A-N."

Something hit me. I looked up at Master Sheng-yen.

The Master was radiating a devilish smile.

That was a perfect summation of Brian.

He w*as* "Brain".

It was like contrapuntal music changing the sequence and positioning of a musical subject to produce a new and related musical meaning. Here, he simply changed the order of letters to spell a word that had ingenious incisive meaning, and yet made it look like an accident. This was without having interviewed Brian, or even meeting him.

I said to myself, "This is remarkable. It is no accident."

My next thought was, "Even though psychic powers are not enlightenment, they can be a symptom. When arising from insight that is definitely in tune with teaching, such a thing is a display of Upia, or skillful means. This is extreme. I never thought such power was possible in these modern times. Surely this Master Sheng-yen is not of the calibre of the ancient Masters, or is he?"

The genius of that simple "mistake" was extreme and I was the only one in the Chan Hall besides Master Sheng-yen that could know this.

One by one, each participant was welcomed by Shifu.

As the number of names on the list began to dwindle, an awareness grew within me that I was being intentionally overlooked.

"Oh please," I thought to myself, "after what I've been through, I'm sick of getting a Zen hard time. I know a Zen set up when I see one, and this is one of them!"

I then recalled what I said in my letter of introduction that I didn't want any gaps in my practice to realize Enlightenment. I began to wish I had said something else.

After the list of participants ended, the Master turned to his monk interpreter and asked, "Is there anyone I missed?"

"Paul, Shifu. You missed Paul," said the monk.

Shifu's face beamed.

In broken English he said, "There is old Chinese saying: 'The light you emit is so bright it leaves a spot before my eyes so I cannot see you.'"

I smiled and bowed while seated.

"Is this a criticism or a compliment?" I silently asked myself.

Given the circumstances of how my life was going, I thought it safer to take it as a criticism. At least then I had something to work with.

During the walking meditation before the next round of sitting, I went up to my room, took off my robe and rokusus and put on black pants and a hooded sweat shirt. This would be my new meditation attire.

The general form of the retreat was very similar to what I was used to, save for the fact that the only use of what was called the kyosaku in Japanese and now called "the incense stick" in English, was only to wake up people overcome by drowsiness when they asked for it.

My overall condition was exhaustion. I felt emotionally and physically drained by what had gone on in Toronto and Doorchester and could barely stay awake.

One of the roommates I had was an animated fellow of Spanish American descent from California. After the final round of meditation during the second evening of the retreat, he told me I needed a massage. I had never, in my 18 years of formal retreats, ever been spoken to in a normal talking voice while a retreat was going on. All communications were by written notes or in extreme circumstances a whisper. It was unthinkable to break the silence of a retreat. Even more surreal was being offered a massage under such circumstances. However, he was a very good natured sort and had a clearness about him.

Brian was also in the room and, only having been to at the most three or four Zen Centre sesshins, had no problem joining in on the conversation.

I put my finger to my lips indicating that we should be silent but this had little effect.

The person offering the massage said, "I can see there's something binding your heart."

Brian said in an off handed way, "You mean this guy is going to have a heart attack?"

The fellow offering the massage said that it was more of an energy thing that could lead to problems.

Taking the way I was feeling into account, and not knowing if this was standard behaviour at one of Master Sheng-yen's retreats, I agreed to have the massage.

The phrase, "When in Rome do as the Romans do," came to mind.

He told me to lie on the floor on my stomach. This was not a position I felt any degree of comfort in given the circumstances, but figured there would be no problem if self defense was an issue. The Californian then stepped onto my back. The way he carefully distributed his weight immediately gave me the impression that he did indeed know a thing or two about massage. After stepping off my back he knelt down, slapped his hands together and vigorously rubbed them, then applied them to my back. There was an immediate and intense burning sensation. This fellow had remarkable powers.

It was at that moment that the bedroom door swung open and one of the monks stepped in.

"What you dooo........?" the monk asked in bewilderment, then quickly shut the door and left.

"This is it," I thought.

"After 18 years and all that's happened I'll be kicked out of a retreat in 'The Big Apple' for consummating a gay relationship on the second night. Nice career ender!"

The next day I felt a great deal better. Furthermore, nothing was said about the night before, so, in the spirit of Chan, I continued on as if nothing had happened.

That afternoon, Master Sheng-yen gave a talk on how to work on a Hua-tou. He said that it should be approached as if it were a beautifully wrapped gift from someone you might fall in love and marry. As it is, you don't know what is inside and yet the time has not come for it to be opened. This intrigue is very useful.

I remembered the beautiful wrapping Barb had done on the large bottle of Canadian maple syrup I brought to Shifu as a gift.

That evening The Master gave further instruction on Hua-tou practice. He said that when you are meditating, you absorb yourself fully in the Hua-tou, and when you are, say, driving a car, you set the koan down and concentrate on driving.

This was a different approach than what I had been practicing and instructing people to do. I could find no need for separation with Hua-tou practice in driving a car or motorcycle for that matter. I also could not find it during the operation of wood working machinery. Everything was the Hua-tou no matter what appeared before you. Of course, I also knew from my own experience that this was the ideal.

However, how many people could just operate a thickness planer or drive a car without the intrusion of irrelevant thoughts that could, if indulged in, prove dangerous or even fatal given the situation?

I put up my hand to ask a question.

"What if the road stops being the road and the driving stops being driving when you are driving," I asked The Master.

The translator monk sitting beside Shifu laughed me off saying, "If …then… what…"

I had a very quick eye for people no matter whether they were a monk or a lay person. This fellow at the time was a one kensho wonder and very bright. He had only been formally practicing for about three or four years and yet being a Chinese Monk and sitting beside Master Sheng-yen gave him all the authority in the Universe. I wasn't asking him the question, but since I had no standing in the Chan Hall, I was fair game for his cockiness. I had to embrace being Master Lin Chi's man of no rank.

Master Sheng-yen smiled.

"Then you pretty good driver!" he said in English.

I wanted to test the waters further. These waters included not just my understanding, but Master Sheng-yen's as well.

Oddly enough, the next morning Master Sheng-yen announced that he would interview anyone who had any questions, and test anyone "for signs of enlightenment".

I asked the head monk for an interview.

During the first round of the afternoon meditation, I was unexpectedly tapped on the shoulder and led to a small room at the front of the Chan hall.

Master Sheng-yen sat in a chair with his interpreter monk at his side.

I was nervous.

After feeling awkward doing a prostration to The Master on the hard linoleum floor, I seated myself in a chair facing both of them. This was a first. All my previous interviews had been done on floor level with mats and cushions.

The Master seemed very annoyed about having to do the interview.

"I have my translator here with me so that I can tell what it is you are saying!" he hissed.

Everything that went on in that room could be clearly heard in the Chan Hall.

I bowed, then said "Koan or hua-tou practice is not something to pick up and put down. When driving, Wu is driving, when resting, Wu is resting, when sitting in meditation, Wu is sitting in meditation. Is this not so?"

He replied that a koan or hua-tou is a method of practice and not to be confused with actual experience. He said it was very dangerous to not differentiate this. He then went on to say that either I had gotten my teacher's teaching wrong, or that teacher did not know what he was talking about.

I knew I had *not* gotten my former teacher, The Roshi's teaching wrong and he must have known this given that he stayed in a monastery in Japan under the same lineage.

It was at this point that I decided that there was great wisdom in playing stupid. After all, being a man of no rank implies neither wisdom nor stupidity. It is the airs we put on and mistake for true self that are the root cause of our suffering. However to appear in this world as an affliction body, we tend to cling to one thing or another. I figured that if I played stupid I would not disappoint anyone including myself. If I played wise and put on a display, I stood to be told I was wrong. Whether I was wrong or not was clearly open to debate so I naturally took the path of least resistance, much like an electrical current. Stupidity if earnestly realized is the initial step to wisdom no matter where your point of perspective is. Starting with a presumption of wisdom is the gateway to clinging and damnation. Although difficult to do at times, playing stupid offers the greater reward. Others then fall into their own traps, and you may emerge from yours.

Shifu ended the interview by saying, "Working on a hua-tou is like looking for a wife".

I could not help but reply, "What if you're already married?"

A playful smile settled upon his face that could not be hidden with his serious manner. He clearly liked what I said.

"Go back to your seat in the Chan Hall!" he ordered.

I bowed, rose from my chair and did another awkward prostration on linoleum, then after bowing, left the room.

"What happened to that nice Chinese grandfatherly monk?" I thought as I settled onto my cushion. "That interview was hell on wheels. I feel like a duck at an N.R.A. convention."

The last thing I wanted to be was a trouble maker; especially as a first-time guest. After all, Canadians are noted for being polite. Now I was outdoing myself as a "shit disturber".

Of course, everything said during the interview was heard in the Chan Hall.

I knew that Brian had no idea what went on other than it sounded like I was totally humiliated by Master Sheng-yen. The bottom line was I really didn't care. The issues were far too large for me to be concerned about image or what other people thought of me.

Had image rather than realizing Buddhadharma been my concern, I would have quit.

However, this whole exposition was not going to get me any followers.

The next interview I had with Master Sheng-yen was during the normal scheduled interview period.

I was used to the Zen Center regimen wherein one was interviewed up to three times a day by the Roshi. There was a lot of one on one contact between teacher and student. Everything else about the Chan retreat was more or less the same, save for the number of interviews with Shifu. It came down to around two, maybe three interviews during an entire seven day retreat.

I was waiting in a line of chairs for my interview. Ahead of me was the roommate who gave me the massage three nights previous.

During his interview I could overhear the conversation. There was no interpreter in the room and it seemed that Master Sheng-yen had no problem at all understanding what was said to him in English. His responses in English didn't seem all that bad either.

When my turn came, I entered the room, bowed and prostrated as was customary, then seated myself.

Thinking that the same protocol applied for this interview as it did for the dokusan interviews of the koan Zen tradition I had spent 18 years in, I began by stating the title of the koan I was working on in the Blue Rock Records.

Suddenly Shifu could barely speak English.

"What you say?" he scowled.

"That is the case in the Blue Rock Records I am working on," I said.

"I don't understand," he replied, as if his mouth was full of vinegar.

Now, if he spent seven years in Japan with a dharma heir of Harada Roshi, he certainly was familiar with how the koan system operated. I thought that this was the way in which he too operated. I had no reason to believe otherwise.

"This is the koan I am working on," I repeated, then offered a brief summary of it.

"You do STORIES," he replied.

I immediately said that they were not stories, and then stopped myself in mid-sentence because I realized that after all, that's what they were.

"Actually, given the circumstances, for the past couple of years I have gone back to working on the koan "Mu".

Master Sheng-yen smirked.

"Oh. And how you practice Mu? You sit there and say, "Mu!–mu! –mu!…"

His words "Mu!–mu!–mu!…" were spoken in a dainty voice, accompanied by little powder puffs of exhalation. He did petite jerks as he said them.

"No," I said.

"Then how you say Mu?" he replied.

I inhaled, paused, and from the depths of my being allowed Mu to rise. This was not at all difficult given the conditions. The volume of the sound built exponentially until it filled the room with an inseparable combination of pain and questioning. The next breath began the word again, this time louder and of greater power.

After doing this three times I stopped and the room filled with equally deafening silence.

The Master sat listening intently with head slightly canted sideways, his gaze to the floor.

At length he said, "Continue on with that practice. But do it quietly and silently. You will distract others from their Hua-tou if you do it out loud."

Opening Mind

That first retreat with Master Sheng-yen was nothing other than an unending series of opportunities to shatter the mold of practice I had been encased in, and move on. This was not always pleasant and took a great deal of courage. I got through the whole thing by entering my refuge of Mu, (now Wu) practice. This refuge was not the same anymore. I was beginning to faintly sense the presence of open portals letting in wondrous light. This was really one small to vanishing verbal step in entering Dhyana's infinite depth framed within a sea of Buddhist Concept I was only beginning to be aware of.

I found out that there were no "subsequent koans" and for that matter, no koan system in Chinese Chan. There was little emphasis on direct student teacher contact and grooming. I immediately realized that this was more natural and less prone to the extreme problems of deception that I had come face to face with in my former training.

If a student or disciple is groomed by the teacher on how to respond and behave, would not that teacher be more easily fooled by a less than enlightened student groomed on how to respond and behave?

You decided what Hua-tou or koan you would work on. If you got results from that hua-tou you did not necessarily go onto another. These hua-tous were methods of practice and not confused with Chan itself.

This was to me a very important distinction I had not previously realized.

It is one thing to go full force into practice and say, "Everything is Mu!"

This is fine to a certain degree. However, to be truly free of distinctions so that everything is indeed "Mu," one cannot *ignore* the mind that generates distinction. If you practice under sweeping generalizations in ignorance of distinctions, your all-encompassing hua-tou is still really a special tool of illumination that can only function undisturbed by distinction, much like a candle flame in a hurricane. It is only designed to survive in the most special and shielded of conditions of sitting meditation. It is useless in all conditions, which in turn makes it absolutely useless, if its nature is not in harmony with its application.

Thus distinctions can rise and fall away freely without the need to pickle the sense of intellect into being a stylistic cloistered preserve inside some dark jar. This is true hua-tou practice.

Another wonderful thing I discovered was the chanting and recitation.

The Heart Sutra was recited - not chanted - in English. At first it struck me as being weak in that it was not chanted with wooden drum and given some meter of word-rhythm. However, after reciting this much longer and more detailed version than what I had chanted for years, I began to realize that it was far superior. The former translation I was familiar with was stylized, dangerously abbreviated to fit a certain meter in order to sound good.

All of Shifu's talks were translated into English. I greatly appreciated the time, care and effort to do so. It impressed me the sophistication of the talks, as well as their hidden knowledge of the English language. Shifu would at times correct the translator with amazing awareness of the nuance of more appropriate English words even though he claimed his English was poor.

Of all the retreats I later had the privilege of attending with Master Sheng-yen, this first one was the only one where he kept extolling the immeasurable virtues of solitary practice and that only those truly fit to practice Chan should attempt it or could make use of it.

I had the feeling I would be doing a great deal of solitary practice in the future, the way things were unfolding.

In that first retreat he also talked about the Sixth Patriarch Hui-neng arriving at the 5th Patriarch's monastery already enlightened. The 5th Patriarch purposely did not acknowledge Hui-neng's realization for over two years although he clearly saw it.

"Why was that?" Shifu asked, and then looked about the assembly of retreat participants.

There were no answers and he left the question open and alive.

Every morning the Chan Hall would be aired out by opening the front doors. These doors were open portals to Queens at 4 A.M. and what was more, Shifu would pass through them to go for an early morning walk

The last day came. My exhaustion had returned during the morning meal and I had problems staying awake during Shifu's morning talk. I heard him say that Chan practice is like riding a great warhorse whereupon the powerful general riding it has the ability to realize Complete Enlightenment.

As I was dozing off, he said from his seat at the end of the long table, "Wake up, wake up." When he had my attention he said, "A fat man riding a donkey of practice can also realize Complete Enlightenment."

I knew he was talking to me because his glance was directed my way, and due to stress I had physically let myself go and put on some weight during the previous two years.

There were compassionate forces at that place that were unmistakable, even though I was given a very difficult time.

Brian and I each bought a book of Shifu's at the Center's gift desk. Upon seeing Shifu pass by, Brian ran after him, produced a pen and got his copy autographed.

He returned excited.

"I've got an autographed copy of a book by a real Chan Master!"

I thought to myself, "Is this what you came for? I'd rather realize his teaching!"

When I returned home I was still in shock. Something very powerful had happened.

A Man of No Rank

The network of friends Barb and I had from the Toronto Affiliate Centre were naturally overburdened by of what had gone on and having distanced themselves from their practice felt they had little to lose. More than a couple seemed eager to prove that practice was a falsehood. This would remove the burden of exerting themselves to come to realize freedom from affliction they undoubtedly desired in the first place.

Brian was one of these people. Of course, he was a professional scientist and frequently mustered up the common and easily recognizable set of empirical markers that are used to debunk anything that does not fit prescribed form. Now, armed with what he perceived happened to me in New York, he began what he thought was a clever set of comments and attitudes designed at skating around his already arrived at conclusion that I too was a fake, but too stupid to realize it. I was very much aware of what he was thinking, and what others thought, but it was impossible for me to stand up and say, "Zen teaching is the absolute way of release from suffering," when I had been demonized by a system that was purportedly the embodiment of Zen itself, and after going to another teacher, was perceived to be publically humiliated.

Many of these friends kept going to the endless meetings at the Zen Centre and were eager to report back what was said about me in my absence. This gave me something of a feeling that there was an enjoyment by some to further stick it to me as a reward for pushing training they felt was not nice and too severe. It was all right for them to read the Zen stories of the great sacrifices made in the past to realize The Way, and yet they wanted for themselves the cushy pseudo Western psychological approach framed within their precious selves that they could come to realization in a more comforting, seemingly sophisticated, modern and self-affirming way.

This trip to Master Sheng-yen with a witness certainly did not help my problem. I was not publically vindicated in any way. At times the thought consumed me that perhaps Master Sheng-yen didn't want anything to do with me because of the controversy that I had brought to light.

Yet my intuitions told me otherwise. Either way, I knew I was in for a rough ride.

On many occasions in the following months and years, I wondered why the ordeal of being demonized and offered as a scapegoat had happened to me. Was I the ego centred deluded tyrant the Zen Centre was telling people I was? Was it a fault of mine that I built things and that I could think and speak in physical scientific terms? Was I really a "show off" that needed to be taught a horrible and severe lesson?

These thoughts were always illuminated by the fact that the institution responsible for the severe "teaching" I was experiencing was all the while teaching something quite divergent from Buddhadharma. It was saying that seemingly severe stories and actions of The Ancient Masters were not necessary. Yet by giving homage to breaking the precepts and calling it "teaching", it was in a very real sense surpassing the severity it was denying as necessary by adding to the equation a living lie.

I tried to keep this group of friends practicing Buddhadharma with the availability of retreats lead by me outside the Zen Centre. However, because they were not told by an authority figure that I was a teacher, it quickly became an issue that nobody was prepared to believe that I knew what I was talking about and that the group didn't want me as a focal point. Therefore, if I tried to schedule a weekend meditation at our place, it became an issue of why it couldn't be at someone else's.

I went along with that concern, and tried going to meditation sessions at other's houses only to find that they were little prepared and really didn't have a clue besides a series of preconceptions of what they were doing.

It was the same power and prestige struggle all over again.

But who was I to say anything?

The worm of cynicism is a very powerful and destructive thing. Its function is to supplant actions of faith and great exertion of realizing wisdom with the rotting stench of asserting that The Great Way and those who refuse to quit walking it are of lesser wisdom than their own. It feeds on the putrefying carcasses of dead dreams and aspirations.

Those that feed themselves to this worm think themselves to be free thinkers unaware that they are completely shackled to the wheel of birth and death by the very thoughts they consider are freeing them. This blindness is so encompassing nothing can be said to any effect.

The dilemma I found myself in, as undesirable as it was, manifested for me as a great blessing because I had a hounding dissatisfaction about my own realization.

It was definitely not that what I clearly could see with my Dharma eye was wrong.

No. That much was self-vindicating. It was the fact that I felt deep affliction from what had happened and could not shake off its effect. This affliction gave me no choice but to enter The Way like I had never done before.

I could not give the fairy-tail story that I received transmission from Master "so and so" and was therefore a certified teacher myself. In fact, what happened to me was quite the opposite. I had been criminalized by the leaders of the group I associated with and yet this criminalization was at odds with the fact that the only reason I kept practicing was that, unlike my accusers, I put my life into practice.

How do you explain this to people?

Once again living in isolation after being surrounded in a social womb that gave my life meaning was a very unpleasant form of rebirth. However the very fact that I was alive and my practice was alive despite this most insidious adversity was a most fundamental vindication.

In order to survive I had chosen to make it a practice of being a man of no rank. This was difficult given that at the Chan Center I was at least ten years more senior in formal practice than the head monk. I could clearly see the condition of people's practice, and had a universe of paradigms with which I could instruct people to enter The Way.

And yet, I was not in any way satisfied with my own realization of Buddhadharma.

But now I had met a Master who intrigued me.

However unpleasant, I deeply felt I could learn a lot from him in the way of transcending affliction for myself and others.

Upia is an interesting thing. It is not something flexed upon those who cannot use it. Those who are capable of using it do so because they themselves choose to exercise the Upia received upon themselves. If this cannot be done then Upia is a useless tool.

False Upia is dangerous. It is used by inferior teachers as a tool on those that "need help" without the student being capable of receiving it in a useful way. It immediately falls into a function of "enlightened" teacher versus "unenlightened" student. This "foxy Zen" is a bungee jump to hell with a severed cord.

However, if the recipient of even false Upia from inferior teachers and teaching lines is bestowed upon a person of capability and potential, they will use it to realize Buddhadharma. In this way, the Universe is your teacher and you cannot fail or fall back from your original resolve by being consumed in the narcotic stink of small successes and vindications so long as you have faith in yourself.

This is called "Turning sewage into gold".

A Bodhisattva

I got a few small organ building and maintenance related contracts that kept me busy enough to keep a friend and myself in the shop. This friend was an excellent improvisational pianist, having trained in Poland. He came to Toronto to take part in sesshins and when things were revealed, left the Centre and began coming out to our place to learn woodworking.

He began clueless but was a quick learner and became very skilled. What impressed me the most was his work ethic. This was in contrast to the fact that I was burnt out and sometimes had a hard time carrying on.

Of course, those who make a habit of standing outside things and offering pearls of "spiritual wisdom" would say that I was clinging to what happened. I was the first to agree. However, I am a human being. What is the religious ideal behind the criticism that I was somehow deficient by being effected by what had gone on? Robothood?

We talked a great deal about music and musical instruments. He was very helpful in keeping me going with his enthusiasm. Most importantly, he would ask questions about Buddhadharma.

I had heard through others that as I had predicted, Baldone Sensei's prescribed psychological "treatment" for Oneson Sensei had not gone the way he had planned and Oneson was being removed as a teacher from the Doorchester teaching line.

Even in light of this, there was yet another meeting orchestrated by Oneson's "yes" men (my old friends) where they put it to a Sangha vote led by Punch that out of parting gratitude for his teaching, they would give him the brand new Toyota Corolla centre vehicle bought and paid for with donations so he could drive back home to The United States in style. As I understood it, he also got a pension from the Doorchester Zen Center for his years of service and was set up as a youth advocate by either the Doorchester Zen Center or certain Zen Center members.

That summer I had to remortgage our house and property to stay afloat.

Dissolving a Horrid Affliction

I told others in our little group about Master Sheng-yen and two or three decided to go to a Chan Center retreat with me.

Furthermore, I told Barb and Angie about the new vistas of practice possible at The Chan Center and they too agreed to go and try it out.

The summer passed and near its end, Barb and I went on a trip to the Agawa Canyon, north of Lake Superior.

One day we rented a canoe and paddled along the open water shoreline of Lake Superior to a small series of Aboriginal petroglyphs painted on a rock face. There we dove into deep crystal clear water.

A week or so after we returned, my musical woodworking friend was staying at our house for a couple of days working on a project.

One evening he got a phone call from his wife that the Toronto Affiliate Centre had called his apartment wanting to speak to him, and that he should get back to them as soon as he could. After returning the call from our place he was told that Punch was diagnosed with leukemia and given only months to live. There would be a chanting service for him in Toronto and Doorchester to pray for his recovery.

I waited for my friends to call me. After all this was serious and by its nature transcended any differences harboured from actions in the past.

I sat in meditation well into the night with the thought of Punch's wellbeing foremost in my mind.

No phone call came.

Deeply concerned with what was going on, I phoned the Centre and spoke with Tibs.

Not asking why I wasn't phoned, I expressed concern about Punch's health.

I was told that as Punch, Tibs, Cottonmouth and Doctor Proctor were returning from their latest trip to Algonquin Park, (I was no longer invited) Punch began to feel very ill. He went to his doctor and after being referred to a specialist was given the diagnosis of leukemia and a very short timeline to live.

I asked when this all happened. It was exactly the same point in time Barb and I were returning from Lake Superior.

I told Tibs to ask Punch if I could go see him.

The next day I got the news that Punch *did not* want to see me.

I was stunned. Was he blaming me for his misfortune? Was there a link? Clearly there was in his mind.

There was something at work here that was linking me to Punch's condition – so much so he didn't want to talk to me. This was more than Zen Centre pettiness and I wanted no part of it.

I began earnestly invoking all things seen and unseen, telling them that I wanted no part of any retribution for what was done to me, and searched my heart to make sure I harboured nothing that would create a linkage to his illness. This devout wish I kept day and night, while in sitting or working meditation.

Sometime later I heard that Punch had undergone a miraculous healing and was in remission. He published a book about his experience and how The Doorchester Zen Center and his dear friends created his good fortune. The Roshi came out of retirement to write a forward to his book holding what Punch had experienced as a testimony of the effectiveness of Zen as it was practiced in his teaching line. Of course, what really went on at the Toronto Affiliate Centre before all this happened was conveniently overlooked in the book, and my name never mentioned.

For The Roshi to hold this miracle up as a result of Doorchester Zen Center meditation was foolhardy. The obvious extension of doing so is that it should work for a similar illness under similar circumstances in the future. Sadly, years later a Zen practitioner did become ill with the same disease, and died despite many practitioners (and my) best wishes.

Long after, I found out that at this point in time The Roshi needed a miracle. He had angered a young student who, unlike most of his students, happened to be able to speak, read and write Japanese. That person contacted people in Japan associated with the late Yasutani Roshi, The Roshi's teacher after Harada Roshi, and found that The Roshi had not received anything in the way of transmission from that teaching line.

So, The Roshi himself did not get transmission.

However, it must be said that a Roshi that did receive transmission displayed remarkable drug and alcohol problems, and most prominently, a Japanese American Roshi who definitely received transmission from the same lineage and was about a decade or more younger than The Roshi was revealed to be another out and out sexual predator.

Compared to these examples who had received transmission, The Roshi was a class act as a teacher. The easily observable personality flaws he exhibited were nothing compared with what some of these others as fully sanctioned Roshis had done.

I remember a teisho wherein The Roshi recounted being in Japan attending the funeral of Harada Roshi. While not naming anyone, he said that a second Roshi was wailing and carrying on excessively.

He asked that Roshi, "If you are free from birth and death, why are you carrying on like this?"

That particular Roshi replied, "This is how I become free from birth and death!"

That's how The Roshi left the story.

Years later while reading the book "Zen at War" I saw a photograph of Yasutani Roshi at Harada Roshi's funeral and realized that this was the incident that The Roshi was talking about. One glance at the picture told me The Roshi's question to Yasutani was valid.

Yasutani's answer was suspect. You could ask the same question about alcohol. There certainly were and still are a lot of Japanese monks who get drunk. Do you think that the answer, "Openly getting hammered on whisky is how I go beyond getting hammered with whiskey," would work? Would it be useful to someone with such a problem?

I also got the feeling that this question did not go down well because it hit the target.

The unfortunate incident with the new student brought into question The Roshi's validity as a teacher. What few seemed to question is the validity of the idea of transmission itself.

This was something not lost on me.

What is being transmitted?

Although The Heart Sutra is recited every day by serious practitioners, it says, "There is no wisdom or any attainment. With nothing to attain Bodhisattvas relying on Prajna Wisdom have no obstructions in their mind. Having no obstructions there is no fear, and going far beyond confusions and imaginings reaching ultimate Nirvana…"

However, wasn't it strange that someone like The Roshi who did not receive transmission put such a high value on giving it?

Is this "no wisdom on any attainment" the opposite of having wisdom and attainment?

Another Retreat

I went to my next retreat with Master Sheng-yen alone.

There was an individual attending who when asked where he was from, said in a profound voice, "RIGHT HERE."

Finding out that I was also going to sit beside this fellow indicated to me that this would be an interesting seven days in Queens.

In the hours before the retreat began, I sat in meditation upstairs before a Buddha figure.

Unexpectedly, Master Sheng-yen walked into the room and looked me over, his vision resting slightly above my head. Nodding a gesture of approval, he left the room.

The retreat began with Shifu going around The Chan Hall asking people how many retreats they had been to. When he got to the fellow sitting beside me, the response was "FOUR".

Shifu shouted, "Don't make joke! How many retreats you been to?"

To my disbelief, the fellow snarled something far worse than, "Screw off!"

Shifu snapped a gesture that seemed to propel the lad out of the Chan Hall.

I was next. I lifted my eyes from in front of my mat and noticed Shifu smiling as if he was enjoying himself. I had never been to a retreat, or sitting for that matter where the teacher was told something far worse than "screw off".

These retreats were not screened and therefore not predictable which meant that outcomes were not assumed and The Master was not sheltered and protected within a narrow band of conditions. This meant that Shifu could handle himself in all situations rather than those carefully predetermined.

He asked me how many retreats I had been to. I wasn't about to say, "Over 50". I had known people and teachers who had been to more retreats or sesshins than me, and were Dharma disasters. This had taught me that life itself is an intense training retreat and that I was taking part in only one. Breaking one's life into daily life versus retreat was a useless and dangerous exercise, much like counting one's kenshos. This was the thought I had before I entered this retreat.

I just raised one index finger in silence.

Shifu smiled, raised two fingers, wiggled them playfully, and then went on to the next person.

The next day I felt a presence beside me while in meditation. Suddenly the wood "incense stick" for striking sleepy meditators snapped cross the lens of my glasses.

"You wear glasses while meditating?" Shifu forcefully asked.

"Sometimes I do, sometimes I don't. This time I just forgot," I replied.

This answer was also greeted with a silent smile of approval before he walked away.

Apparently he had contacted the Doorchester Center and asked about me. He was told I had a serious anger problem. This fact didn't seem to add up with what he saw, so he decided to find out for himself. Apparently I passed the test and met his approval.

The first private interview I had with Shifu was different than all previous.

I sat before him eye to eye.

Unlike other teachers I had sat before, his eyes were the visage of compassion, his voice loving and respectful.

He gently said to me without a translator that he didn't trust the new Zen teacher he spoke with and, with a sad expression said that The Roshi was his friend. He then told me that I was not a teacher yet, and a considerable time will pass before "people will come to you to get something", but that I can help people.

I told him we have a small meditation group and that perhaps it will grow into something bigger. He said, "No. I see it going down to one, maybe two people."

What an unusual thing to say.

Even though it was good to hear that I would become a teacher, this other prediction was not very encouraging.

How was I going to help people when I was so inspiring that I whittled down a group of about fifteen to one or two, and that one or two I had a feeling was Barb and me. It was a strikingly strange prediction that felt like it was not a guess.

I went back to my seat.

Retreats at the Chan Center alternated from one retreat to the next with hua-tou practice, and the practice of Silent Illumination, a practice I had never heard of, except in the Japanese form of Shiken Taza.

Master Sheng-yen introduced the practice of Silent Illumination by saying that it was "The Practice of the Tathagathas."

This was a powerful statement.

I maintained my practice of the Hua-tou Wu, but its character was changing.

I had never heard such exquisite instruction on working on a hua-tou.

"Let your mind rest on the hua-tou. If you have results, simply put them down and return to the hua-tou. Gently investigate it with intrigue."

I began to realize that what I thought was a relatively thoughtless samadhi centered on the hua-tou was really the results of a mind of blocked energy that paralysed thought with the hua-tou as a focus.

What I was now experiencing was the beginning of a natural and very rapid opening of portals that were wonderful and exciting.

I became filled with light. When I worked outside cleaning the windows of the Chan Center during afternoon rush hour right out on Corona Avenue in Queens, everything was silent, empty and still, while manifesting complete motion and noise.

There was no effort or pressure of mind for things to appear as such.

When I entered the private interview room for the last interview of the retreat, Shifu said in a booming voice, "You learn a lot this retreat!"

I said that it was more like things fell away.

The last evening of the retreat we had the usual candies and recounted what was learned during the retreat.

I happened to be sitting very close to Shifu. After receiving my candy, I tried opening it and had embarrassing difficulty doing so.

One of the monks reached to help.

With a quick fluid motion Shifu deflected the monk's hand and took my candy. Holding it in front of my face, he gave it a quick tug and it burst from its wrapper.

His face beamed as he handed the opened candy to me.

I was hit by the force of this teaching.

The next afternoon as I left to get in the cab to the airport, Shifu came out of the front door of the Chan Center smiling, and waved me goodbye.

I had a window seat as the airliner climbed to cruising altitude. The sun was low and its reddened energy spread upon immense columns of clouds. Vista after vista revealed itself outside my window in a most exquisite display of an ethereal realm. Powerful pillars of cumulus rose from their bases far below, bathed in golden orange translucence.

My vision returned to the inside of the plane. Nobody was looking out the window. They were either reading newspapers, working on their computers or dozing off listening to headphone music. All were totally oblivious to the miracle they were privileged enough to be floating through. Several shut the sliding window cover to keep the light out.

Practice is Enlightenment

Return to daily life was now a continuous fusion of retreat experience and ongoing life experience. This was because there was now a vast sea of Buddhist Concept from which to draw upon whereas before, being a koan jockey, only a shell of shallow parameters centering on some form of reward of realization and recognition had been the focus.

From Shifu's teaching I deeply realized that the process and the end are inseparable. Therefore, the process is in itself the reward. The realization of Enlightenment became a useful cherished process rather than a goal to strive for.

However, if everything had come to fulfillment and affliction had been eliminated I would have no need to continue practicing.

This was not the case.

While still being slapped around by good and bad fortune, I was far more fortunate than I realized.

People tend to look at difficulty and misfortune as something standing in opposition to Chan or Dhyana Practice while not realizing that Chan or Dhyana Practice is fueled by difficulty and misfortune. The actual experience of difficulty and misfortune is inseparable from Chan or Dhyana.

This is the forge and anvil whereupon Bodhisattvas are made.

When difficulty and misfortune disappear, The Way disappears.

Thus all adversity is the manifestation of Bodhisattvas when illuminated in correct view.

Why?

Because with adversity illuminated in correct view, there is still somewhere we have to go, something we have to realize. If we content ourselves with whatever we imagine we have realized or attained, we take those realizations and attainments as something to cling to when in truth, there is nothing that can be clung to. By doing so, we fall into the false refuge of attainment. This opens the flaming pit of Samsara.

My life at that time was framed by a serious problem. This problem was that I had been vilified by an institution purporting to represent the teaching of Buddhadharma.

Again, I wondered why this happened to me.

Of course, it is very easy for me to say that I had an evil karma, and that all this is a function of relieving past evil or bad actions through the purification of my own karmic burden.

Although there were those who attempted to destroy me "for my own good", they did not realize that I am actually harder and more critical of myself than they. This can be a dangerous self-defeating practice if not coupled with the Wisdom of Buddhadharma. However, it is more dangerous and self-defeating to *not* practice honest and sometimes difficult self-introspection. Those Zen experts who mouth the words "there is no self" without realizing the nature of The Buddha's "no" do not exercise Manjusri's razor sharp sword of empiricism on themselves. They have stopped practicing still covered, welded, embedded and hopelessly fused in self and other while mouthing phrases and citing texts that say otherwise.

It is a true Chan practitioner's practice to turn this darkness into light.

Introspection coupled with a sense of shame for past actions, thoughts and words born from one's own delusion and selfishness is indispensable in arousing the mind that truly seeks the way.

However, to view all dark and stifling things that befall one having an affliction body as being the just deserts of personal darkness and inferiority is the opposite of Right Attitude contained in the Eight Fold Noble Path.

It is far more useful for the liberation of all sentient beings to illuminate one's predicament, such as the one I found myself living, as an all-encompassing challenge; a hua-tou emanating from a Universe of Compassion that due to its all-encompassing afflicting nature has the power to free all beings from all-encompassing afflicting nature. Thus personal pain, loneliness and suffering flowing from and within one's life situation then becomes the benefit and ultimate liberation of all.

"You Must Take Your Teaching From The Buddha"

We were seriously out of money.

My work as well as Barb's was not producing enough income to pay the mortgages and other losses incurred in the years previous. Furthermore, I was experiencing burn out. Even though a quantum shift had occurred in my practice, I still needed to continue to burn in the light of Chan Practice while being "burnt out" emotionally and professionally. To this end I needed to continue to be a disciple of Master Sheng-yen.

The vistas he presented I found intriguing and self-vindicating.

The third retreat I attended at the Chan Center, I brought my daughter Angie. I was feeling that my work as a father was coming to a close with Angie and that if she could go to a Dhyana Retreat with a Master, I could retire, so to speak. I had pointed her as best I could in the direction of liberation. This was very important to me. What she did with it after this was her business.

It was on the third day of this retreat that Shifu told me something I did not understand.

I arrived in the private interview room absorbed in my hua-tou.

He said to me, "You have a problem".

Hearing these words was like getting a bucket of cold water in the face. It was disjoint from the flow of deepening immersion into a hua-tou that is important at the beginning of a retreat. This had never happened to me before.

Shifu continued.

"You are like a race horse that has been bitten by a snake. Now everything that looks like a snake you cannot trust. Because of this you will not receive my teaching. Instead, you will take your teaching from The Buddha."

I had no idea what he was talking about. It seemed rather odd to come into an interview well absorbed in hua-tou practice and have the Master say something so incongruous that it could completely throw you. I could only think that Shifu thought it was important enough to tell me. However, it was not clear what it was he was telling me, so, fortunately I shrugged it off and returned to my hua-tou. Equally fortunate was that his words were imbedded in my memory.

Was he rejecting me?

People rarely see the immeasurable value in indirect teaching. They correctly believe that honesty lies in delineating what is being imparted in plain words with no margin of misunderstanding; just lay out what is being said so that it maps into the listener's mind with no vagueness. This is a classical mathematics paradigm in that things are definitely things and as such must be clearly defined.

However, what is missed in this direct honesty is the other half of the equation, namely the person who is the focus of the message. In a disciple-master dynamic, the recipient of the message is by definition still manifested in delusion – otherwise they would not have entered the disciple-master coupling. Because of this, the intent and value of what is being said cannot be understood by words no matter how direct and honest. Should specific words and more convergent meaning be used, the disciple will more than likely get stuck on a divergent interpretation of what is said.

If it is spoken by the Master as a truth, then a divergent meaning may now have a reality in the student's mind.

When loaded with the possibility of the recognition of attainment, especially when external vindication after an ordeal is deeply wished (as was my case) such an "honest straight forward telling it like it is" teaching is the most devastating thing a Master can do to a disciple.

I have the deepest gratitude to Master Sheng-yen for teaching me in this honest non-direct way.

This is saying that I have the deepest gratitude to The Buddha.

The important part of this was that I realized the value of this form of teaching in myself. I did not trust that I would not drop Manjusri's Sword and trot off with some certification or content myself with having unrealized potential if I was told I had it. I could not live a life of mouthing the words of Great Masters while still clinging to their dependent meanings. I had in the past, and would in the present reject any certification unless it was from the certitude of my being.

So it all boils down to the classic hua-tou "Who is the Master?"

A Fusing of Minds

I continued to attend two retreats a year when I could. For me there was no longer a hounding necessity to go to every retreat possible since life itself had opened up in a full and natural way as The Practice of Buddhadharma. This was something I had vowed to enter over twenty years before.

There were so many wonderful things I heard during Master Sheng-yen's talks and interviews. Once when my energies were low he told me that sometimes working on a hua-tou was like a cat locked in a room with a dead mouse. The cat starts flipping the mouse and batting it around to make it interesting.

However, that day I thought working on my hua-tou was more like a mouse locked in a room with a dead cat.

During one retreat Shifu gave a talk on Hua-tous. In it he said that the American koan "Who am I?" is not a good Hua-tou. It's parameters of meaning are too direct, personal and simple. This was an observation I had made of that particular koan years before.

Another time after telling everyone that reciting the Buddha's Name or the word "Wu" will not bring you to enlightenment any more than constantly reciting your own name. He then added jokingly that if it works for you, that's fine.

Shifu had a powerful sense of humor.

Once he gave a talk about a matter of practice, then in the afternoon contradicted himself. A woman at the retreat pointed this out to him during question period.

"Shifu," she said, "This morning you said that practice requires great effort and this afternoon you say there is no effort!"

"I'm supposed to be contradictory," he grinned. "I'm a Chan Master!"

Thoughts that are inherently irrelevant can keep a person awake at night. There are also many other things that do so.

During a seven day retreat several participants became very upset that they could not sleep at night.

During one of his talks during the final round of meditation before bed time, Shifu told everyone, "If you can't sleep, just say to yourself, "I am already asleep. I am already asleep…"

Short of Complete Enlightenment, we are still unawakened to our true nature. In a very real sense, we are already asleep.

His young translator monk was quite bright and I was grateful for his (and other's) efforts in translating Shifu's talks from Mandarin. He had realized some small flash of insight and but had a problem of being fueled with high octane arrogance. With a mind still trapped in attachment, it is very difficult being a translator of a Master and not begin to think that this wisdom is your own. This is what can be called "translator's disease".

During one retreat, Shifu addressed the assembly in Mandarin with the translator monk translating. He said that this particular translator monk had a problem with arrogance. I remember marvelling at the genius of this

Chan set-up. Here was a forced confession in front of everyone. It was a mastery of the situation used in the compassion of teaching.

On another occasion I entered the Chan Hall early after lunch to meditate. Shifu was sitting in his place, illuminated by a skylight overhead. As a Zen sesshin monitor I had long developed a penetrating eye for people sitting in meditation. It is something inexplicable. The condition of a person's practice and their clinging to defilements is instantaneously seen without any effort.

Shifu was like nothing I had seen before. He was not sitting in meditation. The Universe, indistinguishable from him was sitting in meditation. There was no focus of him separate. And yet it was calm, nothing special and of the highest dynamism in complete stillness. He is still meditating in my mind's eye, that moment becoming timelessness.

Once he spoke on how being a monk can be an easy life. When he was a young monk in mainland China, old monks would choose to winter in the monasteries with the best food, and tell stories of their experiences all the while not spending much time with any one particular master, especially if that master's training was severe. Such a life had no responsibilities and was not a function of ambition. This absence of ambition included a hounding desire to realize Buddhadharma.

When they got old, and could barely make it to the monastery to winter at, young Shifu and his teenage monk friend upon seeing them hobble though the monastery gates would say, "Here comes another potato to bake in the monastery's crematorium".

To some people's horror, I was the only one in the Chan Hall to find that statement hilarious and burst out laughing.

Shifu looked over to me and gently scolded, "Paul!" in recognition that we shared the same sense of humor.

Another time he spoke of a novice Western monk in Taiwan who thought it was pointless to do hours of prostrations.

"Why do we do this?" he asked Shifu.

Shifu replied, "Because it is a monk's job to suffer."

Upon hearing this I realized that if one is truly practicing, it is a lay person's job to suffer also. However, lay practice is more difficult because within its defining parameters it is far more difficult to plainly see the nature of affliction and the fact that one is indeed afflicted. In lay life one obtains things in order to reduce suffering and "make life easier". A lay person with house, spouse, family and work has more difficulty using the suffering that naturally flows from such parameters without falling into the timeless traps of comfort, reward and escape presented and marketed in normal day to day life.

However, as Master Ta Hui pointed out, if one can use this difficult and slippery path of lay practice, the results are far more powerful than realization in an atmosphere designed to maintain a course in the right direction. Thus lay practice can be a more powerful tool than a life of monasticism.

This observation is even more pertinent when framed in Western culture that has long forgotten its Buddhist roots still submerged under the strata of a history dominated by god toys.

The continuum of retreats framed within the afflicted field of my life went on. I had lost all momentum in procuring contracts for organs and got by on small organ servicing jobs and a couple of additions to pathetically inferior instruments. I was becoming very tired of dealing with churches and church committees who had a primary directive that, because they do whatever they do in God's name, they can break the accepted rules of business practices necessary in normal transactions.

I decided to build three French harpsichords for the private market and only got as far as preliminary case construction. I was just burnt out.

In order to make ends meet to pay my growing debt to the bank, I started building classic furniture for high end retailers, coming up with approximately 14 designs and prototypes.

Once delivered for the wholesale price factor of twice the material cost, without payment for design and prototyping, they were copied and built by the retailer's own larger shops. This saved them an inordinate amount of time, inventiveness and money.

I suppose a small amount of satisfaction could be derived from the fact that my work was so good these "successful" furniture makers stole it. However, satisfaction is one thing, paying banks is another.

One highly successful furniture maker was so artistically devoid of craftsmanship and morally bankrupt that all he did was steal other small shop's designs and make them in his own facility with hired skill and superior (non-skill requiring) tooling. His cost of production was much lower in that he could buy large amounts of lumber at a considerable reduction in price over my ability to store only a couple of hundred board feet.

I began to think that perhaps he knew the right people and got into the right secretive clique because he was always seen with mayors and police chiefs during the highly publicized charitable events he took part in. He hired people who used their own money to put themselves through community college or had learned their skills for minimum wage elsewhere. This also saved him considerable time and money.

Unlike me, he did not spend time teaching people how to use tools, good design, and the innumerable other facets of being a craftsman. There was no explaining his success on his actual abilities.

I suppose I could be faulted on either naiveté, stupidity or both. I could not afford to carry on like this anymore. It seemed that everything I did was a loss.

A remarkable thing happened while all this was going on. During breaks while working in the shop I began scribbling down things about Buddhadharma that came to me without exerting any mental effort.

The writing would become so encompassing I would forget what I was doing. When I once again looked at a clock, two hours had passed as if I had just sat down.

I couldn't stop doing this which added to my financial difficulties because nobody was paying me to write, and the low profit margin projects that I was struggling to get out the door were not getting done.

One morning, after staying up all night to finish a series of cabinets on time, I began doubling over, coughing and throwing up incessantly. I couldn't stop gagging. Along with my lungs having more than their share of sawdust and finishing chemicals, my whole being had had enough of this predicament.

Barb, on seeing me doubling over and coughing up clear bile, told me that this was the end of my woodworking career and that we would once again remortgage the house so that, hopefully, we could get by with only her salary.

The only condition she imposed was that I continue writing.

I told her that what I really needed was to get enlightened.

She looked at me and said, "What you really need is to get lightened!"

Through stress alleviating snacking, I had put on a few more pounds in a relatively short time.

Barb

Over the previous years with Shifu, I had written retreat reports after each retreat. This was something new to me and I loved doing it. However, even if what I wrote was in harmony with Shifu, others did not necessarily see the wisdom. There is nothing wrong with this. It is simply the way things are at places of practice. If they had realized Buddhadharma or had the ability to do so on their own, they would not need to be at a place of practice.

On one hand, Shifu was encouraging me to write and on the other, I got the impression that what I was saying was not always approved by those editing Chan magazine.

That was natural because I had no context to be viewed within.

Since I was deeply in the process of using this vexing predicament as a valuable tool, being politely ignored was in itself an act of compassion.

It was obvious to me that whatever did not bear Shifu's name, Shifu did not concern himself with. Furthermore, since I was at least a decade more senior in serious practice than the head monk at the Chan Center, I decided to keep all my writing to myself.

The most painful of experiences taught me that in such circumstances it is wise to hide your light because there will be a lineup of others within the framework of getting something from an institution that will make every effort to extinguish it. This is nothing new nor is it an impenetrable wall to stifle the mind that seeks the way. It is a natural gate that one must pass through, its inherent nature neither good nor bad unless thinking makes it so. Everything just as it is embodies perfection when illuminated in the light of non duality.

Thus I decided to keep what I had learned and realized secret until things inner and outer, seen and unseen, told me I was ready to teach.

If you are a seasoned monk within the framework of "Oriental" Buddhism, you usually arrive at a Master's place with established credentials and have some degree of seniority.

Coming from a North American Zen teaching line such credentials are not recognised, and in most cases, this is for good reason.

However, I found that being a man of no rank was a powerful method of practice.

Pinebush

It seemed like a flash.

Suddenly the Chan Center bought a country retreat place in a beautiful mountain setting, and retreats were now being held there.

I fondly recall the first December retreat I participated in at that location.

One evening in what later became the dining hall, a warming fire burned behind the glass doors of a woodstove. Large snowflakes gently fell outside the picture window that Shifu was seated in front of.

It was a visage of perfection.

Everything was whole and complete in this world just as it is.

He said, "There is an old Chinese saying, 'People envy the thief eating meat but do not see the beatings he took to get it.'"

This state of perfection does not come without earning it.

I was familiar with country living, engineering, construction and general survival. However, I soon learned that any suggestions I might have on how things would best be done was usually ignored by the head monk. Other people at the center were open to my suggestions and, for them, there was no problem. But the management, for one reason or another, seemed to know better. For that reason I quickly learned to keep my mouth shut and just watch things progress.

Experience is a good teacher.

At the beginning of a late spring retreat, the head monk gave a lengthy talk on the dangers of ticks carrying Lime's disease. He said that it could make you very sick and even cause death.

Half way through that retreat an understandably concerned person came to him with bites on the back of her neck and legs.

He took one look at the bites, laughed loudly and walked away leaving her mind racing with morbid possibilities.

Was this helpful in centering mind on Silent Illumination?

During a retreat such unspoken unease and fear spreads from person to person like a plague without speaking a word.

I decided to stay out of it.

All of it.

I could only watch from the sidelines as to how things were being run.

For the size of the property, the equipment was inadequate. A lawn equipment dealer in a neighbouring city had sold the head monk a large belt driven pseudo tractor, much too small and delicate for the requirements of cutting the lawn, snow removal and various other tasks. Inconceivably, a tractor dealer in Pine Bush that sold serious small tractors and lawn equipment was overlooked.

Knowing small town psychology, ignoring local expertise and help is usually a primal mistake. Strategically not having your servicing facilities close by is another. However perhaps there were circumstances I was unaware of.

An Opening

It was during a fall retreat when I entered the Chan hall and found Shifu standing by my sitting cushion smiling, his gaze fixed slightly above it. I struck up a conversation with him.

He was friendly and open.

Later, midway during the retreat Shifu gave a lecture concerning the creation of those fit to be called Chan Masters. He said they were like swords. As he spoke in Mandarin, the translator monk converted the words into English.

When the monk translated for Shifu that a master is smelted, Shifu stopped and said in English, "No, that is not the right word."

I spoke up and said, "The word needed is "forged."

Shifu was obviously pleased I had offered the correction. Smelted is something being born with the right ingredients. Forging a sword is being forcibly heated until glowing white and repeatedly struck on an anvil causing sparks to fly, after being born with the right ingredients. This is work hardening during the tempering process. It is essential in the making of an effective sword. Ceremonial swords that look and shine like the real thing are not forged. They are useless in battle because they are too soft and dull quickly or their spine is too brittle and they snap. They are incapable as a tool of cutting through the most impermeable.

Is this the Sword of Manjusri?

At the end of that retreat Shifu announced that the position of director of the retreat center was open for applicants. He said that the newly acquired house on the property would be made available for somebody with a wife and child, and that there would be a car supplied as well as a salary and medical benefits.

I was excited. I felt that the job opening was tailor made for me and Barb and that with my experience I could offer a great deal as director.

When I got home I told Barb about the opening. She too found it exciting saying that she would quit her job and we could sell our house and property.

However, I had seen how the retreat centre was being run and also saw that my previous suggestions (all of which turned out to be correct) were not acknowledged.

Keeping this in mind, I wrote an application for the job. I mentioned my then 30 years of retreat experience, my background in physics/engineering, woodworking and construction.

Before I submitted my application, I thought it would be wise to speak with the Head Monk. I told him over the phone that I was applying for the director's opening that Shifu had announced.

He immediately told me it was more of a janitor's position than that of a director. That statement told me who would be making the decisions and that the whole thing was definitely something to stay away from.

I was very grateful to The Buddha to have allowed me the wisdom to cut that application short. This was proven over time to be correct concept and action.

I attended the spring retreat at Pinebush.

On the second day of the retreat Shifu asked each person to state what their practice was.

Feeling a sense of shame for my countless defilements, I said to Shifu that I would like to practice Master Han Shan Te Ching's method of renunciation.

After I had finished speaking, he simply said, "There is nothing to renounce."

During that retreat the young Chinese man assigned to cutting the extensive lawn with the miniature tractor was driving the thing in high gear with the power takeoff on and turning sharp corners. It was like watching a NASCAR race. Even if I wasn't the work supervisor, his driving was scaring the living daylights out of me. This was obviously the first time he had driven a lawn tractor. I told him to slow down because he was going to wipe out and get hurt. He told me he had to get the job done and there was a lot of lawn to cut. In that regard he was right, and his dedication to the job was admirable. However, I felt it wasn't worth becoming an amputee over. After some discussion, we came to an agreement about how the lawn should be cut. We also became good friends.

On the theme of becoming an amputee, the head monk was assigning people with no experience on chainsaws to go into the bush and cut limbs off trees *with chainsaws*. To my horror, these volatile tools were handed out as if they were electric tooth brushes.

There are so many things that can go wrong when operating a chain saw, even when you know what you are doing. I was not the only one horrified. Another senior Western practitioner also questioned the wisdom of making available such potentially devastating tools without at least an introductory course in how to use them. That was the least I could offer.

Retreat interviews with Shifu were now done on a group basis. Private interviews were loosely taken care of by either the head monk or an experienced lay disciple of Shifu's. I was never asked to do interviews but instead found myself constantly in the disciple-of-no-rank paradigm. In this way I was firmly under the dragon's foot with no prestige and no dispensed optics of recognition to feel I was somehow outside the situation. In my case, being of no rank could be equated by some to a rabbit getting both barrels of a twelve-gauge shot gun.

This did wonders for my standing with those who had practiced under my direction in the past. I had received letters from old friends still practicing seriously who had left the Toronto Zen Affiliate and were curious about how things were going between me and Master Sheng-yen. I could not say that I was being recognized and interviewing people or that my presence and experience at retreats were given anything in the way of public recognition or approval. From this lack of "good news" comes the natural extrapolation that I had realized nothing of value and was a Zen idiot.

This was further reinforced by my friend Brian.

He told me, "You know, we all heard what went on between you and Sheng-yen during that retreat," as if it was something I should be ashamed of.

I said nothing concerning this observation. How could I change how he perceived things when he had no will to question what he believed or would like to believe?

To remedy this overall dilemma, I decided to ask Shifu if he would lead a retreat at our place in Mansfield. I had been encouraged to ask him by senior practitioners in New York.

"Ask Shifu to do a retreat at your place! He's very easy that way and would love to do it! This is something he has done quite freely in the past!"

We needed to get our meditation group growing and this would be an excellent way of doing so.

When I put the question to Shifu, he said, "Totally impossible!" and walked away.

He then turned and added, "Nothing is ready," then continued walking.

I thought, "Of course nothing is ready! I can fix that quickly enough given we have a shop building and house that parallels the current accommodations of the retreat center at Pinebush!"

A feeling of bewildered rejection came over me. Was it that he didn't want anything to do with me and Barb because of what happened at another Center? If that was so, why didn't he tell us to leave? I had seen him do that to other practitioners. He had no problem being severe whenever he needed.

This dilemma took a turn for the worse during the last interview of this retreat.

We were all told to ask Shifu a question.

When it came my turn before the assembly of practitioners, I asked, "If the Buddha had mastered Silent Illumination and by that is meant that all illumination has returned to silence, then how is it that he appeared in this world to teach?"

Master Sheng-yen had a heavy cold. He blew his nose into a handkerchief, looked at it causing the head monk standing behind him to cringe, and then flatly stated, "It is because you still stand outside The Teaching!"

I had been struck to the floor.

On the way back to the retreat hall my being became a painful tsunami of doubt.

Out of silence the thought "Maybe I was supposed to have taken that job offer after all," came and returned to silence.

A heron flew low over my head and, despite what had just happened, the thought, "The Romans saw the flight of a bird such as this as a good portent," came into illumination.

That too returned to silence.

I arrived at the porch of the Chan Hall precariously sailing the vastness of Silent Illumination as if there was no tomorrow. There wasn't even a today for that matter. Given half a chance, this sea could become a violent maelstrom of dissonant leaping waves crashing green over the deck, the compass off its gimbals, having plunged overboard into the churning depths below.

On the porch of the Chan Hall was a fellow who was making it his pleasant practice watching the antics of a nest of baby swallows situated in the rafters above the tea table.

As I stood under the nest with cup in hand, he observed one of their little butts protruding over the side of the nest and exclaimed aloud, "OH NO!"

From such a small source, an impressively large stream of bird shit splattered onto my shoulder. I stood unmoved, holding my cup of tea.

After a moment's pause, I closed my eyes, positively nodded my head and quietly said, "Such great good fortune."

Two Bodhisattvas present on the porch doubled over laughing. Once recovered, one kindly came over with a couple of paper towels and mopped up my shoulder, then burst out laughing again.

After finishing my cup of tea, I returned to my seat in the Chan Hall as if nothing had happened.

After the retreat had ended, a fellow sitting next to me at the public interview who had "decades" of Zen and martial arts training at other places said to me, "Man, I wouldn't have taken a shot to the head like the one you took during that interview! I'd get up and leave!"

Being of thick head, I put in my application for the December retreat.

I was accepted, but was told by the Head Monk that all space was taken and I would have no place to sleep.

I told him I would sleep in the foyer of the Chan Hall.

He then said that I could attend.

A Hut to Myself

Dhyana practice was my life.

I had a choice not to continue but realized that this was no choice whatsoever, even though I was definitely not making a living at being a Buddhist.

As my treatment by the Chan Center began to unfold in a strange and questionable way, I said to Barb that if Master Sheng-yen proves to be a fraud, even after ringing so true to my deepest senses, then the world is truly in very desperate shape.

What was missing from this analysis was my own of assessment of myself.

It really didn't matter if Master Sheng-yen was a fraud or not. Ultimately this can be nothing other than *his* private concern.

What really mattered was whether I had realized Buddhadharma for myself and thereby did not need external vindication. Anything short of this would make *me* a fraud.

This fundamental private concern of mine, though very much active, was diluted with a clawing need for an external vindication I expected Master Sheng-yen to give me. After all, I had done everything right up to that point. I had survived vilification and troubling hardship. There had to be the big carrot or lollypop coming my way from the establishment, whatever form it took.

I had on many occasions sat down and took stock of my actions and reactions. This is a natural part of timeless Dhyana Practice and should not be sullied by the greed of the psychology industry to hoard each and every human thought form as if they invented it and had it under patent.

I came to the realization that it was natural to have experienced what had gone on in my life practice and feel deeply hurt and painfully isolated. To *not* feel this way would be an indication that I was dead.

Of course, in the past I had been told that if I had any realization at all, such things should not bother me. This observation always, without fail, came from those dharma gas nebulae who bestow situations on others, thinking they profit from a standpoint of superiority, while not having to test their own reactions and feelings on the receiving end.

I too thought that if I did not have this precious me, I would not feel this pain and rejection. However, I quickly concluded that to do so while manifesting an affliction body was impossible. This was an obvious and deeply intriguing condition that pointed directly to the heart of all Hua-tous.

The only way Buddhadharma is useful to the living is to be able to teach from this natural stress and dilemma. The only way this can honestly and therefore penetratingly be done is from nonattachment to attainment, nonattainment, birth and death without changing the nature of being a living human being.

Therefore it was natural to deeply feel what I was feeling. These feelings were not the forces governing what my actions were, but rather the fuel powering them.

In this way they were useful and everything that I had experienced up to that point was the myriad functioning arms of Avalokitesvara.

The truth was that if I could not make use of this situation for the liberation of others, then the world as far as I could see was indeed in very desperate shape.

Shifu as a separate manifestation could not help me on this one.

I had to do it on my own. In so doing, I was actively changing the nature of how I manifested relative to others, including The Universe Itself.

I came to the conclusion that as far as my standards went, I was not yet ready to teach.

Upon arrival at the Center, I checked the roster of participants. To my joy I saw that an old Polish friend who had lived at the Toronto Affiliate Centre and had been one of my employees at my shop in Mansfield was attending the retreat, along with several other practitioners from Poland. This fellow was also present and witnessed Barb kicking Oneson Sensei for stalking our daughter, and his cowardly 911 call to the police culminating in Barb's subsequent arrest.

This joy began to fade as I recalled that he had not made any attempt to talk either verbally or by written letter to me or Barb since that event, save for a two year delayed letter of thanks for a fairly high quality guitar Barb gave to him before we left the Centre.

When I picked up that letter I could not let it remain in my fingers.

I had long learned to pay heed to these touch and second sight related perceptions that were at odds with what I would like to think. They were not reliable, but then again, the fond thoughts and subsequent trust bestowed upon some individuals from what is considered normal senses I found not to be reliable either.

Despite all this, pleasant thoughts emerged as I saw him walking up the path to the dining hall because a positive and loving heart-mind image of him is what I wanted to think and believe.

When his glance met mine, it was clear to me that the fondness was not mutual. He was not happy to see me. Although he postured a position of respect, our brief conversation confirmed my overall assessment of his condition.

He told me he was always in touch with people at the Toronto Zen Affiliate. Why did he not bother to keep in touch with me or Barb, even though he was a witness to what had happened to her? What he didn't say and do was far more revealing than his words.

When I went to "Check in" with the head monk, I was told that there were no bedroom spaces available, but I could sleep in one of the abandoned summer camp huts still standing on the property from the 1960's. It was December and snow covered everything as a particularly strong cold snap settled in.

"Wonderful!" I said, incongruously enthused.

This response was in accordance with my desire to get my money's worth out of this retreat. In fact I was going to make sure that everyone got their money's worth. This was my degree of professionalism in Dhyana Practice.

I took my sleeping bag and back pack out to the hut and plunked them down on its plank floor. These huts were designed for summer use only. There was no glass or sheet plastic in the large horizontal windows spanning the walls. Just standard mosquito mesh screen. This would help keep snowflakes out, I reasoned. However, the windows did not go lower than about four feet off the floor, so if you situated yourself properly with a given prevailing wind, you were assured of some protection against rapid cooling.

In defiance of this knowledge, I set up my bed in the middle of the floor under a derelict ceiling fan.

The door was screened its full length. I thought that this was good in that at least I could see anyone coming, should anyone besides me be nuts enough to come out here.

When I returned to the Chan Hall after the initial dinner, the head monk took me aside and said, "It's O.K. for you to stay in an upstairs room in the main house. I have assigned you a place."

I cheerily replied, "No! It's fine. I like where I am. Have it all set up!"

He looked at me, paused, then said, "If you change your mind, the room is available."

"Thanks, but I won't need it!" I replied.

If he was going to embark on a tough practitioner route, I might as well make it as difficult and surreal for him as I could.

Before the retreat began, there was a meeting in the dining hall. We were introduced to the newly appointed director. She was a westerner as well as a corporate lawyer who had lived and worked in Taiwan. She even spoke fluent Mandarin.

Although I harboured a sinking feeling that I might have missed an opportunity of career advancement (or actual career existence for that matter) by not taking the job when it was initially offered, I was impressed by her manner and professional way of reaching out for any suggestions any of us might have to make the place work better.

Then my long list of unheeded suggestions came to mind and my thoughts of envy of her position immediately vanished.

After the last round of sitting at 10 P.M., I left the Chan Hall and walked through the snow to my open accommodations nestled just inside a perimeter of leafless wooded area. Nobody except the head monk and (presumably)

Shifu knew I was sleeping out there. I checked the outdoor thermometer that read ten above in Fahrenheit, then crawled into my sleeping bag still wearing my parka and toque.

The wind was fairly strong that night. Laying on my back in dim moonlight, I watched the wind spinning the blades of the ceiling fan above me. I fell asleep.

The retreat progressed.

The most difficult thing about the hut lodging was not that it was cold, but that the Chan Hall was kept unnaturally warm. Perhaps this was because there were a large number of people from Taiwan who wanted it that way in response to the outside thermometer reading and the fact that there was influenza going around. I found the temperature gradient treacherous to accommodate because I was sleeping in a refrigerated climate, yet spending over eighteen hours a day sitting in a tropical petri dish.

Half way through the head monk asked me how sleeping out in the hut was.

I replied, "Great! It gets you out in the fresh air!"

He failed in preventing himself from laughing.

The rough treatment I received as well as the somewhat less than ideal sleeping conditions put me in something of a charged state. I entered a samadhi and was little aware I was eating, working or chanting. Apparently I was also not aware of how loud my voice was when I was chanting.

I had always made a point of not chanting half-heartedly figuring that if you chant, you should chant as though you mean it and believe it. This attitude was what formed the Northern German style of congregational singing that Bach's great choral works arose from. The classic organ of North Western Europe was the powerful exponent of this attitude.

Half way through the evening chant of the second last night the translator monk leading the chanting suddenly stopped during one of the mantras and said in a booming voice directed at me, "WOULD YOU SHUT UP?!"

Everybody in the hall stopped chanting. The silence was deafening. Although aware that I was the focal point of what he had just done, the most wonderful thing was that in my samadhi it was as if it wasn't happening while at the same time it definitely was. This in itself was most fascinating. Thus I wasn't thrown and continued on.

The next morning Shifu addressed everyone. Clearly someone told him what had happened. He was apologetic about the behaviour of a particular retreat participant while avoiding the incendiary use of names. However, to some this could be seen as further condemnation of my loud chanting and practice.

As for the translator monk, he was removed from the retreat.

The retreat ended.

I had stayed out in the ventilated hut for the full seven days. It really was no big deal.

It is hard to say where samadhi ends, or where it begins for that matter. It need not end with the final prostrations of a retreat. What generates the conditions for samadhi is equally interesting.

The head monk and Shifu were kind enough to offer me circumstances to take advantage of.

This is true compassion for which I have to thank The Buddha.

As for me, well, if I really took some nut case sleeping in an open hut during a cold snap in December seriously, then I would be in trouble wouldn't I?

Once during a different retreat someone asked Master Sheng-yen how they could see if someone was in samadhi so they could help them.

Shifu flatly replied, "You can't. Your mind is moving too fast."

It can be said that we all are in samadhi; it is just that we don't know it. Because of this we take our afflicted thoughts as reality. Then things become really serious.

It became self-evident that someone did indeed take me seriously.

After the retreat had ended and everyone was naturally immersed in talking, I noticed my old friend from Poland was taking a series of pictures of me while I was relating to others. After sleeping in the hut for a week, I didn't exactly look like a movie star on Oscar Night.

When I spoke with him it was obvious he had lost his reverential veneer.

After returning home I became very sick with influenza. The infection went into my right eye causing its internal static pressure to build throwing all focus into a blur. Had Barb not taken me to emergency I would have probably lost vision in that eye due to subsequent macular degeneration.

A couple of weeks later, I got a Christmas card. Seeing that the return address on its cover was from my old Polish friend from the last retreat, I opened it with feelings of fondness.

These feelings quickly wilted.

The words "Season's Greetings!" were written upon a strange painting of a surreal insect-like demon emerging from an ink bottle, leaving tracks as it walked cross the page.

Then a picture of me after the retreat fell out of the envelope.

There I stood bloated by three layers of clothes under a winter parka and smiling in the midst of conversation. I had blinked my eyes as the camera's shutter clicked so I looked like a slovenly, homeless, smiling idiot talking with his eyes shut.

Why would he send me such a card and picture?

The obvious answer was that he was being a Polish Fox and this was his "Foxy Zen".

The apparent message of the card and photo was that I was an idiot and didn't know it. Maybe I would learn from his clever teaching.

In order to attend that December 2000 retreat, I drove to Pinebush. This was "Y2K" and it was feared that all automated systems would fail because of a digital oversight.

During that retreat, Shifu strongly suggested I go to the first 49 day retreat to be held at Pinebush.

On the trip back, I saw something in the sky I had never seen before.

Through the translucent cirrocumulus stratiformis cloud appeared two suns. I immediately thought that one was an image produced by the refraction of sunlight through high altitude ice crystals that formed the hazy cloud. However, if this were true, the refracted/reflected image would be of less intensity than the source image, due to absorption.

Both appeared to be of the same intensity. I couldn't tell which was the real sun and which wasn't.

I was so amazed I pulled off the busy major highway and got out of the car to look. What I found equally amazing was that I was the only person who had done this. Nobody else seemed to notice this incredible, obvious anomaly.

49 Days

The 49 day retreat began in May and ended in late June.

It turned out to be an unparalleled opportunity that I was most fortunate to have experienced.

What amazed me at its beginning was that there were two or three Westerners who were accepted to attend who had not even been to one seven day retreat. And here I was, after twenty plus years of seven day retreat practice feeling a sense of unease as to whether I was going to get through the whole 49 days in one piece, given my leg pain that never seemed to subside with time.

One such fellow was a retired United States Navy veteran in his early 60's who had volunteered a couple of weeks earlier to set up the unfinished retreat center facilities and was thinking of taking a permanent maintenance position there. He was technically very proficient and knowledgeable. I found him quite amazing signing up for a 49 day retreat without having been to a previous Chan or Zen retreat, and wondered if he actually had any idea of what he was getting into.

There was another gentleman of the same age and retreat experience who was a Vietnam War veteran. He now was an oil company executive working in Saudi Arabia.

The male retreat participants stayed in a duplex of two dilapidated huts similar to the one I stayed in for the December retreat. There were washroom and shower facilities. Although the weather was still cold, one could live in these facilities reasonably well.

The pathway to these huts was a sea of mud in places. Old plywood covered doors were laid over the muddy sections so that people would not sink ankle deep.

My assigned seat for the entire retreat was beside the navy veteran. I figured this was going to another interesting retreat considering it was his first, and here he was signed up for 7 in a row.

I was relieved that he got through the rounds of sitting with very little pain. In fact, he did so with greater physical ease than I did.

During a retreat, there is no talking unless absolutely necessary. This is because talking is an excellent portal for extraneous thought to envelop the mind. However, if you are engaged in certain work activities, especially involving machinery, a minimal amount of talking is sometimes necessary. As the retreat went into its second week, I had to keep reminding these two fellows about the necessity of silence after they casually started conversations about such topics as the condition of my legs and whether I had arthritis or not. This arthritis thing was something even I never considered!

I found that I could easily retract my senses and practice Silent Illumination, yet if a situation presented itself that required action or some thought, I could enter it without mind cluttering itself in movement. After several more speech incursions it became apparent that a level of cynicism concerning practice was building and that if I followed the rules my presence would do nothing to diffuse it. I could crack the odd joke without losing my practice, and used this to lighten up certain people I knew were getting too uptight to survive the 49 days.

Many people saw this and thought I was a slacker.

Believe me, I also weighed the possibility of being a distraction and detracting from the retreat, so I also naturally became aware of the results of my actions. I was concerned that some were not going to make it through the full 49 days if they carried on in the particular way they were headed.

There were good reasons for this.

The primary one was that many of the tasks became quite surreal. This was because they stood at odds with proper professional practices and many of us were professionals and knew how things should be done.

You had to develop a sense of humour about it, otherwise things could become dangerously strange and explosive. Therefore I perhaps did not appear to be very serious, but that was a big help for others rather than a problem.

On one occasion we were engaged in digging a trench to drain a sizable puddle of water that had seeped into the path to the dining hall. The only problem was, there was little to no height gradient to encourage the water to go where it was deemed by the head monk to go. We were up to our ankles digging and moving mud about with wheel barrows with no observable goal presenting itself. To others not involved in the project, our activity was a source of consternation. One such person present on the veranda the day I was targeted by the baby swallow happened to walk by.

As he passed our activity his brow furrowed.

Seeing this, I muttered, "We're looking for Jimmy Hoffa."

He choked on muffled laughter.

It was a great privilege to be consumed in this retreat with Shifu. I always found his many talks deeply valuable.

During the retreat he said that the reason that Western Buddhist Teachers got in trouble was that they were not monks.

This hoisted a red flag in front of me. My first reaction was that this was not the problem. It was that these people were told they had results when in fact they were far short of the emancipation that is the heart of Buddhist Practice. This applies to monks as well. However, if you take his words one step further, and realize that some, if not all of these colossal failures had shaved heads and wore monk costumes despite the fact that they were not monks, then what he was saying was true.

Now, as far as I know, these frauds all appeared as monks or priests. They did not live the life a Chan monk, but a Meiji Restoration hybrid-married-genus of pseudo monk. To my knowledge, those Western teachers not parading as such but appearing as normal practitioners were not of the same phylum. They taught their teaching without diversion from The Precepts. They did their best without the costume and illusion.

I was not sure why I was being given such a rough time by Shifu and the head monk while others of far less experience, (including the head monk) were treated with positions of authority. I was, however, aware that this lack of recognition was an excellent catalyst for practice that few could appreciate. Here there was no place to relax and no room to fill with attainment. In this way it was ideal. Upia is wasted on those who cannot use it on themselves. However, I was also still aware that carrying on in this situation could be interpreted as stupidity on my part at best, and masochism on my part at worst.

Nobody was getting the custom treatment I was getting. Even fewer it seemed knew it was going on. I ran through my list of self-observations many times searching for something I was doing wrong, an unseen conceit, ignorant things I had said to others that might have set me up, how I practice…

Of course, in all honesty, I did not come up with an empty list of things I was ashamed of and could do better by far, but was still perplexed as to why I was getting treated so. Others were stepping in far bigger cow patties while coursing the barn yard of practice than I was, and seemed to be rewarded all the same.

The only one thing about me that I recognized and had no question about was that I had not yet realized the enlightenment I originally sought and therefore felt not ready to teach. I would and could not settle for mouthing The Sutras and the words of Great Masters with realization still trapped within the petri dish of self and other and the vindication of a Master and his institution.

Once again I was given the job of work supervisor and once again, chainsaws were being handed out by the head monk as if they were electric tooth brushes.

Like any other form of ignorance, some people do not realize the danger of what they are dealing with or getting into, but are more than eager to give it a try because it looks like so much fun. There is simply no percentage in giving somebody a chain saw or an axe (axes are the most popular source of cottage injuries) without at least satisfying yourself that they know how to use it, and if not, then giving them proper training.

The primitive workshop on the property inherited by the Center contained a second rate circular hand saw inverted with its dull blade protruding through a makeshift table. As the retreat progressed, we were asked to use this device in order to rip materials for a project.

I refused.

This poor excuse for a table saw was very dangerous. At least one other practitioner-craftsman shared this view with me.

I had operated table saws for over 25 years on a professional basis. Others with little or no experience began using it readily. After turning it off they would say to me, "See? It's not so bad. What are you afraid of?" They did so because they were told to do so. However, experience gives you the wisdom to see danger. This is a form of teaching. If this teaching based in wisdom is ignored then that act is by definition ignorant. Ignorance is the antithesis of enlightenment, and has definite karmic inflows and outflows.

The warm weather of May necessitated another reminder of the dangers of tick bites.

It was once again mentioned that you could get Lyme's disease and die from being bit by a tick.

Some of these folks had been to only one or two retreats before. I asked myself whether ticks were really that much of a priority, especially the potentially fatal part.

I could sense some practitioner's minds became full of ticks instead of a method of practice.

Of course, it was good to mention that ticks are a little problem and that it may not be a good idea to lie out in the long grass and look at the sky counting clouds, but it was the exact inverse of the chain saw situation.

I figured that people should be warned about chain saws and axes because they can really bite, sometimes fatally, and give the ticks the lack of warning that the chain saws and axes actually got. Then few will be experiencing the living hell of believing that there is a death dealing tick crawling around in their pants during formal meditation in the Chan hall. If they believe there is a chain saw or an axe crawling around inside their pants, then perhaps they might require a little more attention than others.

Right from the beginning, a series of violent storms hit the area. Power lines were down, including the ones that fed current to the retreat Center.

The power was off and people came out to survey the damage. To my horror, a Polish practitioner had heroically climbed up on the rain drenched roof of the shed where the main lines connected the service circuitry of the Center and was removing debris. He did so standing on a maze of rain drenched power lines.

"Those lines can come alive at any moment!" I yelled. "Get off that roof!"

The head monk thought my reaction was hilarious and went into the main house. He returned with a crayon and some pieces of cardboard for me to make signs.

The new director came close and said in a quiet, fear-laced voice, "The liability of this situation is enormous. Thanks for getting him off the roof."

The county road crew arrived. As they removed large tree branches from the road I overheard them say that they hadn't seen anything like the weather that had happened. Being professionals they also made sure not to go near the downed power lines but waited for the electrical company's truck and crew.

The fondest memories of that retreat were the interviews with Shifu, as well as his talks.

Someone was troubled by killing insects and small creatures with a lawn mower.

"Shifu", they asked, "isn't it wrong to use such a device that sucks up and indiscriminately kills all sorts of insects and other living beings?"

Shifu replied, "Insects and living beings do not appear before enlightened people."

During one interview half way through the retreat I asked Shifu, "Master Ta-hui had over 40 awakening experiences. If he practiced Silent Illumination instead of Hua-tous, wouldn't he have lost count? Isn't even results of practice all a dream?"

Guo-gong Fashi, acting as translator, looked at me as if I was crazy, but nevertheless translated what I said.

Shifu smiled fondly.

"Paul has been practicing Hua-tous for 30 years," he told her.

Another time Shifu had given a morning talk about reflecting on impermanence as a method of Silent Illumination and that we would be able to raise any questions that came to us during the afternoon interview with him.

That afternoon I was the only one in the Chan hall "accidently" not asked to go to an interview.

"What kind of a place is this?" I thought. "I have a good question to ask and I'm the only one not asking it."

That night Shifu began his talk.

"Was there anyone missed this afternoon for an interview?" he asked. "Put up your hand only if you have a question, and it better be a good one!"

I was the only one to raise a hand.

"Paul, do you have a question?" asked Shifu.

I stood up and said, "If the universe is completely illuminated and returned to Silence, where do you find impermanence?"

Shifu began to laugh.

"You don't!" he said.

I bowed deeply.

After that exchange, Shifu went on to talk about something else.

Another person raised their hand and asked, "Shifu, I don't think you answered Paul's question."

Shifu looked over to me and asked, "Did I answer your question Paul?"

"Yes. Completely," I replied.

During some of the private interviews, Shifu wore a black face mask. This was to protect him from catching the flu and made him look very much like a Hollywood ninjutsu practitioner. Although I found this humorous, the reason for such attire was also deserving of respect. Everyone at that retreat had the flu in one form or another. Given how terribly sick he was earlier that year, he was literally risking his life giving us all interviews.

After bowing deeply I said, "Shifu, yesterday you said you were going to give a talk on becoming enlightened. I'm not going to wait around for it."

Please know that this was not tritely said nor with any intent of disrespect. What was exposed was and is of fundamental importance.

Poor Guo-gong, sitting beside him as translator was horrified. She couldn't believe my bad manners or that I was saying this to The Master.

Shifu removed his mask revealing a pleased smile, and clearly said in his own English that it was correct to not wait expecting enlightenment. I bowed in return.

I was very moved by the gesture of him taking off his mask to answer me.

Another thing during the retreat that touched me deeply was a talk he gave wherein he said that as far as enlightenment goes, he didn't think he was all that enlightened. However, these were his standards and not the standards of others.

On another day Shifu asked people after his lecture what they felt was the essence of this particular teaching. Various people gave various answers.

After patiently listening, he said, "If that's what you want to take from this, I'll give it to you."

At some time a couple of weeks before this retreat had begun, I wondered how it was determined who should become a Patriarch of Chan.

One afternoon Shifu gave a talk, ending it in English with, "Chan Master is pretty good. Patriarch is better. I would like to be called a Patriarch, so work really hard!"

There was one Polish fellow who was very sincere in his practice. He had left the Doorchester Center and its koan practice and was attending the full 49 days of this retreat. He had also felt that I was a secondary teacher or guide for him, having worked with Polish practitioners in Toronto extensively.

One day he came to me and spoke directly. He was very honest. His overriding problem was that, after years of Doorchester koan practice with all its yelling, interviews and clobbering, he was finding Silent Illumination impossible to get into.

I told him that after the final formal meditation of the day we could talk about it.

Unfortunately, I asked one of my Polish friends from Toronto to help as a translator, since the person needing help's English was still rather marginal.

After the evening sitting meditation was over, we both waited a considerable length of time outside a washroom door while the translator took his time to empty his mind.

I decided to do the interview after dark on an isolated sitting bench located on the far side of the pond on the Center property. In this way we would not distract other practitioners.

It was a clear moonless night, the sky filled with stars.

After wading in darkness along a path through a small segment of forest, we arrived at the pond side bench.

I maintained silence after we were seated to allow everyone's mind to settle.

Then I asked the focus of the interview to tell me about his difficulties.

The translator related my words to him in Polish.

He replied in Polish to the translator, then looked in all earnestness to me for an answer.

When I began to speak, the translator interrupted, speaking in Polish. He came across as knowing everything, frequently spiking whatever he was saying with the word "Shifu".

Now the person having the interview was listening only to the translator while I sat in silence.

It was obvious I had just been elbowed out of the conversation and I immediately realized there was no point in forcing my views.

I sat in quiet disbelief at my translator/friend's behaviour.

Why was this happening?

I realized that whatever was going on had its seeds in the previous winter retreat wherein I was told to "Shut up" in front of an audience that included the Polish Fox.

As words wafted across the pond, I perceived the stars reflected on its perfect still surface. My vision rose to the sky where the same image burned in gentle intensity. Both seemed the same.

I allowed this consuming illumination to enter consuming silence.

Electric Toilets

The overall functioning of the retreat was nothing short of bizarre.

The head monk had sent out all of the lawn cutting equipment to be serviced at the beginning of the retreat. However, this point in time also corresponded to the beginning of grass growing season and everybody with a lawn mower had done the same. Because of this, the centre mowers sat at the dealer until it was their turn for servicing and the grass had grown knee deep.

Furthermore, the violent strange weather continued with many frequent power outages.

I suggested that the Center buy a 5 kilowatt generator and patch it into the electrical service. There was enough money spent for other things less important. This would run the pumps and supply water to all the toilets during a power outage.

Instead, operating on deeper wisdom, the head monk *rented* a 5 kilowatt generator. My Polish translator friend, who was an electrician, took a day to brilliantly wire it into the amateur, improvised and dangerous pre-existing circuitry of the center. It served well in supplying lighting and running the pump that made all the toilets work during a two day power outage.

Once the power came back on, the head monk ordered it removed. I told him this was not a good idea but my advice was ignored.

The power went off again, this time on a weekend. With no running water, the toilets did not work once again. Now the generator was not available for rental.

No announcements were made to not flush the toilets after urination and thereby save water for more important flushes.

There were no backup outdoor latrines and yet there were over 60 people with normal bodily functions. The pump-filled toilets were electrical in nature, probably nuclear powered from Three Mile Island and were filling up with excrement at a rapid rate. Now the only thing that could be done was go down to the river on the property and fill containers full of water and bring them back to the toilets for flushing.

The first expedition was organized by the head monk after dinner. The Center pickup truck and at least fifteen people drove to the river after the sun had long set and began filling anything that would hold water.

I looked upon this exercise with detached humour.

There, in the pitch dark blackness of a power outage the headlights of a pickup truck glowed at the river's edge. As shadowy figures passed in and out of thick darkness I remember saying to myself, "I hope there is nobody around Pine Bush who believes in alien abductions…"

I passed through darkness down to the mysterious luminous activity. The director was standing beside the truck.

"Is it always like this?" I asked.

"Yes," she replied, her voice trailing off and distant.

The box of the pickup was now full of large garbage cans hand filled with buckets of water, each holding about thirty gallons and therefore weighing about three hundred pounds each.

Although they could get the truck downhill to the river in two wheel drive, they found that with about half a ton of water in open containers in the back, the uphill trip to the road on wet grass was impossible. Furthermore, nobody seemed to know how to engage the four wheel drive available.

I decided to offer my considerable four wheel drive trucking experience but was beaten to the call. Like a hero out of the dark, my Polish electrician/translator friend got behind the wheel. I thought, "He doesn't have a clue how to drive a four wheel drive truck!"

After some fumbling he managed to engage the four wheel drive. However, it was in low range. The excessive torque lurched the truck forward and a third of the water sloshed out of the garbage cans into the truck box, and cascaded to the ground. At least half an hour's work by ten people gone in a flash!

He did, however, manage to get the load up to the house.

The power was off for three days.

This exercise was done several times during the day and night with only slightly improved efficiency.

The retreat participant who was a U.S. Navy technician had no problem with the retreat code of silence. He simply broke it. Continuously.

One day he walked up to me one day and said, "This place runs on the Eastern assumption that in order for things to work you let nature take care of things. I am an American. I make things work and to hell with nature!"

I neither openly agreed nor disagreed because to do either would prime a mental sewage system of argument contrary to the reason we were taking part in the retreat.

I kept it to myself that it was ridiculous to try to make things work at odds with nature. It's impossible. Harmony with nature is a Western principal in as much as it is an Eastern principal. There has to be harmony with nature for things to work.

What we were witnessing with toilet management was not harmony with the nature of the situation but rather a dysfunctional circus of events. Those that knew this were repelled by the indifference to The Tao or dharmas of physics and the inability to make congruent choices relative to the nature of the problem nature presented.

I did my best to keep technical people engaged in their practice. They kept coming to me with their concerns.

After 42 days of this it began to appear that I was spinelessly conforming by not joining in the constant cynical observations of those who knew better. The truth was, if you are going to get your money's worth out of a retreat and these things come up, the best attitude is to bear and endure rather than "to bear arms against a sea of troubles and end them".

To openly enter a conflagration of experience versus inexperience and ineptitude turns a place of Chan practice into an ill managed construction site rather than a vehicle to transcend affliction.

After all, we didn't go to retreat to take a course in toilet management.

How can affliction be transcended if it is not experienced?

However, to disregard those of far greater and deeper experience to practice the inept is not Dhyana Buddhist Practice. It is incompetence.

To experience affliction, see its nature and thereby transcend it is to create in an instant The Pure Land here on earth. How can the Pure Land come into being if there is no affliction to form the devout need for its creation?

Is The Pure Land a myth, or is our clinging to the necessary functions of discerning mind misinterpreting the truth of all existence and interaction the greatest of all myths?

Thus, even the incompetence of others can be turned into citizenship in The Pure Land if and only if one illuminates it with Buddhadharma. This is illuminating the cause of affliction and returning it to silence until there is no differentiation of illuminating and silence.

But please know that this most powerful transformation does not change the nature that what is experienced *is* incompetence and contains all of the karmic inflows and outflows that incompetence is noted for.

Becoming A Pirate

It is important to know that a place of true Chan, Zen or Dhyana Practice is like a gift shop run by a pirate.

People naturally come in to shop and perhaps buy something. They do not come in to get robbed. Therefore, people like to have things orderly, nice and as close to preconception as possible, and then leave with something they can tightly clutch in white knuckled grasping hands.

A true place of Chan, Zen or Dhyana Practice appears to be a gift shop, but its sole function is to rob certain customers no matter what their ideas and preconceptions are. It even robs them of their credit card of fixed self and they end up leaving with absolutely nothing. If the robbery is a complete success, they are even robbed of really giving a damn that they don't have a thing to show for it.

This is how one gets to be a Chan, Zen or Dhyana Buddhist Pirate.

Such pirates are extremely rare. They become pirates because they too were robbed and have nothing.

A good Chan, Zen or Dhyana Pirate does not just go around robbing everybody. That is pointless - bad for business. A good pirate knows who to rob, and who to give to. It is rare to meet someone capable of being robbed and becoming a robber. Therefore, most of a Master's activity takes the form of giving.

One evening during one of the first retreats I had the good fortune to participate in with Shifu, he said, "Coming to Enlightenment is rare. In a Master's career, one, maybe two disciples might realize it."

Finding Nothing

On the last day of the retreat with Shifu giving interviews, we were told to present to him what it was that we learned during the previous 42 days.

Most of us had the better part of a day to come up with something but for me, anything I came up with returned to silence.

That afternoon, sitting in the line of chairs waiting for my interview, which happened in groups of seven, I couldn't help but overhear others telling Shifu what they had learned.

Especially voluminous was the amount learned by a Transmitted Dharma Heir.

I heard all of this immersed in Silent Illumination.

When my turn came to enter the interview room we all prostrated together and took chairs before Shifu. Shifu was flanked by Guo Xing fa Shih on his left and the head monk of the retreat centre Guo Yuan fa Shih. On his right was Guo Gong fa Shih, the female monastic and translator.

Each person in my group gave what they learned at the retreat, most speaking in Mandarin.

When it came my turn, I could only ask a question.

I asked why Silent Illumination couldn't be introduced from the standpoint of emptiness in order to cultivate a sense of intrigue within practitioners.

I asked this because there were several practitioners who had become so disengaged they had gone on severe tangents by the end of the retreat.

I knew this because they were telling me so. Some were used to working with all the hell and fury associated with koans in other traditions while others were victims of their own personal incompetence and blamed it on the teaching.

Guo Xing Fa Shih began nodding in the affirmative as I said this.

Then I paused and said, "The only problem is that you have to come from that perspective in order to see its effectiveness."

Shifu said in a matter of fact manner, "Most people practicing here have not realized emptiness."

"I guess I answered my own question," I said.

Shifu then asked me pointedly, "What is it that you have learned at this retreat?"

All I could find within me was a deep intrigue and silence. There was nothing I could find even though I was pressured to do so.

Even his question returned to silence.

Guo Yuan said, "He learned to cut the grass!" and laughed.

Shifu repeated himself more forcefully.

"WHAT IS IT THAT YOU HAVE LEARNED?"

I felt like an idiot but still could find nothing and my intrigue grew.

Shifu then bluntly said, "GO!"

I sat there not knowing if I was supposed to get up and leave because no one else was.

He once again said, "Go," then more gently added, "Besides, the rest of all these interviews will be in Mandarin and there is no use boring you."

As I left I wondered what had just happened. I still couldn't find anything to say I had learned.

Now, it is important to know that all of this was after being a modern Zen koan jockey for over 18 years with acknowledged results, and listening to 42 days of Shifu's talks full of things that could be learned and be rewarded for learning. Surely I could have given a dokusan room answer. Something that was appropriate like saying in a profound voice, "I DON'T KNOW," because in dokusan room logic, that answer would usually work.

However, I could say nothing even though there was an actual desire to say something.

Shifu's question, even when put strongly, simply returned to silence. There was no effort on my part for it to do so. It did it on its own.

Many years before, I had demonstrated the Thundering Silence of Vimalakirti and was passed on the koan with the Roshi's approval. I was well aware of koan-generated appropriate answers and insights. They now revealed themselves as a hamster wheel driven by kensho hunting and the subsequent mental taxidermy of stuffing and mounting. In that game you were aware that silence was the right answer because you stood apart from it by thinking you were one with it.

Conversely, I could have filled my mind and silence with the countless things I did hear at the retreat so that I could rattle them off when asked thereby mistaking them for what they truly pointed to; The Practice of the Tathagathas.

This was different and the urgency of the matter could not leave me nor could I betray it with the Samsaric cause and effect of conditioned scholarly learning and reward.

I later recalled that after Zen Master Dogen was asked the similar question, "What is it that you realized at Master Ju Ching's monastery in China?" he replied that his nose was vertical and his eyes horizontal.

The next day there was an interview with Guo Yuan Fashi. I said to him that I still couldn't find anything that I had learned and that I needed to work on expressing this more eloquently.

He said, "Why don't you go out and enjoy the weather?"

In Chan, there is a famous set of ten drawings called "The Ox Herding Pictures". Each picture represents a stage in one's development of Dhyana Practice.

The first stage is a person looking for the Ox he has faith exists but hasn't seen. The second is getting a glimpse of the Ox's footprints and the third is seeing the ox. The ninth is a circle and the tenth is a sage happily walking through the market.

It is commonly thought in modern Zen practice that the circle representing Sunyata or Emptiness is the realization of kensho.

If Dhyana Buddhism is to thrive in this culture, the whole set of ideas surrounding these pictures must be re-calibrated to its original state of diligence.

Kensho is the third picture, not the ninth.

Complete enlightenment is the ninth picture. The tenth is the highest culmination of Mahayana Buddhism; after realizing Sunyata, teaching in the market place.

The art of teaching Dhyana Buddhism is using differentiation to illuminate oneness. There are many tools to do so as there are perceptions. One of these tools has traditionally been called "The Head Monk".

It must be realized that the job of head monk is like being a lightning rod to discharge the static voltage generated by The Master's Upia upon a disciple.

It is a job beyond competence and incompetence.

It is natural for an accomplished master to live the fact that there is no attainment or wisdom. In this way they can appear to be quite clued out.

This is an advantage.

The Master acts through the Head Monk.

People are fooled by appearances and preconceptions.

The Head Monk may look incompetent, or actually *be* incompetent causing a sea of trouble for the disciple receiving all the attention. Whether he really is incompetent or not is irrelevant. It is a very effective place to teach from, and any karmic outflows originating from the disciple are directed towards the head monk.

This is very handy – an inverse function of the return of merit. In military terms, it is called "drawing fire".

It's like the Master saying to the Head Monk, "We need you to find out how much gasoline is in that fifty gallon drum, and by the way, here's a pack of matches to help find out."

Therefore, it is up to the *disciple* to make the head monk a teacher of Buddhadharma and not just a person with a shaved head causing trouble. It is therefore up to the *disciple* to make this very planet the Pure Land, and not the foaming savage sea of Samsara.

If you have made a vow to deliver all sentient beings, cut off endless vexations and master limitless approaches to Dharma, is this attitude any different no matter who it is you encounter?

Therefore, being head monk is not necessarily a pleasant or easy occupation.

So long as one has a retribution body, there will be affliction. In having a retribution body, it generally goes without saying that one usually has a functioning brain and mental activity. The afflictions of the functioning brain's mental activity are called vexations.

This was true of The Buddha before he realized Parinirvana.

Dying of mushroom related food poisoning, as The Buddha did, could not in any way shape or form be pleasant. However, in the same breath, do you think that in completely realizing the nature of birth and death, even the most terminal and traumatic afflictions are projected into the future in the same way as those who have not realized the nature of birth, death and suffering? Are they even transmitted at all?

What truly is transmitted?

Is The Mind of The Tathagathas any different in its transmission?

Is the True Nature of *your* Mind any different?

The import of Buddhist Dhyana Practice is not results alone.

It is process.

Process and results are inseparable.

This process is the weaving of a conceptual fabric that will create an eventual continual momentum of karma that supports and upholds The Noble Eightfold Path.

That is why studying and learning Buddhist Concept accompanied by Dhyana meditation is so very important.

The texture, weave and strength of this fabric is always in a state of flux.

There are good days and there are bad days.

Initially, the fabric you have so diligently woven can tear, it can become lost, or through negative thoughts and actions, become unraveled. However, you will have the ability to re-do the work at a much faster rate than if you had never woven before. This all depends on the degree, sincerity and quality of your work in the first place.

The worst thing is to do a couple of stitches, either realize or be told that this is now fabric and not just a couple of knots of thread, stand back, savor the results and proclaim that you have just made The Buddha's Robe when actually, it's not even a pair of socks. In truth you're shamelessly walking around butt-naked thinking you are fully adorned and radiant.

If you are sincere and extremely persevering, there becomes a point where this fabric becomes one's own mind, and it is not possible to regress. This does not mean that one has reached the end of development by any means.

It means that one now can truly begin to practice, and every day is a good day.

Even after several true awakening experiences there is still the possibility of regression. Kensho is not enlightenment. It is only an experience still framed within the context of a fixed self in much the same way as a spoonful of water and salt mixed to roughly 35 parts of salt to 1000 parts of water is not the ocean.

Complete Enlightenment is the stage represented as the Circle. The Ox Herding Pictures must be recalibrated to this standard in our collective mind if they are to have any true meaning.

Buddhist concept is not static. It must be proven and used from moment to moment. In this way it is very similar to the science of physics. The dharmas of physics must always be corroborated with the universe, otherwise they are useless. Even though they prove to corroborate, they are not The Universe.

To come to this eventual point is not easy. However those who have not done so, in seeing or hearing of someone who has, may become jealous. In actual fact, were the jealous presented with the same obstacles and difficulties in practice and given a way out, they would invariably take the way out. This is not because those who realize Enlightenment step from one lotus blossom of easy lucky circumstances to the next but rather in loneliness take each sometimes difficult and sometimes repulsive step of walking barefoot through a cattle-filled barnyard into morning light. It is people's ongoing moving minds that occupy these savage realms of easy outs that define the prison walls of Samsara. The situations, the places and the opportunities might be a little different from one person to the next. It is just that most have not yet made themselves ready to use what they experience to annihilate the tyranny of moving mind which shackles the human spirit to the rotating, grinding and merciless wheel of birth and death. Some in effect, never will.

A Dhyana or Chan master treats no two students the same. They spend the most time and energy with those that require the most help, and the least with those capable of walking the distance themselves. Those of great potential receive the last thing anybody wants and few choose to endure.

Many years after Shifu had an enlightenment experience with Master Lin Guan, he practiced with Master Dong Chu. Master Dong Chu's treatment of Shifu was brutal. He would say to him, "You are full of defilements! Do some prostrations!"

When The Master walked into the Chan Hall and saw Shifu doing prostrations, he said to him, "This is a dog eating shit off the floor! You're a smart fellow! Write me an essay!"

After the essay was written and presented, Master Dong Chu threw it on the floor without reading it.

In modern Zen it is a common practice to train and groom Dharma Successors. This dharma that is transmitted as a function of grooming is usually nothing more than mental illness or spiritual halitosis - but it is indeed transmission. It's just that it isn't Buddhist transmission. The people who contract this transmission sound and look enlightened because they have been groomed to do so. Like clothing mannequins in a storefront modeling the Buddha's robe, they entice people to buy an appearance and fashion statement, rather than Buddhahood.

Of course, these days there are Zen teachers who preach that "sniping" at other teachers is not ethical. This of course conveniently puts them in a position above and beyond criticism, because any criticism is therefore "sniping". They site great Zen Masters like Dogen as "sniping" in his criticism of Ta Hui's hua-tou teaching as manifested in Rinzai Zen of the time.

Why would modern teachers say such things? Is this in itself not a form of "sniping"? Is it that they have something to hide, or would like something to hide behind.... something called "position"?

If you are a teacher, you teach. This involves observations and criticisms. There are definite problems with koan system Zen. In China, the collections of koans were not formed to create a practice in and of themselves, but were set down to be kept in questioning mind while entering Hua-tou practice, or Silent Illumination. They were and still are invaluable fuel for Silent Illumination, but not a replacement for Silent Illumination.

Koan practice on its own has definite problems. Added to this is the extra layer of problems made thick by these collections of koans put into a system administered by a teacher. This is amplified interference and is a method of koan practice very different than that practiced by Hakuin Zenji and Ta Hui.

It amplifies having over not having.

What is had and not had? Approval of an authority figure. This has the demonstrated potential to create plastic injection molded clones that will do anything to get ahead and call it enlightenment. Such a system of practice diverges infinitely from questioning in deepest sincerity what a master has said or done that is not yet clear. It is like literary criticism by arts majors who are themselves incapable of writing a play or novel yet still get marks and a degree. Neither of these attainments makes them an artist. Such teaching is a false profession created from standing outside what cannot be stood outside of.

Although this is clear in the Sutras, it is not clear to these teachers. And yet they tell us that to criticise their rarefied condition is unethical and that we should all be sheeple.

For me, the most difficult burden was my unstoppable need to teach in counterpoint with the fear of what happened to me dissuading practitioners from entering The Great Way. For all the world it would be nice to perpetuate the myth I had lived under for almost 20 years, that transmission was something to cling to as real and graspable, that anyone sanctioned as a Zen Roshi was unquestionably authentic and so on.

I was aware of the active ongoing blackening of my name and reputation by those who had not only betrayed me and my family, but Buddhadharma as well. Actually, they had done this so effectively, they don't care anymore. To them I am dead.

In Song of Mind this predicament is mentioned from the perspective of true practice. It says that one should let such libelous criticism be music to one's ears. For years I thought this meant apply it to oneself and if what is said fits, correct yourself. This in itself isn't a bad attitude and deserves the merit it reaps.

Another interpretation arising out of this Mind is that in hearing this music, there is infinitely much to teach.

Receiving Upia

The skilful manifestation of Buddhadharma between Master and disciple is called Upia. One of the ways to defuse Upia is to be of sufficient means to be aware of it, then say to oneself, "Oh, the Master or head monk is doing this to me because they see that I am special and deserving of such harsh treatment! I really am special!"

This is "a tale told by an idiot" and one prone to masochism.

Is it cleverness slamming the Gateless Gate shut on your nose before passing through it?

Because I realized that being a head monk is not a picnic, I became quite interested in investigating *my own* reactions and allowing such things to illuminate *my* defilements.

Therefore, I thanked the head monk for doing his job in the peculiar way he did it.

It didn't matter to me whether he really was incompetent or just feigning it.

The effect of his operating turned me into a ball of highly charged doubt.

In this way the stalled toilets of the 49 day retreat produced gold instead of sewage.

Of course this was at the expense of what appeared well managed and diligent. However, if what you want is an environment well managed and diligently run, then you should become a part of an insurance company or a bank rather than a Dhyana Centre.

It is interesting that even these two examples of diligence are in the process of collectively failing.

When the 49 day retreat began, I was already an ox in a gift shop full of fragile porcelain Buddhas and delicate little Bodhisattva figures all preciously positioned on glass shelves in the most meaningful of scenes.

Because I didn't want to smash anything, I decided to walk as carefully as possible. However, I couldn't keep this up forever because Shifu kept waving red flags in front of me. Still consumed in doubt, I really needed to get out to pasture, otherwise things would get shattered, burned, obliterated.

Was it Shifu's expression of realization to have a gift shop to attach to and preserve much like a Dharma Disney World?

Shifu robbed me. This is what happens to consumers when a pirate runs a gift shop. Since I have nothing left, I too have to be a pirate. Can't help it.

At the time I was still too stunned to realize it.

Now I know that to keep up a store front is fundamental. This is the nature of piracy.

A Dharma Goose

That night after the final interview of the 49 Day Retreat, Shifu talked about a goose that existed in ancient India and was mentioned in the Sutras. Apparently it had a particular enzyme in its beak that could solidify even the slightest traces of milk in water.

He said that it was a pretty smart goose then added, "Are geese that smart in Canada Paul?"

I was aware that I could perhaps take this as a prodding. Should I have gone on about what I learned before that last interview when, in my heart of hearts, I knew what was more important was what was beyond learning and reward? Instead, the whole thing could pass away like last night's dream.

That was because what I had demonstrated was in accord with The Sutras.

Now I can talk about what was learned and it is all the same.

The Bodhisattva Retreat

After the "final examination" of being asked what we learned during the retreat, there was the Bodhisattva Seven Day retreat to complete the 49 day duration.

On the eve of its beginning Shifu made the announcement of who was going to get transmission.

I wasn't one of them.

He also said something to the extent that there were three people present who were capable of carrying on his teaching. Two were monastics, and one was a layperson. Unlike the two monastics, the lay person however, was not going to be told that they were in fact going to get transmission because they would in all likelihood, quit intense practice too soon if they saw the light.

This made my predicament even worse.

It annihilated any place to stand.

I knew I had experienced numerous results in practice over the years. I realized three awakening experiences that were worthy of the name before I met Shifu, and then well over 10 of deeper and varying characteristics within a relatively brief time after practicing with Shifu. After that I was most fortunate to have lost count or really care because I switched completely to Silent Illumination. The first of the three kenshos was recognized by a Zen Roshi after I was clobbered with oak sticks until my shoulders were dark purple at retreats over an 8 year period. In the following ten years, the next two were deeper and of different manifestation, but I didn't tell anyone about them because I realized that what was made of kensho after its experience was not enlightenment. With Shifu I started all over again, and was grateful that he didn't give me any recognition. I also didn't ask for it. However, I regularly tested myself by asking Shifu questions in interviews to make sure I was sailing a proper course. This was very important. Equally important was the fact that after many of these experiences, he would give a talk that reflected exactly the realization I just had. I usually tended to discount what I experienced as not good enough or worthy of attention.

In this way I was very fortunate.

Over the years I've seen a great many practitioners realize results in practice, then become attached to them, and make them something they are not. However, again, it was good to hear Shifu describing a realization a master had in the past that mirrored what I had just experienced. But he always went on to say that that particular master had to experience a great deal more difficulty and trouble before he became truly free of regression's web.

Of course, the power of this seemingly indirect teaching approach is that you never really know if this actually applies to you, or if you are experiencing either a severe bout of wishful thinking or creative analysis. And so you keep investigating yourself, and your reactions in relation to how well you fuse with the method of practice. This you do on your own. A teacher is there to ask a question, and you are there with your karmic butt to get kicked if necessary.

That's the dynamics I operated under.

In the current Zen tradition, it's all done one on one in the interview room. You know when you are being talked to because you are the only one there.

This can have its advantages too, but the problem with having two or three personal interviews a day with a teacher is that it can very quickly become manipulation. It's bad enough that some people want a teacher to tell them how to live, but it's another thing all together for a teacher to manipulate the life of a practitioner.

Conversely, a teacher can run the risk of being manipulated by students when a close linkage in the form of frequent one on one interviews become part of intense practice.

In the seemingly indirect approach of Shifu's Chan, practice was all your own responsibility, and the results were again, all your own. It required a Master who has no need to be confined to a fixed notion of self, and in fact abides nowhere. This is extremely powerful while not rearranging a single daisy in the pasture.

The main test I've always stood by is that one's lack of enlightenment is directly proportional to the way vexations control one's karmic portal of choice. This is directly related to how one sees phenomena, including vexation. If one is blind to the nature of phenomena including vexations, then one's life and what follows beyond is run by vexations. A life being run by vexations and affliction can actually appear to be care-free because all life energy is spent in the pursuit of pleasurable experiences. Because pleasure's existence is defined by the possibility of affliction and suffering, the blind pursuit of pleasure enforces the link to affliction and suffering, further augmenting the lust for pleasure. It is a life engineered by Mara.

This is the nature of addiction.

A life dedicated to realizing the nature of phenomena including vexation and pleasure is a life not lived in cyclic slavery of the pursuit of pleasure and avoidance of affliction. Although it is healthy to experience pleasure, it is also healthy to honestly experience affliction when it naturally emerges. In this way the nature of both phenomena is right before you. Thus the transmission of diseased mind is put in neutral because the mechanism of pursuit is disengaged.

Attending a Dhyana Buddhist retreat is unequalled in the liberation of all sentient beings because it does just that.

Now, it is very important to know that many people, especially those with a number of years of practice and some results under their belt, tend to make a mental projection of themselves as being accomplished practitioners and therefore think they should not experience vexations. However, the fact is readily evident that if they don't consciously experience vexations, they really should because the mind ground that generates affliction is by no means dissolved. Since they manifest through a living body subject to affliction, without realizing it, they are a function of karmic inflows and outflows at a rate that makes general motors look like a cottage industry.

As for myself, after 42 days of Chan Buddhist practice, I experienced vexations and saw that these vexations still had attached to them karmic inflows and outflows because they had a confusing influence on arbitrary choice. Therefore I didn't consider myself to be enlightened. I then began to try to figure out who was, but stopped because such a process didn't have much to do with Silent Illumination. In fact, if I continued doing so, my practice became Silent Elimination.

However, that night after the announcement of who got transmission and everybody had gone to bed, I remember having the thought that I should or could get really upset about being overlooked and all, but, strangely enough, I could carry on as if nothing happened, because, after all, nothing that I wanted to happen did happen. This in itself was quite strange, and cause for joy. There was strong vexation, but even it wasn't worth giving volition to.

This isn't to say that I was totally out of Mara's range.

After leaving the retreat I did experience a very powerful attack of demons. It required all of my skill as a practitioner to ride them out.

Then something revealed itself.

I could dissolve even the strongest of vexations whenever I chose to enter Dhyana Meditation. Mind became clear, profound and motionless with little or no effort. Ultimately the demons that emerged had no power and although Mara could target me, his sights had lost all calibration.

The last seven day segment of the 49 day retreat was different than the first 42 days. Called the Bodhisattva Retreat, it was filled with chanting and the Taking of the Bodhisattva Precepts. Both my wife Barb and daughter Angie attended it.

If I let my mind wander, it was both painful and difficult for me to be a loser yet again. I knew that not getting transmission would be taken by both my friends and enemies as an affirmation of what the Zen Centre did to me all those years ago.

Why did I not get transmission?

I had more years of experience in meditation and retreats than all the people who had received transmission at the end of the 42 day retreat combined.

I was a loser.

One of the winners who got transmission came to me smiling.

He said, "You have been a member here for a long time! How many retreats have you been to, old timer?"

I said that I didn't count them but it was around 20, and then added, "And I took part in and lead over 50 seven day retreats in another Zen teaching line over an 18 year period."

He stared at me in uncomprehending disbelief, then changed the subject.

I didn't make it a habit to tell anyone of my past experience except the head monk, and even that in small doses for good reason. It seemed that the powers that be wanted to keep it that way and I trusted them. I thought that eventually they would find some value in me and use it.

While engaged in Silent Illumination, I began to list the possible reasons I didn't get transmission. This was a phenomenon of thought generated by circumstances and a natural mind function of Silent Illumination, if you let it be.

Was I too straight forward and non-conformist in my interviews?

No.

The things I asked and the answers I gave were neither formula reactions nor asked within a reference frame of image or projected desired results. To be sure, it is far easier to ask questions brimming with honorifics with a decided goal in mind. The questions and statements offered and the way they were offered were honest results of what I saw, and the answers I got from Shifu were not rebukes during the 49 days, nor was I told I was wrong.

Why was I not given transmission like the others?

I had heard a Western transmitted student give a talk and immediately saw that he was still very much a function of thought and duality.

Was I being arrogant?

However, I could not in truth say the things he said. Moreover, I never heard Shifu say anything like the things he said.

Was it because of what happened to me with the Doorchester Zen Center that nobody wanted to give me the spot light? Maybe they wanted to bury me like The Zen Center did. Is it better to promote the fiction of nice things happening to practitioners when they decide to enter The Path no matter what teaching line they decide to join? Is it a good thing to call anything that is called "Zen" good, no matter what is taught under its name?

These considerations didn't stop Master Hui-neng from telling of how Chan Buddhist monks literally tried to kill him.

Being human, it was difficult not being given a reward for diligence in the presence of my wife and daughter. Furthermore, a publication was being prepared about this transmission event and special articles were prepared about the life stories of "the transmitted".

Being a Western participant of no distinction, I was asked to give a brief description of how I entered into practice. I decided to make my story congruent with the import and hype of the magazine. Since it was simply a media event, I treated it as such. I just said that I had practiced Zen before I started with Shifu or something to that effect.

This was obviously what the Powers That Be wanted.

And this was what they were going to get.

The whole import of what had happened caused such a great doubt within me that I quite literally became dizzy if I let it. I had heard that dizziness is associated with doubt, but before this had never experienced it.

This was not the Great Doubt that I had associated with practice.

With that doubt, all things of faith in teacher and one's own self were still untouched.

Here, this Doubt encompassed everything including teacher and self. It would not go away. The only thing that could be done with it was when it came into the illumination of awareness (and it always was illuminated!) it had to be returned to silence. This process was not a dynamic of ease, nor was it a dynamic of tense exertion. It was the dynamic of stellar furnaces that without knowing effort or knowing no effort turn the permeating darkness of space into a continuum of light. This process had naturally begun and the amplitude of the waves generated would take time and careful practice to illuminate and then let go.

I would rather not have experienced this doubt and did not recognize it for what it was. However, it was this horribly uncomfortable and sickening Doubt that was the greatest of Compassion.

During and immediately after that retreat I did not recognize it as being essential in the process of crossing to the other shore. I framed it as an unresolved weakness of either Shifu not vindicating me, or of me not being good enough to my standards and letting this vex me. It was either him or me that was at fault and I could not help but let my mind rest uncomfortably on this doubt as an unresolved menhir of the mind. I could not see that this truly was The Great Doubt of the Tathagathas compassionately and selflessly bestowed upon me by the kindest of Master Teachers while it was in effect. If it was seen as such, its power would have been neutralized.

The weather at the Bodhisattva Retreat became very warm. One evening it rained quite heavily. After the last round of mediation we walked back to our hut dormitory in the spotty on and off lighting of the motion sensor flood light illuminating the path. The smooth plywood covered doors that bridged over the deep puddles of mud were slick with rain. As I stepped onto one of these doors the flat soul of my sandal hydroplaned over its surface causing me to violently catch my balance with my other foot. In doing so I came down full force onto the door with the end of my big toe. A surge of pain ripped through me as someone from behind shouted "Ow!" in empathy.

Just as they said that, I repeated the same cycle and crashed the same toe even harder.

After I lowered onto my sleeping bag/mattress on the floor the initial shock wore off and waves of pain surged. On this note I called it a day and went to sleep.

The next morning I could hardly walk. The toe was swollen and inflamed but I didn't think it was broken.

I hobbled to the Chan Hall and found that I couldn't do prostrations in the normal way because of intense pain, so I improvised.

Later on in the day I happened to notice that the toe had gone from inflamed dawn like red to a darkening night shade of purple/black.

I was too busy with Silent Illumination to care much about it. To me it was the least of my afflictions.

The navy veteran who had sat beside me and heroically lasted for 42 days was at his wit's end. He had gone from great enthusiasm at being a maintenance person and grounds keeper at the retreat center to a stream of never ending criticisms of just about everything done and said. During Shifu's talks he asked questions about small details that really didn't matter. Shifu told him that he was going to start ignoring him every time he put up his hand. The next morning the fellow got into his vehicle and drove away, never to return.

As the retreat began to unwind in its last two days, other practitioners who took the retreat rules more seriously than those who made it a practice (or anti practice) of openly "speaking their mind" to me began to relax.

While at the juice table, one such person said to me, "I don't know why, but I found that practicing with you and around you gave me a very good feeling."

I was very touched, and told him that it was because he had worked very hard these last 49 days.

Shifu was sitting at a table by the window on the opposite side of the room. After the fellow had left, he came directly over to me and said, "I talk too much."

I immediately made a zipping-up gesture across my lips that made him smile. He then repeated saying, "I talk too much."

Of course, the error in English was apparent. Shouldn't he have said to me, "*You* talk too much."?

However, Shifu was not one to make a fundamental structural error in English after having demonstrated over the years that his mastery of the language was far better than he let on. Mistaking "You" and "Me" is a very fundamental speech error that is not a common mistake even with novices.

The differentiation contained in "You" and "me" is also a fundamental Hua-tou pointing directly to the nature of the Universe.

Barb, Angie and me after The Bodhisattva Retreat

Returning With Nothing

Despite what didn't happen, I found the taking of the Bodhisattva Precepts extremely powerful. I, like every other lay practitioner, was given a Bodhisattva "Scarf" along with a traditional sitting robe.

I returned home empty handed and robbed with a robe.

There was absolutely nothing I could say I got except for a couple of souvenirs.

However, I was not confused. My faith in Buddhadharma was not shaken even though it was all one big ball of doubt.

Now it was the only thing I could rely on. Because of this, Silent Illumination continued for its own sake naturally without effort. That is not to say that it was always pleasant or that I was the easiest person to live with. It's just that the practice went on naturally with no effort because there was really no choice.

When there appeared to be a choice, a demon thought would come into light.

It had the theme, "I have been let down. Shifu did not recognise me because of what happened to me. He doesn't want to get involved and ruin a simplistic set of paradigms concerning Buddhadharma that is easy to sell. I am bad news."

This demon was returned to silence with a reply not clinging to the former analysis.

The reply was, "Shifu has placed great trust in me. I could go forward and get printed up somewhere that Zen let me down, and Master Sheng-yen is following suit to save image and a quarrel with another Center. It would be pretty easy to get sympathy, or at least some form of fleeting attention thanks to the sensationalist nature of journalism.

Conversely, Shifu could have put me on a pedestal of quick fame telling the world of the superiority of Chinese Chan versus the particular form of Western Zen I was practicing, with me being a testimonial bearing witness; something I would be more than willing to do. Wouldn't this too be an easy sell and read really nicely in publications in Taiwan?

No, something else was at work here.

Why did all this happen to me?

From birth, I have a responsibility to turn affliction into freedom. Is this not the practice of Dhyana Buddhism called Chan and Zen?

Is this not the Buddha's Teaching?

With these thoughts, the severe affliction that came to light returned to silence while the distinction of illumination and silence dropped.

How I was able to entertain the first vexing thought and illuminate an answer independent of clinging to the inherent pain generated by that initial thought is the fathomless mysterious freedom of Silent Illumination Practice. Through the practice of Silent Illumination, Bodhisattvas clearly speak to you.

A Voice From The Past

About a week after I returned home I received a phone call.

It started with, "THIS IS A VOICE FROM THE PAST!"

I immediately recognized "THE VOICE" as Punch, my monitor friend who had miraculously recovered from terminal leukemia diagnosis and treatment. His words had the air of old acquaintance and friendliness that was at odds with the fact that he had refused to speak to me when he was ill. He, and no-one else from the Toronto Affiliate or The Doorchester Zen Center, had bothered to talk to me since.

This was indeed a first.

Why was he phoning now? Was it because I *did not get* transmission but instead the kick in the groin he thought I deserved?

He started with the question, "How is it going with Sheng-yen?"

"Very well," I replied, assuming that The Polish Fox had reported to him of my being told to shut up during chanting and the fact that I had no rank at the Chan Center.

Now all this was verified by my not getting transmission and any form of vindication. It was open hunting season and I was a Dharma Goose. This was good news to my old colleagues. They need not worry nor lose any sleep about the outcome of their previous actions because now, even the Chan Center was vindicating what they had done by rejecting me.

He continued.

"Besides running the Toronto Affiliate Centre under the direction of our new Female Sensei, we have been asked to go down to Costa Rica to lead the Center retreats there."

"I'm sure Cottonmouth and Tibs would like to see you again too. Why don't you come to Toronto? I can arrange a meeting someplace."

This new fondness had a misinterpretation of events behind it that was directly related to the previous lies The Sensei told of me that conformed to what they wanted to hear. They thought I would come to them like a beaten dog with my tail between my legs, forever at the mercy of this "Great Bunch of Guys".

Since their past opportune actions did not earn my trust or respect, I replied, "Why don't you take the time to come here instead of meeting at some hamburger joint like the last time?"

My friend began to stammer. He wasn't prepared for my response and didn't know what to say.

Finally he managed to mumble, "O.K… I will…" and hung up.

He never did come here. That was the last time we ever spoke.

911

THE HORRID EVENTS 911 BEGAN FOR ME A PAINFUL SERIES OF REVELATIONS on the workings of the world based on empiricism and questioning. I cannot say that I was quick to figure things out on my own. Feeling deeply linked to those who lost their lives and their families and friends, I simply believed what was presented in the news media to be the cause of what had happened. However, things began to reveal themselves in an accelerating fashion that disintegrated, then inverted my view of history to conform with what unseen beings had told me years ago and I chose to ignore. I saw more clearly the actual way the horror of world suffering is brought into the lives of people through the conduits of religion, education, government and institutions posturing to be for the good of humanity.

We are in serious trouble.

Secret Transmission Locked in Neutral

It was around that time that Shifu wrote in Chan magazine that transmission did not mean that those he gave it to were enlightened and that his getting transmission was not that important to him. This was at odds to the fact that he certainly used it to sell himself as a Master because all his literature spoke of him getting *two* transmissions from *two* different Masters.

I still owed the retreat center a set of several offering plates and altar utensils, a replaced handle for a meditation bell and two altar lanterns to illuminate The Buddha as partial payment for the 49 day retreat. Over the next year I completed those items in my shop and applied to the October 7 Day Retreat.

I presented the old timing bell I had made a new handle for to Guo-Yuan Fashi.

He smiled and enthusiastically said, "It's beautiful!"

I noticed on the retreat roster that I was going to be a time keeper, which meant that I was going to strike the little wooden fish drum to begin a round of sitting, and strike a bell to end it when the allotted time was up.

All the timekeepers were told that there would be a time keeper's meeting with Shifu before the retreat began.

Shifu welcomed us as timekeepers and began a demonstration of how to strike the timing bell. I believe this was the first and probably the last time he ever did so. It was not the bell I had worked on and he brandished it about making sure I noticed it was not the bell I worked on.

He then emphatically stated that no timekeeper was to give any form of talk because in the past unqualified people had given talks that were regrettable.

I raised my hand.

"Shifu," I asked, "How should one strike the little wooden drum? Like this?"

I made surprisingly similar small wooden drum sounds by snapping my tongue off the roof of my mouth.

He couldn't help but smile, nodding in the affirmative.

As the retreat progressed it became obvious that several participants were painfully disengaged and bored. On several occasions they sat looking out the large windows in the Chan Hall.

Of course you might ask, "How did I know they were doing that unless I too was looking at them?"

There is a simple answer to this. I could look at somebody and not in any way lose my practice. This is one of the many results of realizing Emptiness as a result of thirty years of Dhyana Practice. It is no big deal, but it is impossible to do when one is still chained to having and not having, boredom and excitement.

Nobody who should have been in charge of keeping an eye on things had said anything and neither Shifu nor the head monk were in the Chan Hall.

Out of compassion and professionalism I could not help but give a talk from my time keeper's seat.

Emerging from silence, I said that the reason we are all here is to practice Chan. The practice of Chan is working diligently with our method of practice as if our heads were aflame. In this way each moment is a jewel rather than a burden.

As I spoke, a woman of some apparent rank at the Center rose from her seat. She was holding the retreat guidelines and in serious mime motioned to me. After I got up and went over to see what her problem was, she forcefully pointed to the paragraph stating that time keepers should not talk.

She didn't listen and use what I said and didn't care to. For her, only a small select few could be her teachers.

I shrugged my shoulders and walked away.

If an institution can't make use of what is offered and is run by those craving status exerting control over what is said and done, they will collectively get what they deserve. This is called Karma. Their prayers for Buddhas and Bodhisattvas to manifest in this world will be without merit because they do not perceive how Buddhas and Bodhisattvas condense in time and space. They will not attract masters worthy of the name but instead stick like glue to shallow paradigms converting all that could be possible and wonderful into a Dharma Disney World.

During the closing talks of the retreat there was an opportunity for practitioners to offer thanks for the privilege of taking part in something as wonderful and rare as a Chan retreat with Shifu.

A female Chinese novice monastic said, "I would like to thank Paul for his talk on Chan practice yesterday."

My glance went to Shifu sitting in his master's chair. He broke into a mischievous smile as if part of a practical joke that had results he relished. He was clearly pleased at what I had done.

It was during the closing remarks that Shifu said, "You can take your normal seat in the Chan Hall, Paul. Your training here is complete."

That was the second last retreat I went to with Master Sheng-yen.

New Vistas

For over twenty years I had remained bottled up in an isolated farm house. I desperately needed to get away.

A kayak is one of the most elegant, seaworthy and economical little boats there is.

I began designing and building a classic skin-on-frame kayak from scrap wood left over from various past projects. Since the maximum speed of a displacement hull is proportional to the square root of the hull length at water line, in order to have a decent cruising speed, I maxed out its length at twenty feet at waterline with a twenty six inch beam and a nice amount of shear for popping through waves. It was primarily a Greenland style kayak with the front cockpit used as either a sealed hold for camping gear and provisions, or as a command bridge for Barb. The solid oak stem extended high above the deck while the stern extended slightly less, in Norse fashion.

The hull covering was ballistic nylon with over nine coats of polyurethane. This made for a heavy boat. However, on the water it was most elegant. Being translucent, its ribs and stingers could be seen, making it appear like a floating Chinese lantern. I equipped it with a retractable oak rudder controlled by rudder pedals like in an airplane. This modern attachment did not detract from the boat's nature and spirit. It allowed the boat to be trimmed in a crosswind without sacrificing power over long distances due to asymmetrical paddling.

One of my friends told me that the retracting rudder mechanism being of wood and hinged was not a good idea because it was wood on wood. This of course would be true except for the fact that he didn't notice that all the bearing joints in the mechanism were machined out of aircraft aluminum and inserted inside the oak components. Since this boat would only see fresh water, hardened aluminum was an excellent choice for bearing material. However, since it had been concluded that I was not enlightened, I decided to leave him with whatever observations he wanted to keep. The same reaction would have probably occurred if it was concluded that I was enlightened.

The maiden voyage was from Honey Harbour to Beausoleil Island in Georgian Bay. This was the beginning of wonderful vistas of open water paddling, island hopping and sitting meditation on some of the most incredible rock formations in the world.

The Inuit design of the traditional kayak is nothing short of genius. With ribs mortise and tenoned into the gunwales, then lashed to hold them in place, the whole frame is flexible yet incredibly strong. This makes for a very sea kindly hull that rides rough water with grace and speed, much like the Norse longboats of a thousand years ago.

Of course, somewhat later, Barb decided she would like to have a go at riding in the front cockpit. To her delight she liked it very much. However, she also considered it beneath her station as commander to paddle. This turned my freedom vessel into something of a galley with me as the engine and her placed in the front cockpit as Cleopatra. In one two day trip I lost ten pounds and began to think that something with a sail might be a little more appropriate.

We had many memorable times gliding past exquisite natural granite sculptures, silently passing through thickets of water grass while watching otters dive and pop up beside us, or floating over mountainous vistas of submerged rock formations. If it rained we were covered by a deck and spray skirt. We felt snug and secure even though invariably we were sitting on seats moistened from the inevitable bilge that managed to get under our spray skirts.

I spent a great deal of time meditating on the enormous granite rocks of Beausoleil Island. These were natural sitting cushions in that you could always find a smooth surface at just the right angle. Each massive rock forming a cliff or a granite plateau had its own personality and spirit. Each has memories and in offering them respect, they always welcome you back.

One evening when in Silent Illumination, I arose from sitting on granite overlooking a small bay that ducks and geese were exploring and realized that there was nothing to attain and nothing to transmit. Laughter rose from within me.

I sent a letter to Shifu. In it I stated that the Buddha wasn't Chinese, but Canadian.

I applied to a retreat and asked for a personal interview with Shifu.

There was a new monk form Singapore, Chi Jun fashi, who was leading the retreat, conducting interviews and acting as translator for Shifu. He was young, bright and scholarly having been a monk for seven or so years.

With Chi Jun fashi there as translator, I prostrated before Shifu and sat at his feet. Since Shifu was seated in a chair, all that filled my visual field when I assumed sitting posture and lowered my eyes was his white socks.

I told him I was writing a book. His feet started moving up and down in joyous enthusiasm. I had never seen such enthusiasm expressed with a strong message of "hurry up!"

"You need a publisher!" he said.

He then asked, "How many students do you have?"

"None," I replied. "You didn't give me transmission and so nobody thinks I am a teacher."

He said, "Finish the book and I will give you transmission!"

"Shifu, wouldn't it be better if you read it first?" I asked.

The smile fell from his face.

"Shifu," I said, "What is there to transmit?"

He then became a visage of fatherly sincerity. In the most gentle and reverential of tones he said, "There is nothing to transmit. It cannot be transmitted."

"Can I teach here?" I asked.

"We don't know what you will say," he replied.

I bowed, then asked, "What do you think of me as a Master?"

In the same gentle tone he said, "There are many fine Masters that are my friends. Once I asked one who is quite famous who he received transmission from? He told me he received transmission from The Sixth Patriarch. You too can say you got your transmission from The Sixth Patriarch."

"Do you still want to read my book?" I asked.

Once again joy radiated from him as his feet began lifting and settling in impatience.

"Send me a copy when it's finished!" he said.

He then rose from his chair and pointed to the floor.

"Prostrate," he ordered.

Without thought I prostrated, then rose to my feet and bowed deeply.

Before I left the interview room, he sternly said, "What is your practice?"

Those were the last words he said to me.

I returned home and quickly finished the book.

He asked the very diligent translator I was in contact with for a translated copy of the introduction and a list of the subject headings of each of the book's chapters.

After some time, I was contacted by the translator. She was instructed to convey the message that Shifu was happy I had finished the book and that when I feel confident in what it says, I should get it published.

That was it.

No offers of publishing, no criticism, no recommendations.

Eager to get the book out and see what response I would get, I published it myself through a do-it-yourself firm in much the same way Shifu self-published his work.

I then sent an announcement of my book to all the affiliates of the Chan Center, supplying a link to the publisher.

The publisher's hit counter indicated that I had close to a 100% response rate. This caused me to naturally expect some form of email, either out of curiosity or at least a complaint.

Instead, absolutely nothing happened. It was rather easy for me to extrapolate several theories as to why this occurred.

Although I knew at the time that the book needed editing, the concepts contained within it were timeless, fresh and correct.

Solitary Retreat

I decided to give Shifu time to read the whole text, and myself an ongoing solitary retreat holiday.

After this strange and less than enthusiastic response, I made a decision to wait and hear from Shifu. I was very tired of relating to political structures only to get a boot to the head. All I craved was to meditate in isolation with Barb, sail around Georgian Bay in our newly acquired miniature sailboat of 1970's vintage, mess around with electrolysis and resonant energy experiments in my shop/physics lab, and continue to scribble stuff down in notebooks.

It was in the fall of 2009 that I got news that Shifu was very sick and would not live much longer.

I sent him an email telling him that I had heard the news about his health and wished it wasn't so.

I then said, "Shifu, years ago you said that for those you had the least karmic affinity with, you spent the most time and effort giving your teaching to, and those with the most karmic affinity with you, you give the least. I consider this the highest of Mahayana Teaching. Shifu, what do you think of my teaching?"

I would have been disappointed had he given me a response.

He didn't.

Sometime later I received from the translator I was working with news that Shifu had died.

This was the only correspondence in any way shape or form from The Chan Center that I had received in over four years.

The news itself caused the emergence of fond memories of a man who had lived his life well, and his presence would be deeply missed in this world.

I decided to go to the funeral service at The Chan Center.

I did not go out of concern for Shifu. To me this would be a lack of realization of The Buddha's Teaching. Within the continuum of death and dying, Shifu had nothing to worry about. However, humanity in its deluded blindness does. This world more than ever needs the Buddha's Teaching. This teaching lives beyond the parameters of religious distortion and spiteful gods whose antiquated messages justify death and destruction on an incomprehensible scale, all in the name of "good". If there was chanting for Shifu's wellbeing, it really was for our collective wellbeing that he, as a Bodhisattva could not and does not exist separate from.

When I arrived once again at The Chan Center in Queens, I was graciously greeted by a female monastic who showed me where I was going to stay. It was Shifu's old office. I put out my mat and sleeping bag where his desk used to be.

The service was projected live from Taiwan on a large screen at the front of the Chan Hall. There was wonderful continuous chanting of Amitabha Buddha's name. This practice I had not taken part in before and found it extremely powerful. The kitchen staff was, as usual, extremely hard working and prepared wonderful vegetarian masterpieces.

There was almost nobody at the Center who recognised me after all these years. Everybody who was present during the funeral services was relatively new, or from Taiwan. So, I was a nobody taking part in chanting. This didn't bother me.

However, I did want to know if there was any message left for me by Shifu concerning my book, and any future association I might have with teaching at the Dharma Drum Retreat Center in Pine Bush. I assumed that after five years of silence from the Chan Center, the seemingly controlled muffling of my book, then receiving a message that Shifu had passed away, there might be someone with a message who wanted to speak with me.

I contacted the translator who sent the message to arrange a meeting. She seemed painfully troubled that I was in New York, and told me it would be difficult for us to get together. This was a person of natural honesty and diligence who was the Bodhisattva who translated the introduction of my book for Shifu.

Within the chanting of Amitabha's Name, it was easy to enter samadhi. This is due to Amitabha's power.

The funeral service also consisted of video recordings of Shifu giving talks. It was good to see him and caused natural fond feelings to rise in my heart.

The funeral service ended slightly after midnight. The translator had arrived at the Center and was functioning as a leader of the ceremony. After the cremation and end of ceremonies, she simply came over to where I was sitting and gave me a long, silent and compassionate hug.

It was at that point I began to realize I was really on my own. There was no message, and she was in a very difficult place to tell me so.

I appreciated her response, but painful feelings of rejection and alienation arose.

"I'm getting burned along with Shifu," I thought.

"Nobody is going to hear this teaching I received, nor does anyone care."

The translator conducted a session where people could come forward to recount memories of Shifu, things he said to them and other interactions.

I could not say anything. Would anybody believe what had gone on between me and Shifu?

This was definitely not the time or the place.

People who preach that enlightenment is not feeling pain, is not feeling the results of having an affliction body and therefore a sense of self at once emerging and generating from it, have not remotely realized Buddhadharma. They are blindly wandering in an amusement park of theoretical practice populated by wax figures that fill their current version of what a Bodhisattva or a Buddha is. You can go a long way in this world so attached, until you inevitably appear in Yama Raja's mirror. Why is this appearance inevitable? It is because, despite all confusions and imaginings of attainment, you have an affliction body and are still attached to it.

As the translator and her husband were leaving the Chan Center, I asked her, "Is my work here done?"

She said, "This ceremony is over. There will be other things you can take part in."

Her husband paused, smiled and said to me in recognition, "It's Paul, isn't it?"

As they both left I heard her say, "Goodbye, Paul."

Her voice trailed off in sadness.

She was a victim of circumstances. I later found that she diligently sent *everyone* a message that Shifu had passed away.

Now I felt that my presence was causing extra vexation for people on top of the nature of a ceremony based upon the seeming discontinuity of life; especially such a luminous life.

I guess it was about two o'clock in the morning when everyone had left. The female monastic in charge told me that the garbage needed taking out for collection next morning and asked me if I could carry out the heavy cans full of the cumulative waste of the three day funeral service.

Without a thought to cling to while experiencing powerful feelings, I simply said "Yes" and did the job. Nobody there was strong enough to carry the stinking load. I was the only one qualified.

A joy rose in my heart that I could do such a thing, while doing such a thing. This is the realization of true freedom, independent of conditions.

When I got home my mind was filled with perplexing finality. I needed some clarification of things. I heard that Guo Xing Fashi, the new Abbot of Dharma Drum Mountain Retreat Center in Pine Bush was going to be in Toronto. I emailed him asking for a meeting.

During the meeting I outlined my situation and that Shifu had only read the introduction to my book.

He began relating to me with the assumption that I thought in terms of Christian paradigms. I gave him the benefit of the doubt concerning the ever present divergence between assumptions of reality and what is actually before one's nose. This gulf of consciousness can create prejudices such as Westerners don't have a clue about Buddhadharma and that Orientals don't have a clue about Westerners.

Then he told me of another person in Taiwan who wrote a book and wanted Shifu to publish it. Shifu told him that he didn't know what he was talking about and said that this person wrote the book to set himself up as a teacher.

Guo Xing fashi then added that perhaps I was the same.

I told him that Shifu said he was happy that I wrote my book and that when I felt confident of what it said, to get it published.

I then told him of my last interview and what went on during it, mentioning that I asked Shifu if I could teach at Pinebush and that he told me that he wouldn't know what I would say."

Guo Xing Fashi smiled and responded that I was in too much of a hurry to teach and that I should go to a retreat. He told me that when he began practice he made a vow that even if it took a kalpa to come to enlightenment, he would persist patiently.

To this I responded, "We don't know what we've done in the past."

He gave no response.

We finished our conversation very pleasantly. I then asked once again, "Is it possible for me to teach at Pine Bush or even here in Toronto?" to which he smiled and shook his head negatively.

Once again home in Mansfield, I vowed to continue my solitary practice and not correspond with the Chan Center for three years. I had been told by Shifu six years earlier that my training was complete there. This corresponded to my own perceptions. I needed to clarify my position in the order of things for myself. I needed to get away from The Circus.

Of course Shifu didn't know what I was going to say. Neither did I.

I still don't.

Shifu tripped me up in that last wonderful interview I had with him. I wasn't ready.

The greatest compliment a practitioner can be given is to not get anything from a Master and to be booted out through the centre gates in winter. This makes for strong teachers.

Why did Shifu secretly vindicate me, and give me nothing in public?

Better still, why, when he later offered me public vindication, did I refuse to take it?

Who was a more severe teacher; him or me?

Is there a fixed enduring reality to the disciple of both these severe teachers?

To grab onto an opportunity offered is a sign of strength. However, it can also emerge from a mind still chained to the dharmas of Samsara; the dharmas revolving around getting and having. True freedom and the open portal of compassion is immediately lost when a position and vindication is taken as a place to rest and say, "I have it made".

I have seen this happen.

No matter if you have had one, two, six, ten or twenty six enlightenment experiences vindicated by a Master, if these become things of having and not having, then the Teaching of The Buddha is only poetic license relative to your own self aggrandized enlightenment. This is nothing other than driving drunk on black ice steering what you think is The Greater Vehicle when in truth you are clutching the wheel of a beer truck.

The hesitancy of grabbing onto opportunity is strength when illuminated in the light of Buddhadharma. If doubt still remains, then one is not content with things being things. Things being things is attachment to dharmas. This attachment is the ultimate blindness inherent in the practice of gods and men. This blindness mistakes concept for The Nature of The Universe.

The unresolved matter of my book that Shifu was so excited I was writing, told me he was glad I did so, yet read only the introduction and chapter headings, still remained. What he did made no sense.

Late one night after I returned from his funeral service, I was going through the material posted on Dharma Drum Mountain's Taiwanese cite. An essay caught my attention. Its form was very similar to the introduction in my book.

As I read on, I said to myself, "Whoever wrote this is very good".

Then an exact and unmistakable line from the introduction of my book appeared. I realized that whoever wrote this introduction had read my book. Going further into the work, I found it was divided into headings that were similar to the headings I presented to Shifu years before.

It then occurred to me that what I was looking at was probably one of the last things Shifu had written.

Although the headings differed somewhat, what he said harmonized with my book.

I now know why Shifu in the mid stages of failing health encouraged me to write and finish my book, yet had only the introduction translated along with chapter headings.

Thus it is revealed that what we taught is no different.

This is the *secret* Transmission of Song of Mind.

To do my best to protect it well, I decided to remain in solitary practice for three more years.

I told a Chan Center friend who used to give interviews during retreats that I needed to get out of The Circus for a while.

The three years I gave myself have long passed.

With the deepest fondness and gratitude, I have said goodbye to Shifu.

Although he really hasn't gone anywhere, now he can retire.

A Dream

You might think this story is all the dream of an idiot before sunrise. If that is the case, then at least it is a noble dream in constant search of awakening, so the idiot need not be pitied. After all, the only way idiots become wise is realizing they are in fact, idiots. The only way an idiot becomes completely wise is when they realize they are a complete idiot. If complete idiocy is realized, then where can there be any wisdom or attainment?

It is taken as a truth that all things obtained in this life cannot be taken with you at life's end. So why do people want to get something from practice? Would this not make practice about as useful as membership in an exclusive golf and country club while exhaling your last breath?

The problem is people make all things into something they are not. This fundamental ignorance is the generator of all suffering experienced within the savage boundaries of Samsara. This is the actual creation of Samsara in opposition to The Pure Land.

This mind of getting something from Zen or Dhyana Practice is nothing but a roller coaster ride to hell. However, freedom from hell necessitates boarding the roller coaster.

Life is inseparable from craving.

Craving and need generate suffering.

A Dream

There is a Way beyond suffering.

This Way is The Teaching of The Buddhas of Past Present and Future.

Is it not more liberating to use this wonderful thing called Dhyana, Chan or Zen Buddhist Practice to enter the great and wonderful process of truly freeing yourself from the clutches of craving that generates suffering?

Now, in the death gasps of this Dharma Ending Age the convulsive birth of a New World Cycle begins.

Lofty institutions and old paradigms crash to the earth.

There is no better time to practice, and no better time to teach.

Master Laughing Cloud is founder and director of The Flower Ornament (www.flowerornament.com), a dynamic place of functional concept and practice arising from The Flower Ornament (Avatamsaka) Sutra. Under his guidance people can enter The Buddha's Teaching through the most fundamental of Dhyana Practices: Silent Illumination.

Glossary

Avalokitesvara

The Enlightening Being (Bodhisattva) of Compassion. Usually taking female form, she listens to the suffering of humanity and offers infinite ways of transcending affliction. Thus she is sometimes depicted with multiple arms, her hands holding such things as tools, flowers, nourishment and drink. She is also beautifully depicted with a hand extended to help the suffering, or holding an urn offering the drink of Amrita, the elixir of Buddhadharma.

Avatamsaka Sutra

The Maha Vaipulia Avatamsaka Sutra (The Flower Ornament Sutra) is one of the largest collections of The Buddha's Teachings.

In homage to The Avatamsaka Sutra it is sometimes chanted, "To know all The Buddhas of the past, present and future, perceive that Dharmadhatu Nature, (the fundamental, highest and most supreme nature of existence), is all created by the Mind."

Bodhisattva

Bodhisattvas are Enlightening Beings. They are Teachers of Buddhadharma who have vowed to liberate all sentient beings before realizing their own Complete Enlightenment.

Buddha

A Buddha is an Enlightened Being. In Mahayana Buddhism, the distinction between the processes of teaching, practice and experience cannot be separated because inherently, no distinction can be found. The distinction of Samsara versus Buddha Realms also vanishes. Buddhas are born into Samsara like all of us, witness and experience suffering, enter The Great Way and come to Unsurpassed Enlightenment. This is the free functioning of Highest Compassion.

Buddhism

Buddhism is not a religion. It is a collection of teachings emerging from the most fundamental of human empiricism. However, when separated from its heart of Dhyana, it loses its essential empirical nature and appears in form as a religion.

To practice Dhyana Buddhism is to find out for yourself the Nature of The Universe, Self and Other. The act of doing so beyond limit liberates all sentient beings from affliction.

This is The Highest Compassion.

Cavaillé-Coll

A 19th Century French organ builder who took applied mathematical and engineering to extreme.

He theorized that in order to produce the most perfect non- influenced speech and tonality, each organ pipe should have enough space between it and the next pipe so that one could walk around it. Furthermore, voicing and winding should emphasize stability through the reduction of natural transients.

However, this whole attitude is at odds with the nature of the organ. As the name implies, an organ is an entity based on the subtle interactions of all its components.

Cavaillé-Coll's 19th Century pasteurization of the organ eventually led to the creation of the electronic organ and synthesizer wherein the same sterilized ideals could be more fully realized at a tiny fraction of the cost. Thus what was a real and living instrument was replaced with a concept-picture of a real living instrument.

Chan

A Chinese lingual evolution of the original Sanskrit word Dhyana.

Dharma

The Buddha's Teaching. Literally meaning The Great Law.

Small "d" dharmas are natural laws that take the form of physical, mental and interpersonal interactions. Thus science and mathematics contain dharmas.

Dhyana

Dhyana with a capitol "d" is the meditative heart of Mahayana Buddhism. It is an Aryan Sanskrit word emanating from Western Mind long obscured by religions. All Enlightening and Enlightened Beings (Bodhisattvas and Buddhas) of past, present and future enter into this natural and Ultimate Meditation.

Dhyana cannot be practiced/realized outside of timeless Buddhist Concept.

Flower Ornament Sutra

This is the English name for The Avatamsaka Sutra.

Heart Sutra

A very beautiful abbreviated version of this Sutra is chanted or recited in Dhyana, Chan and Zen Buddhist Practice. It is also chanted in other Mahayana Buddhist traditions.

Hua-tou

Hua-tou (Chinese) and koan (Japanese) are two words that are used interchangeably.

More precisely, a hua-tou is the heart of a koan. It is neither a function of intellect nor intellect's absence. When mind becomes honed through Dhyana Buddhist Meditation, the peripheral details of the koan drop away, and a great intrigue and urgency continues.

In the early to advanced stages, it is very important to find a reputable teacher to work with.

Kannon

A Japanese lingual evolution of the Chinese name Kwan-Yin. Kwan-Yin is the name the Chinese gave to The Bodhisattva of Compassion. The original Sanskrit name for this Enlightening Being is Avalokitesvara.

Koan

A question emerging from the human condition fueled by a deep desire to transcend affliction.

Such a question becomes a focal point of mind and as such, when coupled with Silent Illumination forms the ever sharpening sword edge cutting through the most impenetrable of delusions.

Koans can be questions that naturally arise from one's own heart-mind generated by life events, or they can be found in historic compilations of Dhyana

Master/Disciple interactions such as The Gateless Gate (Mumonkan) or The Blue Rock Records.

In the early to advanced stages, it is essential to work on koans with a reputable teacher.

Kwan-yin

Kwan-yin is the name the Chinese gave to the Enlightening Being (Bodhisattva) of Compassion.

Mahayana

The great vehicle of Buddhadharma dedicated to the liberation of all sentient beings as opposed to teachings of Buddhadharma centred on liberating oneself. In truth, it is impossible to truly liberate oneself without the liberation of all sentience because all sentience is generated and defined through the self.

Manjusri

The Enlightening Being (Bodhisattva) of Wisdom. He is commonly depicted holding the infinitely sharp delusion cutting sword of Buddhadharma while seated upon a tiger.

Mara

The Lord of Delusion, Craving and Temptation.

Mara offers things craved as a portal of choice thereby ensnaring practitioners in resultant suffering. This is the heart of addiction. When one has had enough of Mara's manifestations, one may enter the Practice of Buddhadharma. Thus it could be said that Mara is an Enlightening Being.

Moving mind

The mind of perception and thought. By clinging to perception and thought, consciousness is deluded into mistaking these mind functions as the true nature or reality of The Universe separate from Self. This is the generator of karma, and therefore rebirth. When this fundamental attachment drops away, the true nature of The Universe and Self is realized without negating or obliterating the natural and necessary mind of perception and thought. If anything, through the practice of Dhyana Buddhism, both of these wonderful human faculties are honed to a far greater usefulness.

Mu

Chinese Wu. The most frequently used koan because of its inherent simplicity. It's nature draws into question the notions of having and not having, giving and getting, enlightened and not enlightened. Thus it draws into the razor sharp sword edge of Buddhadharma the nature of Mind, Self, Other and Universe.

The case of the koan Mu is as follows: A monk in deepest seriousness asked Master Chou Chu (Japanese Joshu) "Does a dog have Buddha Nature?" to which the Master replied "Wu".

Unfortunately, Wu and the Japanese equivalent Mu have no exact translation in English. The word is most commonly translated as "no". More accurately it means "has not" or "doesn't have" which is an indirect negative. This indirect negative is far more powerful than the polarity generated by a direct negative and adds greatly to the koan's potency. Through the unavoidable dependency of words, those speaking either Japanese or Chinese associate this indirect negative and therefore have a more open window to beyond. When those not speaking either language focus on the word "mu" this is lost. Mu then becomes a pseudo mantra and a thing of attachment unless overridden by strong life-questioning.

Nirvana

The cessation of karma and all phenomena. This cessation is not the cessation dependent upon activity as an opposite, nor is it the cessation of Self.

Prajna

Wisdom cultivated in harmony with Dhyana Buddhist Meditation.

Runes

Sharing similar magical power and intuitive meaning as symbols found in Egyptian hieroglyphics, they are currently attributed to being created by The Celts within a time frame encompassing roughly the last fifteen hundred years. However, the use of recurring magic symbols used by the ancestors of The Celts goes back to a past discontinuous within the current accepted historical paradigms.

Samadhi

Single pointed mind revealed through dhyana meditation. All meditation converging to a state of samadhi is realized through dhyana, the act of meditative concentration. Thus yoga contains dhyana that will lead to samadhi. Engineering, physics, mathematics, music, craftsmanship and art also generate dhyana leading to a form of samadhi.

There are many different forms of lesser samadhis experienced in fierce Zen training, such as warrior samadhi, the powerful liberating experience of transcending hellish battlefield phenomenon including fear and pain along with an inexplicable controlled release of super human energy (Chi). However, this liberation is dependent on being immersed in the hyper charged realm of the zendo or battlefield. Thus battlefield samadhi is very commonly mistaken for Buddhist Dhyana or Zen Samadhi because it is far easier to experience.

The Supreme Samadhi of Buddhist Dhyana Samadhi inevitably requires no mediation and no special circumstances. It is simply realizing the true nature of The Universe, inseparable from your own Self Nature. This is the experience of Buddhist Enlightenment.

Samsara

The living realm of birth and death into which we are all born. The experiences within this realm are predicated by cyclic pain and joy framed within a blindness generated by clinging that in and of itself offers no escape. When one's karma matures and one has had enough, escape is deeply desired. This opens the gate to Buddhist Enlightenment.

Sangha

A group of arduous practitioners of Buddhadharma.

Sanskrit

The mother tongue of The Aryans. The body of Buddhist Concept including The Sutras is recorded in Sanskrit.

Language is a window of the soul.

Called "an Indo European language" Sanskrit shares the same basis as Latin, Welch and Germanic Languages including English. The divide between the history of Europe and India is an artificial creation of Judeo-Christian prejudice now becoming revealed through unpolluted scientific empiricism. What was called Northern India two thousand years ago and beyond included much of what is now Afghanistan. The Aryans entered India from the north and in time influenced the languages spoken there.

The language is highly precise and therefore scientific. The Vimana Shastras written well over six thousand years ago speak in engineering terms of energy manipulation and flying machines that our current science is only beginning to understand.

Silent Illumination

The fundamental practice method of Dhyana Buddhism. It has been called "The Practice of The Tathagathas".

While immersed in sitting meditation, perception and thought naturally come into awareness and are returned to silence. Illuminating through awareness of perception and thought and its return to silence is the active process of non-attachment to craving and subsequent suffering.

After some mastery of this method of practice, perception and thought outside of sitting meditation in and of itself returns to silence while exerting no effort to do so. Here perception and thought are unpolluted and at a very high level. One is able to respond spontaneously without clinging to special situations or images. One appears completely normal: nothing special. Others cannot see this because they are attached to thought and perception. Thus they are easily fooled by images and marketed media.

In the early to advanced stages, it is highly important to practice under the guidance of a reputable teacher.

Sunyatta

Inseparable from form and precisely form, inseparable from emptiness and precisely emptiness, it is beyond the dependent meaning of words. Loosely and inadequately translated as "Emptiness", its nature is embodied in the koan "Mu" and the practice of Silent Illumination.

Swastika

An ancient runic form symbolizing a vortex, the natural flow of volition, energy and matter. It is the form spiral galaxies manifest and is found over the hearts of many Buddha figures. In The Flower Ornament Sutra (Maha Vaipulia Avatamsaka Sutra) countless practitioners of Buddhadharma naturally congregate to form swastikas on hearing The Buddha's Teaching.

Tathagathas

The Buddhas of past present and future. Shakyamuni Buddha is the current Tathagatha for whom a history and timeline is associated. Previous to him, there were countless Buddhas who are ascribed Sanskrit names and taught in previous world cycles. The future Buddha is Maitreya.

This Buddhist model of a very long timeline of world cycles wherein humans have lived is at odds with the modern pseudo scientific view based upon highly filtered evidence and prejudicial paradigms. It is the current pseudo-science model taught in Judeo-Christian ignorance that is now crumbling.

The Four Noble Truths

The Four Noble Truths of Buddhism are:

1) The nature of life is that we are afflicted.
2) Craving causes affliction.
3) There is a Way through which one can transcend affliction.
4) That Way is the Path revealed through Buddhist Teaching.

The Precepts

There are Ten Buddhist Precepts regarding right conduct.

The first five are practiced by lay practitioners and all ten are practiced by monastics.

The first five are:

1. Refrain from killing.
2. Refrain from stealing.
3. Refrain from improper sexuality.

4. Refrain from lying.

5. Refrain from taking intoxicants.

The Sixth Patriarch

It has been said that The Sixth Patriarch of Chan (Zen), Master Hui Neng, was the greatest Chinese Master. Secretly given the symbols of Zen Transmission by the 5th Patriarch, Hui Neng lived in the forest with a band of hunters in order to evade attempts on his life by jealous monks.

One monk in particular vowed to retrieve the robe and bowl from Hui Neng, and went searching for him.

When the time was ripe, Hui Neng presented himself with the robe and bowl.

Sitting the robe and bowl before him, Hui Neng told the monk that if this is what he wanted he could take it. The monk could not take what he originally sought and cried out, "Master, I did not come for a robe and bowl. I came to realize the Buddhas Teaching! Please instruct me!"

Hui Neng gently said, "Think neither good nor evil. What was your original face before your parents gave you birth?"

At this, the monk realized Enlightenment.

The Sutras

The teachings attributed to Shakyamuni Buddha, the last great teacher in historical record to be called A Buddha. However, there are other Sutras, most notably the Platform Sutra of The Great Chan Master Hui Neng, Chan's (Zen's) 6th Patriarch.

In the Buddhist pantheon there are countless historical Buddhas preceding Shakyamuni. The latest scientific, empirical unbiased historical inquiry points to a human history far exceeding ten millennia from which an original language similar to Sanskrit was spoken by the Aryan Race who created both European and influenced Indian languages.

The scope, perfection and unsurpassed profundity of The Buddhist Sutras indicate that these works are as old as humanity itself. They have not simply been preserved. Their profundity has been *realized* through the ages by teachers and disciples inseparable from Buddhas and Bodhisattvas, thus keeping alive their compassionate truth.

The Three Jewels

The Three Jewels are the teaching manifestations of Buddhadharma. They are Buddha, Dharma and Sangha.

Upia

The skillful means of a Master in teaching a student.

Yama Raja

The Lord of Death.

Following death, Yama Raja holds a mirror in front of the deceased. What the deceased sees based on their past continuum of choices taken forms the next choice of impermanent rebirth into heavenly, hellish, demonic, angelic, ghostly, animal or human realms. This is an animistic representation of karma.

Zen

A Japanese lingual evolution of the Chinese word Chan.

These days Zen is marketed as something independent of Buddhism. This has proven to be not only dangerous, but a myth as well.

Zen is Buddhism, Buddhism is Zen.

Zen is Dhyana Buddhism.